MORE PRAISE FOR *PEAK*

"I love the Joie de Vivre Heart icon that Chip uses to illustrate how a passionate corporate culture breeds happy employees, which leads to satisfied customers, which results in a profitable and sustainable business."

—**Sir Richard Branson**, founder and chairman, Virgin Group Ltd.

"Late in his life, Abe Maslow imagined how his iconic hierarchy of needs could be translated to the collective, especially to companies, but he never fully realized that vision. Chip Conley has channeled Abe's point of view and made it relevant to the business world. There is no person on the planet better versed in how to create a self-actualized organization than Chip and *Peak* is his virtuoso manifesto."

—**Michael Murphy**, cofounder, Esalen Institute

"*Peak* was one of the sources of inspiration for Life@Facebook, our new comprehensive approach to caring for our people and those who matter to them."

—**Tudor Havriliuc**, vice president, human resources, Facebook

"The world could use more conscious capitalists who realize the most neglected fact in business is we're all human. Chip Conley's *Peak* is one of the most practical and inspiring books of this new era of stakeholder-centered businesses. This was required reading for many of our top execs."

—**Kip Tindell**, cofounder and chairman, The Container Store

"WeWork truly resonates with Chip's *Peak* principles as we believe our mission is to create a world where people work to make a life, not just a living. As a fellow former hotel industry CEO, I have the utmost admiration for Chip's approach to leadership and how it translates into success."

—**Michael Gross**, vice-chair, WeWork

"Within this engrossing, inspiring, and all-around wonderful book is the gripping story of an extraordinary company facing the most trying circumstances imaginable and emerging stronger than ever. If you want to build a great business, work in a great business, or simply understand what greatness in business is all about, you need to read *Peak*."

—**Bo Burlingham**, editor-at-large of *Inc.* and author of *Small Giants: Companies That Choose to Be Great Instead of Big*

"There aren't many books that do a more brilliant job of showing how both a company and a leader can create loyalty and differentiation by just applying a little common sense psychology. Like most wonders of the world, *Peak* is both simple and complex at the same time, but, most importantly, it's effective as a way of seeing business and life."

—**Leslie Blodgett**, founder and former CEO, bareMinerals

"Chip Conley has captured something special here. *Peak* shows how to apply fundamental human principles toward building a great company and offers poignant insights for all leaders."

—**John Donahoe**, former CEO, eBay

"What do Yvon Chouinard, Timothy Leary, and a company where one-third of the employees clean toilets for a living have in common? As brilliant entrepreneur Chip Conley will teach you in this groundbreaking book: Abraham Maslow. Essential reading for anyone trying to create an organization with meaning."

—**Seth Godin**, author of *Purple Cow* and *Tribes*

"Chip's book is a rare combination of poignant story, potent theory, and prescriptive action steps—it is applicable to both public and private sector work."

—**Gavin Newsom**, lieutenant governor of California

"Chip Conley proves that Abraham Maslow's brilliant theories regarding work and leadership cannot only be applied in the real world but, when embraced, often lead to enormous competitive advantages. Chip's book is an instructive guide for any leader who seeks to build enlightened organizations that tap the potential of employees and capture the hearts and minds of customers and shareholders."

—**Deborah Collins Stephens**, coauthor of *Maslow on Management* and *The Maslow Business Reader* and cofounder of The Center for Innovative Leadership

PEAK

PEAK

CHIP CONLEY

How
Great
Companies
Get Their
Mojo from
Maslow

REVISED AND UPDATED

WILEY

For general information about our other products and services, please contact our Customer Care Department within the United States at (800) 762-2974, outside the United States at (317) 572-3993 or fax (317) 572-4002.

Wiley publishes in a variety of print and electronic formats and by print-on-demand. Some material included with standard print versions of this book may not be included in e-books or in print-on-demand. If this book refers to media such as a CD or DVD that is not included in the version you purchased, you may download this material at http://booksupport.wiley.com. For more information about Wiley products, visit www.wiley.com.

ISBN 978-1-119-43492-4 (paper)
ISBN 978-1-119-43493-1 (ePDF)
ISBN 978-1-119-43494-8 (ePub)

Printed in the United States of America

10 9 8 7 6 5 4 3 2 1

Contents

Foreword   xi
Introduction   xiii
Preface   xxi

Part One: Maslow and Me

1	Toward a Psychology of Business	3
2	Karmic Capitalism	17
3	The Relationship Truths	31

Part Two: Relationship Truth 1: The Employee Pyramid

4	Creating Base Motivation	45
5	Creating Loyalty	61
6	Creating Inspiration	77

Part Three: Relationship Truth 2: The Customer Pyramid

7	Creating Satisfaction	99
8	Creating Commitment	119
9	Creating Evangelists	135

Part Four: Relationship Truth 3: The Investor Pyramid

10	Creating Trust	159
11	Creating Confidence	175
12	Creating Pride of Ownership	187

Part Five: Putting the Truths into Action

13   The Heart of the Matter   201
14   Peak Leadership Practices   215
15   Creating a Self-Actualized Life   235

Appendix: *Peak* Managerial Assessment   247
Notes   251
References   259
Acknowledgments   267
The Author   271
Index   273

To Abraham H. Maslow, whose lifetime of learning offered a precious gift to the world.

And to my Joie de Vivre crew, who "sought the peak" with me every day.

FOREWORD

I first met Chip Conley at an event where we were both speaking in 2007, just one year before we hit $1 billion in gross merchandise sales at Zappos.com. When he presented his concepts from *Peak*, I was instantly struck with how similar our philosophies about building a brand and business were. I later found out that we were both passionate students of the field of positive psychology—essentially, the science of happiness—and that we had both applied our learning to our respective businesses as well as our personal lives. I felt like we were kindred spirits.

At Zappos, our goal is to wow our customers, our employees, our vendors, and ultimately our investors. We strive to deliver the very best customer service and customer experience, and ultimately our brand is about delivering happiness to the world. Our hope is that 10 years from now, people won't even realize that we started selling shoes online, and perhaps 20 to 30 years from now, there may even be a Zappos Airlines that's focused on just delivering the very best customer experience.

Our number-one priority at Zappos is company culture. Our belief is that if we get the culture right, then most of the other stuff, like building a long-term enduring brand, delivering great service, and finding passionate employees and customers, will happen naturally on its own.

Building a brand today is very different from building a brand 50 years ago. It used to be that a few people got together in a room, decided what the brand positioning was going to be, and then spent a lot of money buying advertising telling people what their brand was. And if you were able to spend enough money, then you were able to build your brand.

Today, what you do and who you are matter much more than what you say. Your brand is the combination of everyone's experience with your company, which is ultimately a byproduct of your company's culture.

A company's culture and a company's brand are really just two sides of the same coin. The brand may lag the culture at first, but eventually it will catch up. At the end of the day, every brand is basically a short cut to emotions. All of the world's greatest enduring brands ultimately appeal to one or more human emotions. *Peak* provides a great framework for thinking about how to accomplish that.

One of our core values at Zappos is to *Pursue Growth and Learning*, so we offer many different classes to help our employees grow both personally and professionally. We are such a fan of Chip's work that *Peak* has become required reading for many of our employees, and our training team now offers a class specifically designed to cover all the concepts from the book that you are now holding in your hands.

Every employee and visitor to our headquarters in Las Vegas is offered a free copy of *Peak*, and we even have posters on the walls of our headquarters in Las Vegas to serve as a daily reminder to our employees to always keep Chip's modified version of Maslow's Hierarchy in mind.

If you're interested in building an enduring brand and business, this book will be one of the best investments you'll ever make. I encourage you to do what we've done at Zappos: get a copy for each and every one of your employees. This book is one of the rare few that can help you and your employees grow both personally and professionally.

Tony Hsieh, CEO of Zappos.com (ceo@zappos.com)

P.S. If you're ever in the Las Vegas area, I would like to invite you to come and tour our headquarters to observe firsthand many of the concepts from *Peak* in action. To schedule your tour, just go to https://www.zapposinsights.com/tours.

INTRODUCTION

Books teach me. Even my own. Writing a book helps make sense of what I've learned at the congested crossroads of psychology and business. And I enjoy sharing the wisdom found on the journey. You're welcome to think of me as your crossing guard at that confusing intersection.

It's been 10 years since *Peak* was published and I'm thrilled the book is still a favorite with so many people, and in so many different industries and countries. This updated edition offers new insights from me, as well as many examples of new companies—from Facebook to WeWork—that use the *Peak* model in their organizational strategy. You'll also find a whole new chapter on *Peak* Leadership Practices (Chapter Fourteen) and a new Managerial Assessment tool regarding the Employee Pyramid in the Appendix.

Quite a bit has changed for me in the past decade. Just six months after *Peak* came out in 2007, it was clear we were entering the Great Recession, not long after recovering from the dot-com bust. Who knew my company would experience two once-in-a-lifetime downturns in the same decade? Déjà vu. Joie de Vivre (JdV). Don't worry, this isn't a French lesson; let's just say I felt a whole lot of déjà vu at JdV between 2008 and 2010.

During difficult times, it's natural to feel paralyzed and to operate exclusively in survival mode. Most of us are working in infectious fear factories, where risk aversion runs rampant at a time when creativity, innovation, and teamwork are more needed than ever. That's where you, the leader, come in. W. Edward Deming, father of the total quality movement, once said that the primary duty of every leader is to remove fear from the workplace. But organizational wellness doesn't emerge simply from the absence of fear. Fear must be replaced with a positive spirit of fulfillment and vitality that comes from the principles outlined in this book. What's true of the companies we love is true of the leaders we love. They are deeply admired for being passionate, smart, resilient, trustworthy, original, and humane—the same qualities we admire in people.

Joie de Vivre made it through that difficult time. But I had a health scare in late 2008, which woke me up to the fact that my new calling was to primarily be a writer and speaker. Of course, that was confusing to me, and everyone around me, as we thought I'd be the owner and CEO of my company for at least another 25 years. Ultimately, I sold Joie de Vivre, the brand and the management company, in mid-2010. But I kept ownership in much of the hotel real estate, and provided guidance to the new ownership team (led by John Pritzker of Geolo Capital, whose father started the Hyatt hotel chain). This gave me time to sort through my emotions after my heart literally stopped at age 47, which led me to write *Emotional Equations.*

In March 2013, I was approached by Brian Chesky, the CEO and cofounder of Airbnb, at the time a small start-up home-sharing company. He and some of the young execs had read *Peak* and were intrigued by how it might apply to Airbnb's business model. Brian asked if I wanted to "democratize hospitality," which sounded pretty nifty to me. But I only wanted to do it part-time since I'd just launched a business, Fest300 (now part of Everfest), to share my passion for the world's best festivals. Not surprising, the part-time consulting gig turned into a full-time obsession and leadership role for this "retired" CEO. Fifteen hours a week became 15 hours a day. How many chances do you get to disrupt your favorite industry? For me it happened not just once—as a boutique hotelier long ago—but a second time, at the forefront of the *sharing economy.*

My initial title was Hospitality Guru, which in a few weeks morphed into Head of Global Hospitality and Strategy. Brian said he liked the way my mind worked strategically and also asked me to create a Learning and Development department. Over four years, I oversaw more than a half-dozen departments and key initiatives for the company before moving into my Strategic Advisor role—and back to blessed part-time status. But what a fascinating journey it's been! We weren't really called a hospitality company in early 2013, and we were thought of as a travel tech start-up with a design focus. Today, we offer more accommodations than the top three hotel companies in the world combined—Marriott (including their Starwood acquisition), Hilton, and Intercontinental—and our private market valuation has surpassed $30 billion.

Today, I also see pyramids on whiteboards all over Airbnb's headquarters and our more than 20 offices around the world. But I remember just four months into my tenure, when Brian asked me to lead a three-day retreat for Estaff—our dozen-person senior leadership team—and I introduced the principles of *Peak* to develop our 2014 strategic initiatives. It's been a true peak experience to see the business model I developed applied at such a deep level to a fast-growing, high-profile company playing on a global canvas. Airbnb was going to succeed whether I was there or not. But I do feel a certain joy and honor at how my contribution helped this fledgling and extremely talented leadership team earn *Inc.* magazine's Company of the Year cover story in December 2014, and Glassdoor's Best Places to Work award in December 2015. And, I do believe the underpinning of *Peak*'s humane approach to business has helped Airbnb steer clear of some of the cultural, personality, and strategic challenges that have hurt the reputations of other sharing economy companies.

While it turned into a huge disruption in my life, I'm glad I said yes to Brian. Many hoteliers couldn't see Airbnb coming. But I recognized that Brian's investment in the company's culture, and the fact that home sharing was addressing an unrecognized need for travelers—living like a local affordably—meant Airbnb had the potential to go big. As I point out in Chapters Seven through Nine on the Customer Pyramid, established companies can miss innovation if they get too fixated at the base and address only the expectations of their core customers.

A more mobile populace leads to changes in lodging needs. There's a growing number of mostly Millennials choosing to be "digital nomads," living parts of the year in places like Bali or Baja, and the rest of the year in cities such as Boston or Austin. These folks are less interested in being upwardly mobile and are, instead, outwardly mobile. Equipped with a laptop and a smartphone, a Wi-Fi connection and a coworking space, these freelancers, entrepreneurs, and other modern merchants are not typically weighed down by home or car ownership.

My Baby Boomer generation saw work and leisure as an "either/or" proposition. With an occasional sabbatical to moderate workaholism, the global nomad phenomenon is "both/and"—enjoy a great life while doing work on the road. Add in the "bleisure" trend, where business travelers tack on a few extra days of leisure to an interesting destination, and you see an upward trajectory in the extended-stay lodging market. Nearly 60 percent of Airbnb's room-night demand in many major metropolitan markets is guests staying a week or longer, whereas the average length of stay for most urban hotels is less than three days. Thinking about the expectations, desires, and unrecognized needs of these new kinds of travelers has helped Airbnb deliver a level of guest satisfaction that far exceeds the hotel industry average (based upon net promoter score as the common metric). This is part of the reason we've grown so quickly.

Over the past decade, I've been introduced to so many business leaders who are also "peakers." What's been surprising is how universal this *Peak* model is, no matter the industry, geography, or culture of the company. Some might be surprised that investment bankers are also intrigued by this humanistic approach to business, yet Merrill Lynch has invited me to give eight speeches to their various employees and customers around the world.

But it's another investment bank, Houlihan Lokey, that woke me up to the biggest realization I've had about my Maslovian model since I wrote the book: *the two lines that define the boundaries between the Survive, Success, and Transformation levels of the Employee, Customer, and Investor pyramids are not fixed.* When I was leading a workshop for Houlihan Lokey's top leaders, one astutely pointed out that, depending upon the industry and the economy, the bottom of the pyramid that defines survival could represent 80 percent of the pyramid. For example, investment bankers are money-obsessed. So, the base of their employee pyramid takes huge precedence. But, interestingly enough, both Merrill Lynch and Houlihan Lokey execs have agreed that the next two levels of the pyramid (Recognition and Meaning), while thin in the world of investment banking, represent the differentiators for an employer. This is where loyalty is created with their slightly mercenary bankers. As one exec said to me, "*Peak* helped us see that many of our bankers are stuck at the success level of the pyramids, not seeing the disruptive transformation available at the peak." I call this "the illusion of being ahead" that afflicts many established companies and execs, who are just coasting along based upon historical momentum.

A completely different company, on a completely different continent, reinforced the message of the movable lines in the employee pyramid. Liderman is one of the largest security firms in Latin America, with more than 12,000 security guards, mostly in Peru and Ecuador. Its average employee makes as much in a month as the Houlihan Lokey investment bankers make in an hour. Yet,

Liderman CEO Javier Calvo Perez Badiola, who also calls himself the "guardian of the culture," told me at a *Peak* seminar in South America that their employee pyramid is dominated by money as well, because their guards and their families are living paycheck to paycheck. But, just as with the investment bankers, Javier—who is one of the most *Peak*-focused execs I've ever met—recognizes that you create a unique, loyalty-driven culture higher up the pyramid. This is part of the reason his company is consistently ranked one of the best employers in Latin America. Conversely, in many non-profit, governmental, or educational institutions, the money slice of the pyramid is very thin and the meaning at the top is what predominates. So, these new insights have proven to me just how adaptable the *Peak* model is to just about any institution.

In my travels, I've met many inspired business leaders—some at conferences, others in the cliffside hot springs at Big Sur's Esalen Institute, and even some at the annual Burning Man event in Nevada. Bill Linton is an inspired idealist and, for 40 years, has been a pragmatic entrepreneur growing his life sciences company, Promega, to approximately $400 million in annual sales with a reputation that is world-class in the biotechnology world.

Bill and I are birds of a feather. Because we're both "Burners" (those who enjoy making the Burning Man pilgrimage each year), and because we consider Maslow as so fundamental to how we see life and business. Bill explains, "In the early 1990s, Promega's board and management team started exploring our purpose and meaning of being in business. As a model that reflects a path of meaningful growth, we chose Maslow's hierarchy and began to develop our purpose with corporate 'self-transcendence' as our aspirational goal. It was exciting and helpful to discover *Peak* and its insights. All our corporate leaders received it. Chip provides an excellent resource in how a business can access and practice a way of operating that brings greater reward for all parties involved. We have put the concepts into practice throughout the organization for the past two decades with excellent outcomes."[1]

Khalil Gibran said, "Work is love made visible."[2] So true. *If* you're on the path of living a calling and you're in a habitat that supports that path. Tragically, only a small percentage of the world can say that. So, I'd like you to consider a one-month trial of the following exercise based upon the classic question we ask each other as strangers. When someone asks, "What do you do?" answer not with your profession, job title, or company. Tell them what creates meaning for you. This gives people a window into your occupational soul and it may also prompt them to ask a deeper question of themselves.

Or, they may just think you're a crackpot when you answer like I do: "I am a crossing guard at the congested intersection of psychology and business," or "I dispense wisdom and uncover blind spots," or "I help people do the best work of their lives." A doctor could answer: "I fix people," or "I listen," or "I help people heal themselves." My friend and colleague Debra Amador DeLaRosa helps people cultivate their unique stories and says, "I am a Story Gardener." And Vivian Quach, who I featured at the start of my 2010 TED speech and has been cleaning hotel rooms in my first hotel, The Phoenix, for more than 30 years says, "I am the peace of mind police." Who are you?

Finally, I share the following letter from someone whose life has been positively affected by this book. Receiving these kinds of letters keeps me motivated to continue writing about my experiences in business and in life. Thanks, Gabe! My next book, *Wisdom@Work: The Making of a Modern Elder* celebrates what the young and not-so-young have to offer each other.

Dear Chip,

I know that you're a storyteller, so I hope you can take some time to read and enjoy this one. It's a little long, but I assure you it's worth it.

My first job in hospitality was running an elevator.

Despite being a college graduate, the only entry-level hotel job I could find was as a host of a rooftop venue at a new boutique hotel. Being last in the pecking order, every night it was my job to run the independent elevator that took guests up and down 27 floors to and from the hotel's popular rooftop.

I was extremely embarrassed by my job. I had entered the hospitality world because of my love for creating experiences for those around me, and despite already having success in the service industry and travel booking, here I was confined to a tiny space for hours at a time. Something had to change.

First, I timed each elevator trip. Thirty-two seconds. I began to practice different ways to introduce myself and create a routine of relaying the basic facts and information required before they reached the top, always leaving room for a joke or some improvisation. I'd even recommend drinks at the bar, views around the rooftop, and give them my own business card for table bookings. After a while, guests began asking for me instead of the hosts that were actually working the venue.

I'd made the most of my "elevator pitch," but I had yet to focus on another opportunity: the way down. In fact, most of the time I spent in that elevator alone, so how could I take advantage of that time?

When I told my parents I'd found a job, I decided to hide some of the details from them (specifically the moving metal box), but they still knew I was at the bottom of the food chain. As a gift, my mom sent me a book that she said would help me once I got to where I wanted to go. The book was called Peak, *and I would read it every trip down in that elevator a half a minute at a time before hiding it in the emergency compartment as the doors opened for the next guests to go up.*

Because of Peak *I began to see more and more value in my job as well as those around me in other departments of the hotel. I also began approaching relationships with coworkers and guests more genuinely, enhancing my network and accelerating my development as a leader. It also provided me with a level of confidence in my decision-making that would serve me well when I got my shot.*

Over the next three-and-a-half years, I worked from the elevator to management. While a lot of my own personal motivation led to my success, it was your book that prepared me for when I got my shot and provided a context from which I could evaluate and contribute to the overall leadership of the venue and hotel. I also decided to return to school for my master's, focusing on customer service psychology and business management before joining an up and coming hospitality group in 2015. I have since left that job and have been traveling around the world and preparing for beginning the next chapter of my life, one that introduces self-actualization, or perhaps my own "joie de vivre."

I hope you enjoyed the story and continue to influence young professionals and companies poised to impact the world. Oh, and I can't wait for that next book, either.

Best,

Gabe Huntting

PREFACE

Deep down I always knew that business could be done differently. I founded and grew my company, Joie de Vivre Hospitality, with this rebellious spirit. But it wasn't until I was rocked to my foundation with a desperate economic downturn that I was truly able to see the power of my principles.

Celebrated restaurateur Danny Meyer told me he wrote his book *Setting the Table* because it helped him move from the intuitive to the intentional in how he ran the Union Square Hospitality Group. Brazilian CEO Ricardo Semlar has said he wrote his books *The Seven-Day Weekend* and *Maverick* to address one of his director's questions about whether what works in practice for their company could also work in theory. I decided to write *Peak* because it allowed me to combine three of my greatest interests: writing, psychology, and business. Writing this book required me to reconcile how Joie de Vivre has successfully interpreted one of the most famous theories of human motivation into how we do business. But my learning was most profound when I discovered dozens of other peak-performing companies that have also consciously and unconsciously relied on Abraham Maslow's Hierarchy of Needs. It wasn't just my little company that was fond of Abe's pyramid. Yet, taking all of this learning and turning it into a book was quite a task. Thankfully, at a very young age, I knew I wanted to be a writer when I grew up, so all the time spent researching and writing just helped connect me back to a lifelong aspiration. I guess that means I'm now grown up.

This book is about the miracle of human potential: employees living up to their full potential in the workplace, customers feeling the potential bliss associated with having their unrecognized needs met, and investors feeling fulfilled by seeing the potential of their capital leveraged. Celebrated author Fred Reichheld says, "The fundamental job of a leader is to be a role model, an exemplary partner whose primary goal is to help people grow to their fullest human potential."[1] Great leaders know how to tap into potential and actualize it into reality. My hope is that whether you are a start-up entrepreneur or in management at a Fortune 500 company, you will be able to use the theory in this book to maximize your own potential as well as the potential of those around you. Don't get discouraged if this theory feels a little foreign. At Joie de Vivre, we weren't perfect, either. I can't say we acted on this theory every day in every one of our more than 40 businesses, but the process of educating everyone in the company about these principles made a big difference in our lives.

I might have called this book *How I Survived the Great Depression and Created a Great Company and Great Relationships Along the Way*, but I don't think my publisher could have fit that on the cover. It seems trite to say that companies are just communities of relationships. But common sense suggests, and empirical studies show, those organizations that create deeper loyalty—with employees, customers, and investors—experience more sustained success. In this age of commoditization, one of the truly differentiating characteristics of leaders and companies is the quality and durability of the relationships they create. *Peak* (a much more succinct title) will help you create peak experiences with those you work with so that these flourishing relationships will help you sustain peak performance.

PART ONE

MASLOW AND ME

CHAPTER ONE

TOWARD A PSYCHOLOGY OF BUSINESS

If we want to answer the question, how tall can the human species grow, then obviously it is well to pick out the ones who are already tallest and study them. If we want to know how fast a human being can run, then it is no use to average out the speed of the population; it is far better to collect Olympic gold medal winners and see how well they can do. If we want to know the possibilities for spiritual growth, value growth, or moral development in human beings, then I maintain that we can learn by studying the most moral, ethical, or saintly people.

ABRAHAM MASLOW[1]

Pop.

That word conjures up some nostalgic images for me: my dad who doubled as my Little League coach, a style of music I couldn't get enough of, the Shasta Orange I used to drink by the six-pack.

At the end of 2000, as we were enjoying the second millennium celebration, the word *pop* had a new meaning to me: it was the sound of champagne flowing, of good times continuing to roll, of prosperity anointing me with a hero's halo.

I had a lot to be thankful for. My company, Joie de Vivre Hospitality, had grown into one of the three most prominent boutique hoteliers in the United States. My first book of any note, *The Rebel Rules: Daring to Be Yourself in Business,* which included a foreword from my demigod, Richard Branson, was hitting the shelves. And *USA Today* had just profiled me as one of 14 Americans, along with Julia Roberts and Michael Eisner, to be "watched" in 2001. Every indication was that my life, my company, and my budding career as an author were all heading in the right direction—up—and the New Year would be a welcome one. Little did I know that the real thing to watch in 2001 would be that I didn't jump off the Golden Gate Bridge.

I went from being a genius to an idiot in one short year. You see, *all 20* of my company's unique hotels were in the San Francisco Bay Area. Yes, you can tell me all about the value of geographic diversification, but in the late 1990s, there was no better place, with the possible exception of Manhattan, to operate a hotel. I had learned long ago that a company can be product-line diverse or geographically diverse, but it's hard to be both. Rather than be a Holiday Inn with replicated product all over the world, we consciously chose the opposite strategy as we built our company. We would focus our growth in California and create what has become recognized as the most eclectic, creative, and handcrafted collection of hotels, lodges, restaurants, bars, and spas in a single geographic location.

But that pop I heard around New Year's was more than just champagne. It was also the sound of the bursting dot-com bubble. It was the pop heard around the world, but nowhere was it louder than in my own backyard. I won't bore you with the details, but even before the tragedy of 9/11 sent the worldwide travel industry into an unprecedented tailspin, San Francisco and Silicon Valley hotels were experiencing annualized double-digit revenue losses because of the high-tech flameout. Bay Area business leaders didn't want to admit that we were as addicted to electronics as Detroit is to cars or Houston to oil, but in 2001, during that first full year of the new millennium, we came to realize that we were going through withdrawal.

It turns out the millennium was sort of the midpoint of the seesaw. The Bay Area had partied for five good economic years in the last half of the 1990s. But just like if you drink heavily for five days approaching New Year's you might also suffer through a five-day hangover, our region experienced a comparable nausea in the first five years of the new millennium. That seesaw hit the ground really hard. My business, my confidence, and my self- worth all took a precipitous fall.

What do you say to a journalist who asks, "How does it feel to be the most vulnerable hotelier in America?" I knew I was feeling rotten, but I didn't realize my melancholy was being observed on a national stage. The reality is my company, after 15 years of rising to the top of the hospitality industry, was suddenly undercapitalized and overexposed in a world that had changed overnight. I never realized that after founding Joie de Vivre at age 26, and dedicating 15 years to building it, there was a risk I could lose everything. Most industry observers thought we were done for.

It wasn't just the dot-com meltdown or 9/11 that led to a truly troubled travel industry. A couple of wars, an outbreak of SARS (severe acute respiratory syndrome), and a very weak worldwide economy from 2001 to 2004 didn't help. It seems as if everyone wanted to stay close to home. The San Francisco Bay Area was ground zero for this great depression for American hoteliers. In the history of the United States since World War II, no hotel region in the country had ever experienced the percentage drop in revenues the Bay Area experienced in those first few years of the new millennium. And because Joie de Vivre operated more hotels in the region than any other hotelier, we faced a classic thrive-or-dive dilemma.

I remember sitting on the dock of my best friend Vanda's houseboat in Sausalito, facing the sparkling city of San Francisco across the bay on a crystal-clear morning. It was low tide, which exposed all of the mud and muck of the shoreline. It felt familiar: my business was at low tide. Vanda certainly knew it and, being the poet aficionado she is, she read me a line from a Mary Oliver poem, "Are you breathing just a little and calling it a life?"*

I was speechless. I'd been holding my breath ever since I'd heard the pop of the bubble bursting. I had a moment of clarity. This downturn was proving to be a true stress test for my business, but it was also a stress test for me personally. I'd been joking with my Joie de Vivre leadership team that we were becoming a faith-based organization. We truly believed this downturn wouldn't last forever, but with each passing quarter, things only got worse. The pressure made me feel like *I* was going to pop. I realized I needed to stop holding my breath. Speechless, yes—breathless, no.

A couple of days later, when I was experiencing a bit of malaise, I snuck into the Borders bookstore around the corner from Joie de Vivre's home office. I needed another Mary Oliver fix or some form of inspiration. A CEO in the poetry section of a downtown book-store on a weekday afternoon? I felt like I should be wearing sunglasses and a disguise. Somehow I drifted over to the psychology

---

* Excerpt from "Have You Ever Tried to Enter the Long Black Branches" from WEST WIND: POEMS AND PROSE POEMS by Mary Oliver. Copyright © 1997 by Mary Oliver. Reprinted by permission of Houghton Mifflin Harcourt Publishing Company. All rights reserved.

section of the bookstore; maybe it had something to do with my mental state.

There among the stacks I came upon a section of books by one of the masters of twentieth-century psychology, Abraham Maslow. I started leafing through *Toward a Psychology of Being*, a book I'd enjoyed 20 years earlier in my introductory psychology class in college. Moments grew to minutes, which grew to hours as I hunkered down, sheepishly looking over my shoulder every once in a while to make sure no one was watching. I couldn't put the book down. Everything Maslow was saying made so much sense: the Hierarchy of Needs, self-actualization, peak experiences. In the midst of the crisis that was threatening my business, which was challenging me personally as I had not been challenged before, this stuff reminded me why I started my company.

When you name your company after a hard-to-pronounce, harder-to-spell, French phrase meaning "joy of life," as I did, you must have different motivations than the typical Stanford MBA. The goal I set for myself just a few years out of Stanford was to create a workplace where I could not only seek joy from the day-to-day activities of my career but also help create it for both my employees and customers. I'd done a short stint at Morgan Stanley investment bank and realized that my aspiration in life was not to climb the typical corporate ladder. After deciding against a career in investment banking, I'd spent a couple of years in the rough-and-tumble world of commercial real estate construction and development and realized that spending all day negotiating through adversarial relationships wasn't my idea of a good time, either.

It was on my twenty-sixth birthday that I finished the business plan for Joie de Vivre. At that point, I'd become a tad disillusioned with the traditional business world and was considering a career as a screenwriter or massage therapist (I did training in both). Starting a boutique hotel company was my last option before I took an exit off the business superhighway. What inspired me about the hospitality world was that if we got our job right, we made people happy. And as a boutique hotelier, I could tap into my creativity to do things that I could never do in building an office tower. I remember telling an MBA friend back in 1987, when he was helping me paint my first hotel (I didn't have the budget to hire a professional painting contractor), that Joie de Vivre was my form of self-actualization (we'd both been exposed again to Maslow in a business school class called Interpersonal Dynamics, which all of us deridingly called "touchy-feely").

Each day during the early part of 2002, when there seemed to be no limit to the depths the San Francisco hotel industry could fall, I would come home from work weary and a little battered and crack open another Maslow book. I even had the opportunity to read his personal journals from the last 10 years of his life. I started using some of his principles at work. I came to realize that my climb to the top wasn't going to be on a traditional corporate ladder; instead, it was to be on Maslow's Hierarchy of Needs Pyramid. During the next few months, I began to mentally compost this book—throwing everything into the bin I had experienced and everything I was learning—while giving my business mouth-to-mouth resuscitation based on Maslow's principles.

A BRIEF PRIMER ON MASLOW

> *A musician must make music, an artist must paint, a poet must write, if he is to be ultimately at peace with himself. What a man can be, he must be. This need we call self-actualization. . . . It refers to man's desire for self-fulfillment, namely to the tendency for him to become actually in what he is potentially: to become everything one is capable of becoming.*

—ABRAHAM MASLOW[2]

Abraham Maslow is probably the most recognized and quoted psychologist in corporate universities and leadership books. In best-selling business books by legendary authors Stephen Covey, Peter Drucker, and Warren Bennis, you find many limited references to Maslow's seminal work. The influence of his thinking is everywhere. Author Jim Collins (*Built to Last, Good to Great*) wrote, "Imagine if you were to build organizations designed to allow the vast majority of people to self-actualize, to discover and draw upon their true talents and creative passions, and then commit to a relentless pursuit of those activities toward a pinnacle of excellence."[3]

Maslow believed human beings had been sold short, especially by the traditional psychology community. Freud's perspective on the human psyche was a kind of "bungalow with a cellar," with his main psychiatric focus being on people and their neuroses, which often came from childhood traumas. B. F. Skinner pioneered the idea of *behaviorism* in psychology, based on the premise that we could learn a lot about humans by studying lab rats (think of the bestseller *Who Moved My Cheese?*). Maslow came at this from a very different angle, focusing more on people's future than on their past. Instead of studying just people who were psychologically unhealthy, he began reading about history's acclaimed sages and saints to look for commonality in their outlook and behavior. Maslow focused on the "higher ceilings" of human nature rather than the basement cellar. Of course, this all made sense: in sports, in the arts, and in business, we study peak performers to understand how to improve our own performance. By recognizing that all humans have a higher nature, Maslow helped spawn the human potential movement in the 1960s and 1970s. And even the U.S. Army picked up on his theory when their internal Task Force Delta team turned Maslow's "What man can be, he must be" into the phrase "Be all you can be," which became the advertising slogan in its recruiting campaign.

The foundation of Maslow's theory is his Hierarchy of Needs Pyramid, which presumes that "the human being is a wanting animal and rarely reaches a state of complete satisfaction except for a short time. As one desire is satisfied, another pops up to take its place. . . . A satisfied need is not a motivator of behavior."[4]

Maslow believed that each of us has base needs for sleep, water, and food (physiological), and he suggested we focus in the direction of fulfilling our lowest unmet need at the time. As those needs are partially fulfilled, we move up the pyramid to higher needs for physical safety, affiliation or social connection, and esteem. At the top of the pyramid is self-actualization, a place where people have transient moments called *peak experiences*.

HIERARCHY OF NEEDS PYRAMID

SELF-ACTUALIZATION

ESTEEM

SOCIAL / BELONGING

SAFETY

PHYSIOLOGICAL

A peak experience—comparable to being "in the zone" or in the "flow"—is when what *ought to be* just *is*. Peak experiences are transcendental moments when everything just seems to fit together perfectly. They're very difficult to capture—just like you can't trap a rainbow in a jar. Maslow wrote, "They are moments of ecstasy which cannot be bought, cannot be guaranteed, cannot even be sought . . . but one can set up the conditions so that peak experiences are more likely, or one can perversely set up the conditions so that they are less likely."[5]

This was pretty fascinating stuff. But as much as I searched for books on Maslow, I couldn't find one that applied his theory to the universal motivational truths that define our key relationships in the workplace.

Although I knew I wouldn't find a book that would say, "Here's how you can get out of your funk and create peak experiences at Joie de Vivre," I began to wonder: if humans aspire to self-actualization, why couldn't companies, which are really just a collection of people, aspire to this peak also? Maslow wrote, "The person in the peak experience usually feels himself to be at the peak of his powers, using all of his capabilities at the best and fullest. . . . He is at his best, at concert pitch, the top of his form."[6] Why couldn't that same sentiment be applied to my company? What does a self-actualized company look like? And how could Joie de Vivre "set up the conditions so that peak experiences are more likely"?

I started studying Maslow even more deeply. I learned that this rebel with an IQ of 195 was elected to the presidency of the mainstream American Psychological Association in his latter years. His studies of exceptional individuals like Abraham Lincoln, Albert Einstein, and Eleanor Roosevelt helped him to realize that there was a "growing tip" of humanity who could prove to be role models for the rest of us. He called these individuals *peakers* as opposed to most people who were considered *nonpeakers*. The characteristics of these self-actualized people included creativity, flexibility, courage, willingness to make mistakes, openness, collegiality, and humility.

MASLOW IN THE WORKPLACE

In the summer of 1962, Abraham Maslow spent a few months at Non-Linear Systems (NLS), a digital voltmeter factory just north of

San Diego, California. His goal was to see if the characteristics that defined the self-actualized person could also apply to a company. He saw industry as a "source of knowledge, replacing the laboratory . . . a new kind of life laboratory with going-on researches where I can confidently expect to learn much about standard problems of classical psychology, e.g., learning, motivation, emotion, thinking, acting, etc."[7] In essence, Maslow wanted to see if the science of the mind could be translated into the art of management.

Andrew Kay, the owner of NLS, relied heavily on Maslow's 1954 book *Motivation and Personality* to create a more productive and enlightened workplace. He believed, based on Maslow's theories, that employees satisfied their deeper social and esteem needs when they could witness the fruits of their labor. Kay noticed that his workers were more productive at the end of the assembly line, where finality of the assembly provided a sense of accomplishment. Kay dismantled the assembly lines, created small production teams that were self-managed, offered stock options, and created a post called the "vice president of innovation." These teams were even allowed to choose the decor of their private workrooms—a pretty revolutionary approach during the era of the Organizational Man, more than 30 years before the first dot-coms sprouted.

Maslow was fascinated with how NLS used basic theories of human motivation and applied them in the workplace. He went on to publish a book on business called *Eupsychian Management* in 1965, but the inaccessible title doomed this effort, as did the fact that many of his ideas were probably ahead of their time (the book sold only 3,000 copies when it was first printed). Maslow's interest in business didn't wane, as he spent his last couple of years as the scholar-in-residence at the Saga Corporation on Sand Hill Road in Menlo Park, California, just off the Stanford University campus. (A couple of decades later, this street became the number one address for the world's leading venture capital firms.) I only wish Abe Maslow had lived to a proper age (he died in 1970 at 62 years old) because I might have had the opportunity to meet him: just eight years after he died, I was regularly running along Sand Hill Road as a freshman on the Stanford water polo team.

Although Maslow's impact in the workplace took decades to gain widespread acceptance, many business pioneers beyond Andrew Kay took his theories to heart. Charles Koch of Koch Industries got an authorization to reprint the long-forgotten

Eupsychian Management for his senior executives as they built the country's second largest private company. Lee Ozley was a consultant to Harley-Davidson's president, Rich Teerlink, during the 1980s and 1990s, when the company was struggling to survive. Ozley had studied with Maslow as a graduate student at the University of Wisconsin and believed the key to Harley's renaissance was aligning the employees' intrinsic motivations with the needs and priorities of the company. Harley's reengineering of its company and its unique approach to creating a cult brand with its customers can be partially traced back to Maslow's theories. Senior leadership in diverse companies from Whole Foods Market to Apple to Pinterest also credit Maslow's influence with helping develop the foundational elements of how they operate their businesses.

Maslow's message struck a chord with many business leaders. In essence, he said that with humans, there's a qualitative difference between not being sick and feeling healthy or truly alive. This idea could be applied to companies, most of which fall into the middle ground of not sick but not truly alive.

Based on his Hierarchy of Needs, the solution for a company that wants to ascend up the healthy pyramid is not just to diminish the negative or to get too preoccupied with basic needs but instead to focus on *aspirational* needs. This idea is rather blasphemous for some. The tendency in psychology and in business has always been to focus on the deficits. Psychologists and business consultants look for what's broken and try to fix it. Yet, fixing it doesn't necessarily offer the opportunity for transformation to a more optimal state of being or productivity.

TAKING MASLOW TO HEART

It seems natural that corporate transformation and personal transformation aren't all that different. In this era when more and more individuals have undertaken deep personal change striving for self-actualization, it's not surprising that this has also become the marching orders for many companies. Employees are looking for meaning. Customers are looking for a transforming experience. Investors are looking to make a difference with their investments. We often forget, especially in today's high-tech world, that a company is a collection of individuals. As my friend Deborah

Stephens wrote in *Maslow on Management* (which helped to resuscitate *Eupsychian Management*), "Amid today's impressive technological innovations, business leaders sometimes forget that work is—at its core—a fundamental human endeavor."[8]

As a guy who runs his company in the shadow of the iconic Transamerica Pyramid, it's only fitting that I would become so pyramid-obsessed. Maslow's pyramid offered me a way of rethinking my business at a time when the brutal travel economy demanded it. During my first 15 years in business, I'd found that having an organizing philosophy I could live and teach to my team helped drive Joie de Vivre to success. Best-selling author Malcolm Gladwell (*The Tipping Point* and *Blink*) told the *New York Times* that part of the reason for his books' successes is, "People are experience-rich and theory-poor . . . people who are busy doing things . . . don't have opportunities to collect and organize their experiences and make sense of them."[9] I came to realize that Maslow's Hierarchy of Needs would become my organizing structure for understanding the aspirational motivations in my workplace and in the marketplace. It would be the road map for the next chapter in my company's history.

Using Maslow as our inspiration, we created a new *psychology of business* based on not just meeting the tangible, foundational needs of our key stakeholders but, more importantly, focusing on their intangible, self-actualizing needs. I came to realize that creating peak experiences for our employees, customers, and investors fostered peak performance for my company. This book illustrates that new psychology of business and tells the story of how Joie de Vivre transcended its challenging situation during the first five years of the new millennium and not only survived but thrived. It's all about where you put your attention. Are you focused on the base or on the peak of the pyramid in your relationships with your employees, customers, and investors?

Whereas our biggest hotel competitors, who had much deeper pockets, experienced bankruptcies and lender defaults during the big hotel downturn of 2001–2004, Joie de Vivre grew market share by 20 percent, doubled revenues, launched our most successful hotel ever, was named one of the 10 best companies to work for in the Bay Area, and reduced its annualized employee turnover rate to one-third of the industry average. How is it that Joie de Vivre, seemingly left for dead during the worst hotel downturn in 60 years, avoided the fate of its peers and began the most successful period in its history? I attribute it to the Maslow-inspired management philosophy we adopted and practices we implemented during our darkest days. This stuff works. But you don't have to wait until your company is experiencing a crisis to implement it.

The subtitle of this book, *How Great Companies Get Their Mojo from Maslow*, speaks to the idea that today's most successful companies consciously and unconsciously use Maslow's principles of human motivation every day. *Mojo* means a lot of different things to different people, but if you check slang dictionaries you'll find that it refers to a narcotic or some kind of magic spell. From my perspective, mojo is the secret ingredient that gives life and vitality to your organization. *Peak* is dedicated to helping you and your company build and sustain high-performance relationships with your employees, customers, investors, suppliers, and the community.

How This Book Is Organized

The book is organized into five parts. The first part, "Maslow and Me," includes the book's initial three chapters and provides background on how I developed a new management theory for Joie de Vivre based on my study of Maslow during those difficult days in the new millennium. I describe this theory using what I have termed the *Relationship Truths Pyramid*. The theory represented by this pyramid is what we successfully adopted as our guiding principle for Joie de Vivre's relationships with employees, customers, and investors. The Relationship Truths Pyramid comprises three smaller pyramids, each of which focuses on a different workplace relationship.

The second part of the book, which contains Chapters Four through Six, details the *Employee Pyramid*, the first of the three smaller pyramids that make up the Relationship Truths theory. The Employee Pyramid focuses on what it takes to apply Maslow's theories to create a deeper and more meaningful relationship with your workplace associates. Some of America's most-respected employers, from Genentech to Google, are profiled in these chapters to illustrate how they apply the Hierarchy of Needs to creating a more self-actualized employee base.

The third part of the book, which contains Chapters Seven through Nine, describes the *Customer Pyramid* and illustrates how cult brands create more self-actualized customers and speak to their unrecognized needs. I have provided concrete examples of companies such as Netflix, Harley-Davidson, and Apple, which have reached the peak of this pyramid. In Part Four of the book, Chapters Ten through Twelve, I describe what I have termed *the Investor Pyramid* and apply the concept of the Hierarchy of Needs theory to a company or entrepreneur's relationship with investors or those to whom the company or entrepreneur is accountable. The former CEO of Medtronic describes how his company used its relationship mojo to become the darling of investors with one of the fastest rising market capitalizations on Wall Street in the 1980s and 1990s. Venture capitalists and small entrepreneurs also report how they create sustainable relationships based on basic human nature. Maslow was convinced that the process of creating a new enterprise was a classic path toward self-actualization.

Throughout Chapters Four through Twelve, I provide *peak prescriptions* to help managers, CEOs, and leaders of any organization build workplace relationships focused on the peak of the pyramids, where performance is maximized or actualized. These *read it in the morning, use it in the afternoon* tools apply universally to any situation involving leaders and employees and can be implemented by executives in a multinational company, entrepreneurs in a new start-up, executive directors of nonprofit organizations, and others in positions of authority.

The final part of the book, "Putting the Truths into Action," has just three chapters: one focusing on the heart or company culture that keeps the three components of the Relationship Truths Pyramid cohesive, another on the leadership practices supporting a Peak-performing company, and the final giving some perspective on how to use the pyramid in your own work life and create peak experiences outside of work, as well.

Because this book covers such a wide array of topics, and some only briefly, at the end of each chapter you'll find a list of relevant books, articles, and studies that I recommend based on the subject of the chapter.

Can organizational life rise above the darker premises behind Freud's psychoanalysis and B. F. Skinner's behaviorism? I believe that it can and that there is a better way for organizations to interact with their employees, customers, and investors. In a world where brainpower and teamwork have surpassed brawn and individualism, there is no doubt that Maslow's legacy is exceptionally relevant today. The airwaves are populated by Dr. Ruth, Dr. Laura, and

Dr. Phil, so why not turn our attention to Dr. Abe and his resonant message of our potential as humans? It's possible we can't afford not to. Plato has been quoted as saying "We can easily forgive a child who is afraid of the dark. The real tragedy of life is when men are afraid of the light." I hope *Peak* helps you to shine your light just a little brighter and, by so doing, catalyzes those around you to shine brighter, too. We all deserve to be peakers.

RECOMMENDED READING

Flow by Mihaly Csikszentmihalyi
Maslow on Management by Abraham Maslow
Motivation and Personality by Abraham Maslow
Need, Greed or Freedom by John Whitmore
The Art of Possibility by Rosamund Stone Zander and Benjamin Zander
The Caterpillar Doesn't Know by Kenneth Hey and Peter D. Moore
Toward a Psychology of Being by Abraham Maslow

CHAPTER TWO

KARMIC CAPITALISM

Behind every managerial decision or action are assumptions about human nature and human behavior.

DOUGLAS MCGREGOR, *THE HUMAN SIDE OF ENTERPRISE*[1]

Against all odds, my first hotel became a smash hit. In 1987, at the ripe old age of 26, I bought a virtually out-of-business no-tell motel in San Francisco's gritty Tenderloin district. My slightly delusional business plan was to turn The Phoenix into San Francisco's official rock 'n'roll hotel so that I could rub elbows with famous musicians, build a business that would enable me to utilize my creativity, and design a workplace where I could live the *joy of life* every day.

Cheap Trick? Bad Company? While those were some of my favorite bands during my younger years, they also described the clientele I inherited. The hotel's biggest corporate account was Vinny (and his girls)—at least until we renovated the place and terminated the pay-by-the-hour option, which constituted most of the hotel's business. Based on a classic niche marketing plan, a lot of chutzpah in our sales efforts, and a bit of luck, this 44-room motel soon became an internationally acclaimed crossroads for the creative.

I have innumerable stories I could tell about my experience running The Phoenix: babysitting Sinead O'Connor's new child, serving Linda Ronstadt breakfast in bed, loaning cuff links to JFK Jr., and asking Courtney Love to wear a bathing suit when she used the pool are just a few—but they're perhaps more appropriate for another book. The reality is, shortly after a pull-me-up-by-the-bootstraps renovation, the reopened, over-achieving 1950s ghetto motel attracted people on the rise or fall. We were the haven for Nirvana, Pearl Jam, and the Red Hot Chili Peppers (who, on more than one occasion, all stayed in the hotel at the same time) on their way up, as well as the first choice for Devo, Johnny Rotten, and the Ohio Players, who'd all seen better days.

But of all the guests we've hosted at the infamous Phoenix, there's only one who's ever engaged me in a dialogue about Maslow: Timothy Leary. The well-known Harvard psychology lecturer and icon of the rebellious children of the Vietnam era was in the twilight of his life when he started regularly spending time at the hotel in the early 1990s—a demographic outlier among the twenty-something tattooed set who hung out by our hotel pool. At one time identified by Richard Nixon as the most dangerous man in America, Leary was an enigmatic pop star in the 1960s and 1970s. He became an advocate of psychedelic drug use for the purpose of turning on, tuning in, and dropping out, a mantra the hippie generation gladly appropriated from him.

My one and only lengthy poolside conversation with Leary was about Maslow, long before I was reacquainted with the Hierarchy of Needs a decade later in my time of need. Both had been in Boston teaching psychology in the early 1960s, and although Maslow was a bit of a square compared with Leary, he appreciated the latter's iconoclastic and optimistic personality. In our conversation, I told Leary about my odd career path from the potential riches of a Stanford MBA grad to the relative poverty of a budding rock 'n' roll hotelier. I'll never forget his words: "You chose the path of self-actualization. This is what you're supposed to be doing. And based upon your relationships with your staff (he'd noticed me hugging some of the housekeepers), it looks like you're creating self-actualization for the people around you, too." Ever the idealist, he told me that Maslow wanted to see more capitalists like me. Leary whispered, "I might get shot if some of my friends heard me say this, but businesspeople probably have the greatest potential to transform the world for the better."

More recently, in reading over Maslow's journals, I get a sense that Timothy Leary was echoing what Maslow believed. Maslow had an interest in the idea of mass therapy and found that the business world was the most efficient and profound place to reach the greatest number of people. This interest in applying his motivational theory to the in-the-trenches business lab rather than to the ivory-towered university experimental lab had a profound effect on how he spent his last few years. Maslow wrote, "What conditions of work, what kinds of work, what kinds of management, and what kinds of reward or pay will help human stature to grow healthy, to its fuller and fullest stature? Classic economic theory, based as it is on an inadequate theory of human motivation, could be revolutionized by accepting the reality of higher human needs, including the impulse to self-actualization and the love for the highest values."[2] In his utopian sort of way, Maslow believed that good managers created good enterprises, which created good communities. In other words, good business can create good karma.

Over the past few years, I've been fortunate to engage in deep conversations with business leaders at conferences all over the world. Take most of them away from the transactional day-to-day details of their work life, give them a moment to have some observation time, and you'll often find a budding philosopher underneath that suit. Based on these conversations, I've arrived at four key premises for this chapter:

1. Every company is organized based on a certain premise of human nature.
2. Most companies aren't very conscious of this fact and operate based on an outdated or short-term perspective, even though sustainable results might be better served by a different business approach.
3. Companies have a habitual "tendency toward the tangible," which means that financial results usually get more attention than relationship issues.
4. More and more business scholars and consultants are making the intangible of relationships and the human spirit more tangible, and many successful companies are leading the way with respect to how they reorganize themselves to pursue both profits and happiness.

THE WORKPLACE AS A MIRROR

How we set up our workplace mirrors our assumptions about human behavior and the world we want to create. As employees, most people have little direct say about this, often to their disappointment. Those of us who are managers or leaders, however, have a great deal of influence on how our workplace is created. Mostly these assumptions are unconscious or at least unspoken. Unfortunately, most work mocks human capacity.

Maslow and his associate, management theorist Douglas McGregor, believed that business leaders needed to take a closer look at these assumptions if they wanted to create a more successful workplace. McGregor wrote, "Next time you attend a management staff meeting at which a policy problem is under discussion or some action is being considered, try a variant on the pastime of doodling. Jot down the assumptions (beliefs, opinions, convictions, generalizations) about human behavior made during the discussion by the participants. Some of these will be explicitly stated. . . . Most will be implicit, but fairly easily inferred."[3]

McGregor identified two contrasting assumptions about human nature: what he called "Theory X" and "Theory Y." If you believe in Theory X, you likely subscribe to a mechanical or highly hierarchical approach to management in which people need to be watched and controlled because they inherently dislike work and want to be directed. The theory of human nature consistent with Theory Y is that people are motivated to work and enjoy controlling their work environment if certain conditions are satisfied. Of course, although most of us would wholeheartedly express our support for Theory Y, the reality is that most businesses are still organized according to Theory X. Top-down employee reviews, time clocks, and 90-day probationary periods when you start a new job are just a few examples of how Theory X lives on, even within some of my hotels. I find that when I speak to leaders of other companies and call attention to this point, they often realize that the environment they have created for themselves, their employees, customers, and investors is, in fact, at odds with the things they say they hold dear as personal values. Have these people, many with good intentions, purposely created a workplace with values in contrast to their own? Of course not. It is more likely a situation of failing to stop, self-analyze, and consciously change course.

Much of what we do in the workplace is inherited from past generations at home, at school, and at work. It is incumbent on us to walk *our* talk, not that of our grandparents, our professors, or our early employers. Whether you hold an entry-level position or are the CEO of the company, do you know which theory your workplace is based on? Just asking the question might shake things up, as the act of getting conscious may wake you up to the potential misalignment of your company's habits to your own perspective on human motivation.

WHY ARE WE SO FOCUSED ON THE SHORT TERM?

For me, walking my talk means that I use my business as a vehicle for making a better world. I like to use the expression *karmic capitalism,* which suggests that business can have a transformative effect in our lives, both personally and in our impact locally and globally. If capitalism has a habitual tendency toward the short term, the concept of karma is spread over many lifetimes. Karma applied to the business world means that individuals in companies consider the long-term effect of their actions—on the environment, the community, their relationships, and themselves. A little New Age? Perhaps. But during the first decade of the new millennium, we witnessed the karmic consequences of the actions of Enron and Bernie Madoff, among others. They experienced the biblical version of karma: reaping what they sowed.

Stephen Covey, in his best-selling book *The 7 Habits of Highly Effective People,* uses the metaphor of the "emotional bank account" to describe "the amount of trust that's been built up in a relationship."[4] Successful leaders recognize that they can't constantly make withdrawals from their business relationships. You have to create balance by making deposits—in the form of giving people something they want or need—if you are going to make withdrawals from your relationships. Prosperous farmers do this with their land. Harmonious spouses do this with each other. Socially responsible companies do it with the community. During the post-9/11 downturn that challenged the global hospitality industry and all of Joie de Vivre's hotels, one of the critical things that helped the company not just survive but thrive was our ability to tap into the long-term relationships we'd created with loyal guests and corporate accounts. In the darkest days of that time, our vice president of sales, Peter Gamez, and I would not just make sales calls in the traditional sense. We would go see longtime customers and express directly our need to make a withdrawal from that emotional bank account we'd built up over the years. The emotional bank accounts we had with corporate customers had a positive balance that enabled us to make these withdrawals, largely because our customers understood and appreciated that we hadn't price-gouged them during the good times of the dot-com boom. We undertook other activities to draw on our reservoir of good will in the bank account, including sending a letter to the most frequent guests of our hotels telling them that we needed their help during these challenging times and asking them to spread the word about us to their friends and families. Sounds a little like George Bailey in *It's a Wonderful Life*, doesn't it? In our own way, we were hoping our "townspeople" would show up, cash in hand, just like they did at the end of that classic movie.

Karmic capitalism is just another way of saying "what goes around comes around." When you make a conscious decision to live your work life this way, it completely alters your perspective on how you make business decisions and how you treat your business relationships. And it has the potential to reorient the logic of our economy so that human capital is valued with the same kind of reverence as financial capital.

There is an ongoing conflict in companies between the theory espoused by legendary economist Milton Friedman, who advocated "fundamentalist capitalism" (a strict focus by corporations on maximizing shareholder value), and what I believe are more enlightened leaders who embrace the philosophy of the long view. In *Built to Last,* Jim Collins and Jerry Porras empirically proved that companies focused on core values and a sense of purpose are more successful in the long term than those that are purely profit driven. Yet, we continue to see company after company make decisions that sacrifice long-term performance and value to meet short-term goals such as quarterly earnings. Why? We live in a world that's often distilled down to cryptic, monosyllabic texts or tweets sent moment to moment from our so-called smartphones. The business world often feels much more short term and transactional than long term and transformational. The quickening pace of change has created almost a rent-a-relationship approach to how we *do* business (sounds a little like the past life of the pay-by-the-hour Phoenix Hotel before Joie de Vivre came along). Many business leaders have built their enterprises on the pure Friedman form of capitalism that seems to align with the harried pace of life we Americans have adopted. Especially in the post-9/11 era, we equate professional success with personal satisfaction and fulfillment. Yet, the tendency of companies to focus on the short term and toward purely functional relationships is directly at odds with what surveys show about the aspirations of American businessmen and businesswomen.

How do we explain this paradox? We know that profit maximization has not exclusively been the driving force of exceptional companies.

John Bogle, who founded the Vanguard Group, the second largest mutual fund company in the world, lamented in his book, *The Battle for the Soul of Capitalism,* the fact that stock market investors have increasingly taken a short-term, profit-taking perspective toward their investments. He says investors have moved from an "own-a-stock" approach to investing to a "rent-a-stock" perspective, as the average length of holding a stock has tumbled from more than six years to approximately one year. Yet, similar to Collins and Porras, Bogle cited that "[mutual] fund managers who hold companies for the long-term and allow intrinsic value to build over time have provided higher returns to their clients than managers [who] hold stocks for the short-term and trade them whenever Mr. Market offers them a tempting but momentary price."[5] America's most well-respected investor, Warren Buffett of Berkshire-Hathaway, lives by this theory of focusing on the eternal, intrinsic value of a company.

James Sinegal, cofounder and long-time CEO of Costco, has consistently received flack from stock analysts who believe he's paid too little (he makes a salary equal to only 12 times the average pay of his line-level workers) and that his employees are paid too much. He says, "Wall Street is in the business of making money between now and next Tuesday. We're in the business of building an organization, an institution that we hope will be here 50 years from now."[6]

Mihaly Csikszentmihalyi writes in his book *Good Business,* "We have learned to develop five-minute and even one-minute managers. But we would do better to ask ourselves what it takes to be an executive who helps build a better future. More than anything else, we need *hundred-year managers* at the helm of corporations."[7] Maslow would agree. He wrote, "There are many qualities of enlightened management, which become very, very clear and very easy to understand if one asks the manager, 'Do you want this company to grow even after you're dead?'"[8]

We know that people in general want to make an impact, create a legacy, and do something that feels truly substantive. These people—our colleagues, subordinates, supervisors, customers, and investors—long for a connection to others and something bigger than themselves. I believe they want to transcend the base of the pyramid.

SATISFYING OUR TENDENCY TOWARD THE TANGIBLE

Okay, you may be thinking that talking about new management philosophies, karma, pyramids, and the like is easy here in hippie-dippy San Francisco, from my enlightened hotel company with the funny name, but that the real world doesn't work that way. The classrooms of graduate business schools and the corridors of Wall Street still focus on market fundamentals more than human fundamentals because business has a natural tendency toward the tangible and rewards short-term performance. Accountability, one of the keystones of business, is easier to measure when it comes to results as compared with relationships.

Recently, both academicians and business leaders have been looking for ways to make the intangible, long-term values in business more tangible. Author of *The Loyalty Effect*, business consultant Fred Reichheld acknowledges that the "pursuit of profit dominates corporate and individual agendas, while accountability for building good relationships gets lost in the shadows." But he goes on to say, "The growth of any organization is simply the accumulated growth of the individual relationships that constitute it."[9] He and his partners at Bain & Company have created a simple measurement, the *net promoter score* (NPS), which allows companies to turn the intangible of customer loyalty and the associated word-of-mouth proselytizing into something business leaders can measure. Companies as diverse as Enterprise Rent-a-Car and Intuit are using this tool as a means of determining whether they're building long-term relationships. Some things are so big, they're almost impossible to measure. The motivation of the human spirit is hard to calculate but easy to witness. Remember MasterCard's "Priceless" commercials? How can you compare the cost of a baseball bat with seeing your child hit his or her first home run in Little League? Yet, in the business world, accountability, which literally means "the ability to count," defines how we value things. But is the inability to easily measure something a valid excuse for dismissing its value? Many business schools worldwide teach the old adage "If you can't measure it, you don't focus on it." But as Maslow asked in his book

Eupsychian Management, "Where do you put consumer good will and consumer loyalty in your balance sheet?"[10] As mentioned in the book *Karaoke Capitalism,* economist Jonathan Kendrick's work shows that the overall ratio of intangible to tangible resources in modern companies has shifted from 30:70 to 63:37 during the past 70 years. We all know that the value of intellectual property has risen exponentially in our knowledge economy, but how would a company show this on a simple balance sheet?

Consider your laptop. Twenty years ago, 80 percent of the cost was the hardware, and 20 percent was the software. Today, it's roughly reversed: the intangible soft stuff inside your computer is four times more valuable than the tangible hard stuff that encases it. Could this be a metaphor for the way in which companies themselves are evolving?

There is a new field of psychology called Positive Organizational Scholarship (and an interesting book by the same name) that is looking for ways to make the intangible more tangible in the workplace. Academicians have found a means of systematically measuring the capacities and processes that give life and strength to an organization. What they have discovered is that there is an interconnected ecology of relationships found in the most successful organizations: *Companies that cultivate an environment that allows for peak individual performance are rewarded with peak company performance.* They have been able to show that qualities like creativity, integrity, trust, optimism, and teamwork have a profound impact on productivity, customer retention, and product quality.

THE PURSUIT OF HAPPINESS AT WORK

The pursuit of happiness isn't mutually exclusive of the pursuit of profit. Bill O'Brien, former CEO of Hanover Insurance, once said, "Our traditional organizations are designed to provide for the first three levels of Maslow's Hierarchy of Needs: food, shelter, and belonging. Since these are now widely available to members of industrial society, our organizations do not provide significantly unique opportunities to command the loyalty and commitment of our people. The ferment in management will continue until organizations begin to address the higher order needs: self-respect and self-actualization."[11]

In creating the Declaration of Independence, Thomas Jefferson and our founding fathers rephrased English philosopher John Locke's dictum of "life, liberty, and property"[12] to something that was a little more karmic. They could have chosen different words: the pursuit of wealth or intelligence or even safety. But they chose the pursuit of happiness to cap their mission statement. You can do the same for your company. In fact, companies around the world are changing their work rules and company customs to assure they are more consistent with human nature. These enlightened companies are proving every day, as they strive to reach the peak of their own pyramid, that they can optimize their relationships with employees, customers, and investors while simultaneously generating outstanding financial results. What are the assumptions that define how your workplace is organized, and how is the pyramid integrated into your company's values?

John Mackey, founder and CEO of Whole Foods Market, talks about the upward flow of human development. John is well known among the company leadership of Whole Foods to whip out a Maslow pyramid to make a point about his company's business model. He believes both profits and personal happiness are best achieved when not aiming directly for them. They are the result of a collection of other activities that inspire your employees and yourself to a consciousness of the interdependencies we have with each other. So the Whole Foods Market working model flows entirely from these assumptions. That's why you see line-level employees having a significant say in everything from what kinds of benefits program they'll have to who they should hire, while receiving stock options and complete transparency of wages and salaries throughout the company.

Another example is Yvon Chouinard, the founder and owner of Patagonia, whose book, *Let My People Go Surfing*, sums up his philosophy not just about the workplace but also about the nature of people. This large private company doesn't believe in time clocks and rigid schedules. In fact, when a surf swell is on its way, you may see a mad dash out the door of both line-level employees and senior executives. In return for the flexibility, fairness, and care the company demonstrates, Patagonia's employees exhibit deep loyalty to the cause (and that's how they think of their environmentally friendly company) on which they work, resulting in little turnover and extremely high employee and customer satisfaction.

There are even examples of more traditional companies embracing Maslow-like management philosophies. The multibillion-dollar energy giant AES has consciously built its assumptions about people into its business model. Cofounder Dennis Bakke writes about this in his book *Joy at Work,* where he says most companies haven't evolved from the industrial mentality of management. Bakke started asking more fundamental questions of his organization, like "What if we eliminated the employee manual or detailed job descriptions?"[13] Based on the response to these questions, he reorganized the company into autonomous teams that were given unprecedented decision-making flexibility that spoke to the leadership's trust in the judgment of its people. These family-like groups helped improve interpersonal relationships in the company while enhancing learning and a sense of meaning for the employees.

Finally, I have to mention the ultimate in Theory Y management styles: Ricardo Semlar's Semco, based in Brazil. Semlar has written about his unique company in *Maverick* and *The Seven-Day Weekend,* two books that dare to ask the question "Why?" This and Semlar's management philosophy question everything that is taken as a given in running a company. Semco's employees are encouraged to choose their own salaries, set their own hours, and have no job titles.

MAKING THE HIERARCHY OF NEEDS TANGIBLE

As Joie de Vivre was struggling with the post-dot-com, post-9/11 downturn, as I was facing the greatest challenge in my professional life, as my competitors were declaring bankruptcy and the press was predicting Joie de Vivre was next, I was immersed deeper than ever in Maslow's theory of human motivation. One night I experienced a moment of clarity: I needed to make Dr. Maslow's theory tangible in my company.

I don't know if you've ever been part of a company that's suffered through a catastrophic period. All workplaces have fear ripples that move like concentric circles out from those places in the business that are most unhealthy. Well, in a difficult time, it's like you move from throwing small pebbles in a pond to throwing a few boulders. The ripples become tsunamis unless you do something to focus people's attention on a more positive outcome. During our company's tsunami, when every part of our business was threatened by tidal waves, I decided to turn our attention to how the Hierarchy of Needs could be our tangible operating model for sustainable success.

The question was: How could I translate Maslow's pyramid into something actionable for my team? I found an answer in James MacGregor Burns' book *Leadership,* which describes two types of leadership: "transactional" and "transforming." Burns writes, "The relations of most leaders and followers are transactional—leaders approach followers with an eye to exchanging one thing for another. . . . Transforming leadership, while more complex, is more potent. The transforming leader recognizes and exploits an existing need or demand of a potential follower. But, beyond that, the transforming leader looks for potential motives in followers, seeks to satisfy higher needs, and engages the full person of the follower. The result of transforming leadership is a relationship of mutual stimulation and elevation that converts followers into leaders and may convert leaders into moral agents."[14]

I wish I had written that! This short excerpt captured everything I had been thinking about as to how I could lead us out of our current challenges. What a provocative way of thinking of my job as the CEO. It's almost like a transactional leader is leading from the bottom of the pyramid while the transformational leader is leading from the top.

In studying Maslow's pyramid, I started to realize that the five layers of his pyramid—physiological, safety, social/belonging, esteem, and self-actualization—really represented three states of being. At the base of the pyramid, where we find physiological and safety needs, we do our best to *survive.* Basic survival is where we place our attention. In a company, this means that the organization is just focusing on the basics of running the business. It is treading water, but potentially in a pond full of fear ripples growing into tsunamis. In this situation, a transactional leader may focus on just the basics. For example, he may cancel the company holiday party (as many of our competitors did) in a downturn to sustain cash flow and save money. Nice short-term move, but possibly the opposite of what this company's culture needs to surf the tsunamis.

As we move up Maslow's pyramid, we strive to succeed in our social relationships and in our esteem. These third and fourth levels of the Hierarchy of Needs represent what many people and companies strive for. It's the stuff that gives us pleasure as individuals or brings us a sense of accomplishment as a businessperson. It is satisfying but not necessarily transformative. Most individuals and companies do not strive beyond this level, despite the fact that they might have the ability and opportunity to reach a more subtle but powerful kind of success, which exists at the very top of the pyramid.

At the top of Maslow's pyramid, a less tangible but very powerful state exists that enables us to transform ourselves and our relationships with others. This idea of self-actualization as applied to the workplace means a company can live up to its full potential and, just like Superman, leap small buildings in a single bound. That's what Joie de Vivre needed to do during the biggest U.S. hotel downturn in 60 years. We couldn't afford to purely survive during the tsunamis; we needed to transform our relationships with our employees, customers, and investors so that we would come out of the downturn with heightened momentum and a new sense of purpose.

Once I drew the Transformation Pyramid with these three levels of survive, succeed, and transform, I was able to communicate the natural progression from what's tangible at the bottom of the

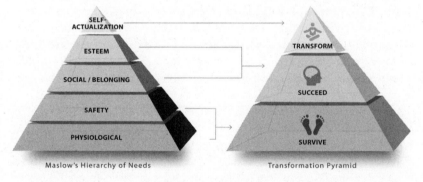

MASLOW'S HIERARCHY OF NEEDS EVOLVES TO THE TRANSFORMATION PYRAMID

TRANSFORMATION PYRAMID

pyramid to what's intangible at the top. It became easier for me to then translate how Maslow's Hierarchy of Needs could be applied to the three most crucial relationships found in the workplace with employees, customers, and investors. It is clear that there are essential base needs in each of these relationships, and if you don't satisfy those survival needs, you can't move up the pyramid. Yet, just focusing on those base needs will never allow the relationship, or the company, to succeed and transform into its greatest potential.

Of course, this Transformation Pyramid is a wonderful model for life. Many of us are redefining success as something more intangible, more meaningful: the idea that we can transform ourselves and the world through the work we do. But this head-in-the-clouds approach can feel disorienting without an organizing principle for how to get there. By imagining that there's a progression from survival to success to transformation, one can have confidence that transcending those tangible basics in life is a path worth taking. Or as Anaïs Nin once wrote, "The day came when the risk it took to remain closed in a bud became more painful than the risk it took to blossom."[15]

In the next chapter, I will tell how I turned this Transformation Pyramid into the template that allowed Joie de Vivre to create much deeper relationships with our three key stakeholders: our employees, customers, and investors.

RECOMMENDED READING

Good Business by Mihaly Csikszentmihalyi
Joy at Work by Dennis Bakke
Karaoke Capitalism by Jonas Ridderstrale and Kjell Nordstrom
Leadership by James MacGregor Burns
Let My People Go Surfing by Yvon Chouinard
Love and Profit by James Autry
Maverick by Ricardo Semlar
Positive Organizational Scholarship by Kim Cameron et al.
"Rethinking the Social Responsibility of Business," *Reason Magazine* (October 2005)
The Battle for the Soul of Capitalism by John Bogle
The Human Side of Enterprise by Douglas McGregor
The 7 Habits of Highly Effective People by Stephen Covey
The Ultimate Question by Fred Reichhel

CHAPTER THREE

THE RELATIONSHIP TRUTHS

Relationships are all there is. Everything in the universe only exists because it is in relationship to everything else. Nothing exists in isolation. We have to stop pretending we are individuals that can go it alone.

MARGARET WHEATLEY, *Leadership and the New Science*[1]

Spiderwebs are both the strongest and the most fragile structures in the world. Pound for pound, spiderwebs are stronger than steel, yet they can stretch to nearly 40 percent of their length. They can also break with just the touch of a finger.

The construction of spiderwebs was an apt metaphor for relationships long before the World Wide Web became our new medium for meeting and greeting. Relationships can be resilient or tenuous. They can stretch when tested, or they can break at the first sign of heavy winds. Joie de Vivre faced a hurricane in the post-9/11 world.

With my industry in a downward spiral, I felt like the prey caught in a web, stuck in circumstances that felt almost insurmountable. Fortunately, my nightly dose of Maslow gave me some hope that by tapping into basic human motivation, Joie de Vivre could capitalize on the relationships it had built over the years and create even stronger ones to transcend the challenges of the moment. By focusing on the construction of our relationship web with employees, customers, and investors, I came to discover the Relationship Truths, or three pyramids, that became the foundation of our success story.

Using the principles I will briefly outline in this chapter and explore more deeply in the next nine chapters of the book, Joie de Vivre was able to leverage these truths so that, as the proverbial Bay Area hotel revenue pie shrunk, our slice of the pie grew dramatically.

JOIE DE VIVRE'S WEB OF RELATIONSHIPS

My company is composed of a complicated web of relationships. We operate more than 40 businesses that generate nearly $250 million in annual revenue. We have created a unique name and identity for each business that is part of the Joie de Vivre family. We are an owner in just under half of the hotels, but in not one of them are we a majority partner. Of the hotels in which we have an ownership stake, there are more than a hundred different investors representing more than a dozen different ownership entities. That's the simple part.

The rest of our hotels are owned by everyone from Wall Street investment firms to small-time local real estate owners. In each of these hotels, we are a third-party manager, just like Hilton might be with a hotel they manage that bears their name but which they do not own. From the perspective of our employees and customers, most don't know which ones we own versus which we purely manage. But I can tell you, the owners certainly know.

All in all, we have nearly 30 different ownership groups to whom we're accountable. This is not unusual for a hotel management company. What was unusual in the previous decade is that the world fell apart, and regionwide hotel revenues dropped by an unprecedented 50 percent in Silicon Valley and nearly 35 percent in San Francisco over a three-year period. Imagine your company's revenues being cut in half virtually overnight. All of Joie de Vivre's hotels were located in this worst-in-the-nation region, and many competed in the same geographic or price submarket. One thing a downturn will teach you is which relationships in your life—both inside and outside of work—are secure and which ones are not.

If any of us on the Joie de Vivre leadership team forgot for a day that relationships were at the heart of our business, we were quickly reminded of the fact by one of innumerable nervous or agitated investors or owners. Each of these ownership groups wanted to feel like they were our top, and in some cases our only, priority.

Understandably, with their money at risk and the dire hotel economy only getting worse, these investors needed constant assurance that we were focused on their hotel. Further complicating things, they needed to trust that another one of our Joie de Vivre properties down the street wasn't cannibalizing their business.

We faced a similarly difficult challenge navigating the web of our employee and customer relationships. Some of our hotel employees are represented by unions. Others are not. In some cases, there are four different unions representing various job classifications within the same hotel. And of course, nearly half of our employees are immigrants to the United States and speak English as a second or third language, so there are a variety of cultural factors at work. As for our customers, our largest corporate account represents less than 2 percent of our total revenues, so we have a lengthy list of individuals and groups to whom we're accountable as our regular patrons. It's not like we can sign one corporate sales agreement to change our fortunes overnight, as might be the case in another industry.

I became supremely aware of how far we could stretch our relationships during the downturn. Most economists think of employees as "units of production," customers as "units of consumption," and investors as "units of investment." I came to realize that there is no one unit of production because employees are influenced by their motivation, capacity, and the tools we've made available to them, and their results are a function of these influencers. Similarly, not all customers or investors approach their relationship with a company in the same way. In sum, many business observers view these units as fixed commodities (like steel) when, in fact, they truly are flexible (like a web), depending on how these relationships have been nurtured or spun.

THE VALUE OF RELATIONSHIPS IN THE WORKPLACE

As I was preparing to write this book, I read nearly a hundred books and scholarly articles on the nature of relationships in the workplace. One of the most fascinating articles was cowritten by a business school professor and a management consultant (Ranjay Gulati and David Kletter) in the *California Management Review*. This article, "Shrinking Core, Expanding Periphery: The Relational Architecture of High-Performing Organizations," posits that "winning companies define relationships in a very consistent, specific, and multi-faceted manner."[2]

Gulati and Kletter conducted a survey of Fortune 1000 senior executives for their article to understand the nature of "relationship-centered organizations." What the results showed is that sustained performers are set apart from their competitors by a higher willingness to engage in activities that increase the longevity of their relationships, both internally and externally. This was particularly true in a downturn.

From a Hierarchy of Needs perspective, however, we witness what seems to be a natural tendency for companies and people to get stuck at the bottom of the pyramid when faced with an economic recession. Fear breeds the need for safety and security. And this race to the bottom of the pyramid can lead to a downward spiral of declining employee morale, customer satisfaction, and financial performance.

In a troubled time, more than two-thirds of the top-performing firms (top 25 percent) in Gulati and Kletter's survey devoted their primary focus to heightening their awareness of their customers' needs while the bottom-performing companies devoted more of their attention to cutting costs and shedding underperforming assets. Gulati and Kletter conclude that it is just as important for a company to manage, monitor, and measure their relational capital as it is to do the same with their financial capital. In fact, one could argue that the relational health helps create the financial success.

When you talk to successful business leaders about some of their greatest career memories, you often hear them talk about the deep relationships they created in a downturn. The shared experience of authentically facing vulnerability and the sense of connectedness that comes from a focused team can create a true self-actualizing experience in the workplace. We observe this behavior from enlightened leaders and successful companies. Unfortunately, too many companies and business leaders, when faced with mounting financial pressures, take the opposite approach: they create a bunker mentality with senior leaders providing no face time to the troops or customers.

But being smart in today's workplace means understanding and interacting with people. Daniel Goleman, the best-selling author of books on emotional intelligence, says, "After analyzing 181 competence models from 121 organizations world-wide, we found that

67 percent of the abilities deemed essential for effective performance were emotional competencies. Compared to IQ and expertise,
emotional competence mattered twice as much."[3]

Goleman also found that feelings are contagious—positive even
more so than negative. The limbic system of the brain is character-
ized as an open loop, and it relies heavily on connections. The
mood of an organization has a causal effect on everyone within that
organization. This scientific research just reinforces my comment in
the last chapter about the fear ripples or tsunamis that can occur in
a company. Creating good *psychohygiene* in your company is one of
the most valuable steps you can take, especially during difficult
times.

When Joie de Vivre's hotels started seeing double-digit revenue
drops in 2001, I didn't sequester myself and my leadership team
inside a cocoon, analyzing our strategy, organizational processes, or
how we needed to cut expenses. Our senior leaders spent as much
time as possible interacting with our line-level employees and
managers, our regular customers, and our loyal investors.

You may remember I've mentioned Fred Reichheld, the Bain &
Company consultant who has written a number of books on the
value of loyalty. His first book, *The Loyalty Effect*, persuasively argued
that companies obsessively focused on employee and customer
loyalty created greater economic growth and reduced recruiting,
sales, and marketing costs. This makes so much sense because most
of your new employees and customers cost the business in their
early years and become more profitable over time. Reichheld was
able to show that an increase in customer retention rates of just
5 percent could increase profits by 25 to 95 percent, depending on
the industry. And these companies typically grew revenues at more
than twice the rate of their competitors. He writes, "Quite likely the
only possible source of sustainable competitive advantage in the
new economy will be the bonds of loyalty you generate. . . . Human
capital, unlike other assets, does not depreciate over time. Like
good wine, it actually improves with age."[4]

Perhaps the quintessential example of the importance of workplace relationships is Southwest Airlines. Author Jody Hoffer Gittell
wrote in *The Southwest Airlines Way* about how the company has
created a bundle of mutually reinforcing organizational practices
that allow it to have spectacular internal and external relationships.
Through statistical analysis, the author was able to show that
relational coordination led to shorter airplane turnaround times,

greater employee productivity, fewer customer complaints, and fewer lost bags. The book also shows that in post-9/11 times, when most of Southwest's competitors were in true downward spirals financially and culturally, Southwest had an organizational resilience that allowed it to rise to the occasion. It was the only major American airline to show consistent profitability during this trying time. Gittell sums up the book with the following thoughts, "For Southwest's leaders, taking care of business literally means taking care of relationships. . . . They believe that to develop the company, they must constantly invest in these relationships."[5]

Based on all this evidence, you'd think that the number one investment modern companies would make is in their relationship architecture and processes. Yet, former Xerox Corporation Palo Alto Research Center director John Seely Brown (coauthor of *The Social Life of Information*) says companies have instead invested 95 percent of their spending on business processes, and only 5 percent has gone toward supporting ways to mine a corporation's human capital. Once again, the tangibles of processes overrule the intangibles of people.

INTRODUCING THE RELATIONSHIP TRUTHS

In Chapter Two, I introduced the organizing principle of the Transformation Pyramid, which suggested that Maslow's Hierarchy of Needs could be distilled down to three essential levels: survive, succeed, and transform. We use these three levels to consider the true motivators for employees, customers, and investors, as these are the most important stakeholders in most businesses. I have organized these stakeholders into three pyramids that I call the *Relationship Truths*. We will examine each of these pyramids in the light of survival, success, and transformation over the next nine chapters. But let me first give you a summary of the key principles of the three pyramids and what lies ahead.

Companies often misjudge the true motivations of their employees, imagining that compensation is their primary aspiration. Similar to Maslow's placing physiological needs at the base of the pyramid, *money* (or, more broadly, the full compensation and benefits package) is a base need but also a base motivation for most employees. Loyalty and inspiration are fostered further up the pyramid. *Recognition* needs to be viewed broadly; it's about not

RELATIONSHIP TRUTH 1: THE EMPLOYEE PYRAMID

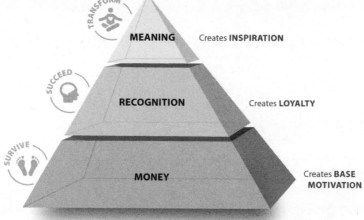

only knowing someone's name but also their talents, goals, and dreams. At the top of the Employee Pyramid is a concept that few employers talk about or even think about (because it's less tangible than the subject of money). Finding *meaning* in one's work—both in what you do daily and in the company's sense of mission—creates a more inspired employee. On each of these three levels of the Employee Pyramid, you'll see a duality that gives you choices about how you address this particular need. For example, there are two ways to address the issue of money: through looking at the wage or salary and through the traditional or unique benefits you offer. Similarly, there are both informal and formal means of recognition. Finally, meaning can come intrinsically from what an employee does, or more broadly, from what the organization does.

Just like money is at the bottom of the Employee Pyramid, *meeting the expectations* of customers is the survival need for this second Relationship Truth. Most companies spend too much time just trying to achieve basic customer satisfaction at the bottom of this pyramid. Purely creating customer satisfaction won't necessarily tame your customer's tendency to wander in an increasingly promiscuous marketplace. Tapping into customers' *desires* can be a means of creating differentiation, which can be your cure in a progressively commoditized world. When customers' desires are met, they are substantially more likely to come back for more, and they tell others.

RELATIONSHIP TRUTH 2: THE CUSTOMER PYRAMID

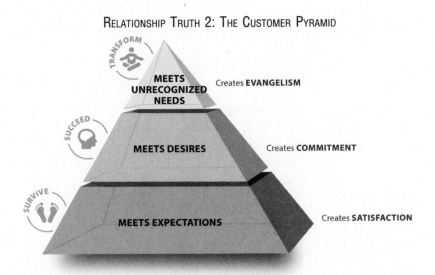

Frederick W. Smith, the chair and CEO of FedEx, sums up the top of this pyramid: "We thought we were selling the transportation of goods; in fact, we were selling peace of mind."[6] Most companies think too narrowly about who they are and whom they're serving. Rarely do they consider searching out and meeting the *unrecognized needs* of their customers. Instead, at best they create focus groups to listen to their customers' conscious wishes. But companies like Airbnb, Apple and Harley-Davidson have become highly successful cult brands by creating self-actualizing experiences for their customers.

There would be no employees or customers if there weren't a capital source for the business. This Relationship Truth addresses what a company can do to meet the needs of its investors. Many of us think that the only need an investor has is to make bucketfuls of money. No doubt investors' base premise is that they want to ensure a strong return on investment. To facilitate this, they need to have *transaction alignment* with the company executives or, in a start-up, with an entrepreneur. Establishing parallel goals will create *trust*.

Yet, just being aligned on the key goals for a particular investment creates a short-term, transactional relationship. Moving beyond this basic survival level is the idea of creating a collaborative partnership in which an entrepreneur or company and its investor see the relationship as being the core to why they do business together as opposed to having the transaction or business act as the

RELATIONSHIP TRUTH 3: THE INVESTOR PYRAMID

TRANSFORM

LEGACY   Creates **PRIDE OF OWNERSHIP**

SUCCEED

RELATIONSHIP ALIGNMENT   Creates **CONFIDENCE**

SURVIVE

TRANSACTION ALIGNMENT   Creates **TRUST**

glue that keeps this relationship alive. At the core of *relationship alignment* is the idea that an investor has built deep *confidence* in the people they are investing in, and they have likely built a close personal relationship as well. On this level, an investor's social and esteem needs may be met. Finally, at the top of the Investor Pyramid is the transformative nature of what investing can mean in making a difference in the world. A self-actualized investor is one who sees the *legacy* in his or her investing, whether it's in some breakthrough of a new product that will revolutionize an industry, in the socially responsible results of what the company does, or in how this investment and the investor's counsel can help a mentor relationship build with a budding entrepreneur so they can live up to their full potential. When investors invest in this manner, they experience *pride of ownership.*

THE POWER OF THE PYRAMID

What's common about each of the pyramids is they move from tangible elements at the bottom to intangible elements at the top—just like the Hierarchy of Needs goes from food, water, and sleep to the peak experience of self-actualization. And you'll see that what's created at the top layer of the pyramids is something meaningful, whether it's inspiration, evangelism, or pride of ownership.

Pyramids provide a powerful metaphor for progression that is different from a ladder or some other geometric shape. Pyramids get narrower at the top, which seems to suggest that it is more challenging the higher one ascends. Certainly, the traditional corporate pyramid suggests that the narrowness at the top means there's only a small collection of folks running the company (hopefully that narrowness isn't a reflection of the nature of the minds at the top).

Each of these three pyramids has a survival base, a success-oriented midlevel, and a transformative peak. Human beings cannot survive by spending all of their time on self-actualization without attending to their physiological needs. Similarly, some nonprofit organizations focus the whole employee experience on the sense of meaning that's created in the workplace—at the risk of losing employees because their compensation doesn't cover their rent. And some creative start-ups focus too much on imagining their customers' unrecognized needs—at the risk of neglecting the base expectations of their customers.

The reality is that most companies have the opposite problem. They spend too much of their time focused on the base of the three pyramids, thinking that moderately motivated employees, barely satisfied customers, and transactionally driven investors will transform them into an industry leader. Transformation happens at the peak of the pyramid, and it cascades down from there. Unprecedented loyalty comes from the peak experiences we've been able to create for our employees, customers, and investors. I intuitively have always believed, but now empirically know, that what people remember in business isn't the mundane day-to-day details; it's the peak experiences that create lifelong inspiration, evangelism, and pride of ownership. Peak experiences create lasting impressions.

These Relationship Truths are the relational mojo that makes diverse companies from Starbucks to Google successful. These three pyramids will provide you the opportunity to create a dialogue in your company about how you address the self-actualizing needs of your employees, customers, and investors. Most business leaders want to consider new ways to think about their key stakeholders. The Relationship Truths provide a language to make the intangible more tangible.

Most of us spend our lives focusing on what *is,* but Abe Maslow reminded us to focus on what *could be.* This transformational perspective is just as relevant to a company as it is to an individual. Maslow expressed how relevant he believed companies could be to the transformation of the world when he wrote, "This is the simplest way of saying that proper management of the work lives of human beings, of the way in which they earn their living, can improve them and improve the world and in this sense be a utopian or revolutionary technique."[7]

For me, the Relationship Truths were heaven sent. They proved that I didn't have to be the supreme leader trying to solve all of the organization's problems unilaterally. I could engage our talented operations managers and senior leaders in a discussion about how we were addressing the true human motivations of our employees, customers, and investors. And the more empathic our people became about these motivations, the easier it was for them to feel empowered to create solutions.

RECOMMENDED READING

Emotional Intelligence by Daniel Goleman
Love Is the Killer App by Tim Sanders
"Shrinking Core, Expanding Periphery: The Relational Architecture of High-Performing Organizations" by Ranjay Gulati and David Kletter, *California Management Review* (Spring 2005)
The Loyalty Effect by Fred Reichheld
The Maslow Business Reader by Abraham Maslow (edited by Deborah Stephens)
The Soul of the Firm by C. William Pollard
The Southwest Airlines Way by Jody Hoffer Gittell

PART TWO

RELATIONSHIP TRUTH 1: THE EMPLOYEE PYRAMID

Work is about daily meaning as well as daily bread; for recognition as well as cash; in short, for a sort of life rather than a Monday-through-Friday sort of dying. . . . We have a right to ask of work that it include meaning, recognition, astonishment and life.

STUDS TERKEL, *WORKING*[1]

CHAPTER FOUR

CREATING BASE MOTIVATION

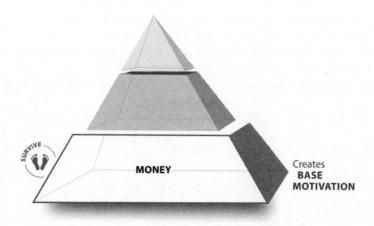

*Money isn't the most important thing in life, but it's reasonably
close to oxygen on the "gotta have it" scale.*

ZIG ZIGLAR, AUTHOR AND MOTIVATIONAL SPEAKER[1]

I had one talent in my younger years that bordered on Olympian. Throw me into a backyard swimming pool with a collection of other kids, and I could hold my breath underwater longer than any of them. I would challenge my fellows to the Big Gulp, submerge, and watch them turn a slight shade of blue before they raced to the surface a half-minute later. I don't remember at what point I found out that the Olympics did not award a medal for this stunt—and that only magicians and madmen did it in their adulthood.

As an adult, I came to realize that many entrepreneurs also practice the Big Gulp when their business requires them to stop taking a salary. I stopped taking a salary in April 2001, thinking it would just be temporary and San Francisco hotel occupancies would start recovering once the dot-com bubble burst was behind us. I was wrong; the length of the tourism depression that afflicted the San Francisco hotel industry made the Big Gulp that I took in my youth look like what it was: child's play.

During the next few years, I became painfully aware of both my employees' and my own base needs on the Employee Pyramid. As our revenues dropped, so did our net income. Soon after 9/11, we were faced with a moment of reckoning. As we approached our typically slow winter season ahead, the only way we could survive as a company was if we trimmed our payroll. Where was that going to come from? Layoffs? Reduced wages for our room attendants and bellmen? Or were we going to take a different approach that acknowledged something that few CEOs seem to address? When the going gets tough, the people who can least afford payroll cutbacks are the people at the bottom of the compensation pyramid. So instead, I continued my Big Gulp of not taking a salary and convinced our senior executives to take a 10 percent pay cut for at least two years. And all of our salaried employees (who typically make more than our hourly wage earners) accepted a pay freeze for more than two years.

I came face-to-face with my own base needs as I went without a salary for more than three and a half years. I cashed out all of my retirement savings to cover the monthly payments on the two mortgages on my home (I added one mortgage early in the downturn), and I invested everything I had in covering the cash losses of Joie de Vivre and those hotels that we owned. Those outside of the company might have perceived that I was wealthy, but my experience isn't unusual for many real estate entrepreneurs in a downturn: asset rich and cash poor.

Perhaps more than anything else, the experience of being flat broke and having to borrow money from friends rekindled my empathy for the challenges paycheck-to-paycheck workers face every day. Those of us at the top of the traditional corporate hierarchy tend to think that we earn the big bucks because our jobs are so stressful, but I can tell you that those at the bottom of the hierarchy experience a "just-getting-by" type of stress that most CEOs couldn't even imagine.

Although news headlines are filled with public company CEOs who make multimillion-dollar bonuses on the backs of their employees during hard times, my story isn't that unique. Many business leaders, especially entrepreneurs, face these tough choices. If you're a karmic capitalist interested in preserving a long-term enterprise full of trust with your employees, you make the right choice and acknowledge that your lowest-paid employees deserve the greatest support during the most difficult times.

American broadcaster Edward R. Murrow once said, "The obscure we eventually see, the completely obvious takes longer." Boy, is this true in my industry! Why is it that hotels value their hangers more than they do their employees? The captains of the hotel industry have been smarter at securing their clothes hangers to the closet poles than they have been at holding onto their employees. The average hotel has something between 75 and 100 percent turnover annually, which is truly embarrassing. I'm proud to report that Joie de Vivre's turnover hovers around 25 percent—partly because of how much we focus on the people issues in our company.

Founder and former CEO of Four Season Hotels and Resorts Isadore Sharp says, "Designing service to help busy people make the most of their precious time can be challenging. Because we can't pre-check it or sample it, production and consumption are simultaneous. Those few moments of service delivery are a company's make-or-break point, when reputation is either confirmed or denied. And the outcome in our industry normally depends on front-line employees: doormen, bellmen, waiters, room attendants—the lowest-paid people, and often, in too many companies, the least motivated. These front-line employees represent our product to our customers. In the most realistic sense, they are the product."[2] Hotel owners spend millions on architectural monuments to differentiate their physical product, yet rarely do they spend the time or money to consider what investing in their people could give them as a competitive edge.

THE BASE OF THE EMPLOYEE PYRAMID

Although the base of the Employee Pyramid is Money, this needs to be considered more broadly than just the size of the paycheck and the variety of employee benefits. Most companies are moderately savvy about paying a competitive basic wage or salary. Therefore, it's likely there's not significant differentiation between you and your competitors when it comes to your pay scales. First, ask yourself if your base pay is sufficient for your employees to feel that their survival needs are being met, and consider how much worry about job security exists in your workplace. As Maslow taught us, your employees can't focus on their higher needs when they have an empty stomach and fears about how the rent is going to be paid. Most American employees find that their wage or salary does pay the rent, so it's really the tangible and intangible benefits that differentiate you as an employer in the eyes of your employees. With this in mind, as I talk about money in this chapter, know that I will be addressing the full compensation package, including unique benefits, with respect to most of my comments. And we will climb the Employee Pyramid over the balance of Part Two by focusing on the recognition and meaning needs of employees in the next two chapters.

As the CEO of a company that's composed of 85 percent hourly wage earners in arguably the most expensive part of the country, I know that the compensation package is critical for our employees. In fact, I started thinking about this Money-Recognition-Meaning pyramid even before I got reacquainted with Maslow in the hospitality downturn because during the late 1990s, we were regularly having our employees cherry-picked by dot-coms recruiting in a robust San Francisco economy with just a 1 percent unemployment rate. I remember one employee who was making $12 per hour as a front-desk host (we call front-desk clerks *hosts* because it's a better description of their role). She was offered nearly $50,000 per year to join the customer service phone force of a new, cash-rich dot-com. This employee called me, almost in tears, apologizing for the fact that she was going to leave the company, but once she told me about the woes of trying to make ends meet on her wage, I completely sympathized with her decision.

During the dot-com boom, we had to increase our base wages at twice the inflation rate (as rental housing costs were rising 20 percent per year), develop unique compensation perks beyond the wage, and focus our efforts on providing recognition and meaning—benefits that were so powerful that they helped our employees feel good about staying in their jobs. We were obsessive about listening to our employees as we tried to understand what would make them more likely to stay without breaking the company piggybank. Maslow believed that you could learn a lot by the "grumbles and complaints," as he acknowledged, "human beings will always complain."[3] Our Joie de Vivre team knew that once we started hearing "higher-level complaints," like what kinds of classes we were teaching in "JDV University" or how often we had fun company events, we had moved our employees beyond the base of the pyramid mindset.

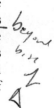

GOOGLE IS PEAKING

My company, and industry, is the exception to the rule in an increasingly white-collar America. Your company may look more like Google, a high-tech company with few employees who are stuck at the bottom of the pyramid. Google is a very Maslovian company. It pays competitively, but this is not why people join the company, especially after their splashy and profitable initial public stock offering already passed long ago. One key differentiator at the base of the Google employee pyramid is the over-the-top benefits and perks it offers, from the free company cafes with gourmet organic cuisine to deeply discounted massages to free car washes. The company almost thinks of its corporate campus as a well-run luxury resort with Google employees as the guests. In fact, the better Google treats its "guests," the longer they're likely to stay (both in number of years and in hours in the day).

The first time I walked onto Google's headquarters campus in Silicon Valley (known as the "Googleplex"), I felt like I'd discovered Shangri-La University. The average age of the multicultural employee base seemed to be around 26. The first thing I noticed were the two Endless Pools with two Googlers swimming against the current. Just beyond that was a sand volleyball court with an outrageously competitive two-on-two match between beach-boy-looking techies. Then there was the large open-air farmer's market of fresh produce that employees could stock up on. There were a few dogs roaming around on the grass as Google employees, each with their own laptop, were talking in the sun. Is there a value to all of these small perks? Clearly there is, because when you can take a free shuttle to work in luxury buses with Wi-Fi, have free recreational opportunities all over the campus, receive free gourmet meals at one of 11 upscale cafeterias, can visit one of five free on-site doctors, and have the comfort of free child care, the net result is that Google employees can start the workweek with $80 in their wallet and can end the workweek with exactly the same amount. As one of my Google friends says, "They make life simple for us." The company even offers unlimited sick days to its employees.

Google is also well-known for their "Search Inside Yourself" mindfulness programs cocreated by Chade-Meng Tan, who wrote a bestselling book by the same name. Now, any company can tap into these programs because the Search Inside Yourself Leadership Institute (https://siyli.org) offers workshops on mindful leadership.

Not surprisingly, one of Google's chief competitors for employees, Facebook, has also pursued a comprehensive approach to thinking about the base of their employee pyramid. They invited me to speak at their global assembly of HR leaders as they launched a new initiative, Life@Facebook.

Vice President of Human Resources Tudor Havriliuc explains, "*Peak* was one of the sources of inspiration for Life@Facebook, our comprehensive approach to caring for our people, as well as those who matter to them. We felt it was important to do much more than offer competitive compensation, so we built programs and provided resources to help our employees in the most important areas of their lives: community, family, health, time-away, financial future, personal and professional growth, and perks of convenience. As a result of this new approach, 96 percent of people at Facebook believe or strongly believe the company cares for them."[4]

Corporate generosity with perks isn't limited to Silicon Valley. Promega, based just outside Madison, Wisconsin, has offered a deluxe fitness center on their corporate campus since the 1980s as well as mindfulness offerings—from yoga, massage, and meditation—since the 1990s. Their campus is based upon the premise of bringing the outside in with natural materials and a connection with the local landscape. Employees are offered garden space for personal use and the company garden helps create a healthy menu in the corporate dining spaces. Lastly, they've experimented with a program called ESI (Emotional and Social Intelligence) Bootcamp that helps employees learn skills for self-awareness in the form of empathy, discernment, and courage.

I've been fortunate to give hundreds of *Peak* speeches on six continents and to witness some remarkable stories of companies that have adopted a *Peak* operating perspective. But no company has impressed me more than Liderman, one of the largest security companies in South America. As you can imagine, the South American security business is fraught with challenges given the variety of issues that CEO (and Guardian of the Culture) Javier Calvo Perez Badiola cited for me: police corruption, organized crime, low pay, and low regard by the general public. Liderman, which has now been ranked the Best Place to Work in Latin America, took this very seriously as it really hurt their recruiting efforts. Incorporating all kinds of *Peak* programs, they came up with a dozen different initiatives that bolstered their employees' sense of being valued at work. Some of the more notable ones include:

- They created a radio show for the graveyard shift (when many security guards work) that reached out to more than their employees, and became the most popular late night show in the country, which helped amplify Liderman's core values.
- They developed a course called "Value Your Spouse" that helped the almost-exclusively male guards learn how to treat their mates better, and a "<u>Lunch with your Family</u>" program where the boss visits the guards and their families at home, bringing a meal and presents for the kids.
- They moved up payroll dates to the 12th and 28th of each month so employees felt like they were getting paid earlier than their friends at other companies, and it helped them to pay the rent and other first-of-the-month bills earlier.

In sum, the best companies in the world—whether they employ expensive software engineers or security guards—tailor their compensation and benefits package to meet the unique needs of their *colaboradores* (the Spanish word for *contributors* and one that I use often since work is meant to be an inspiring collaboration).

BIGGER THAN MONEY

Many recent studies have shown that the majority of companies expressed confidence that increased compensation was the *best way* to retain their employees. I couldn't disagree more. Employees' perception of the value they receive from their work is complex. How do you value giving up your work friends or the beautiful surroundings or the flex-time benefits or the comfortable relationship you have with your direct supervisor? On the margin, money is not a primary motivator once employees have moved beyond their basic needs. Peter Drucker said, "We have known for 50 years that money alone does not motivate to perform. Dissatisfaction with money grossly demotivates. Satisfaction with money is, however, mainly a 'hygiene factor.'"[5]

Frederick Herzberg's well-known writings about intrinsic versus extrinsic benefits have suggested that money is a foundational need that shouldn't be ignored, especially in a low-wage industry. But he also writes, "Ask workers what makes them unhappy at work, and you'll hear about an annoying boss, a low salary, an uncomfortable work space, or stupid rules. Managed badly, environmental factors make people miserable, and they can certainly be de-motivating. But even if managed brilliantly, they don't motivate anybody to work much harder or smarter. People are motivated, instead, by interesting work, challenge, and increased responsibility. These intrinsic factors answer people's deep-seated need for growth and achievement."[6]

Former Harley-Davidson CEO Rich Teerlink and his internal consultant Lee Ozley write in *More Than a Motorcycle* about how they mixed Maslow and Herzberg into the powerful compensation cocktail that helped jump-start the company's fortunes two decades ago: "Gaps existed between the *theory* behind Harley's compensation practices and the *reality* of the company and its workers. Harley's next task . . . was to come up with a new compensation theory that squared better with reality."[7]

Based on deep discussions within the senior Harley leadership team, the organization decided that four deeply rooted psychological pillars would define how the company viewed its compensation policy:

1. Give employees the opportunity to act on their intrinsic motivation whenever possible.
2. Realize that salaries and benefits are only a part of a totality of rewards and recognition.
3. Fairness is an integral part of whether employees feel well compensated: fairness compared with workers at other companies and fairness relative to fellow Harley employees.
4. Make sure rewards and recognition for Harley employees or teams are congruent with the overall company goals.

We could all learn a few things from Harley-Davidson. The company has one of the most loyal workforces in American business. A few years ago, I had the good fortune of being a consultant to Harley-Davidson regarding a new development project it was considering. From what I witnessed, I can attest that they are an outstanding example of the truism that the biggest differentiator between an average company and a great company is the motivation of the people within the company. Harley-Davidson got it right by aligning compensation and recognition in a way that both motivated its employees and was congruent with the company goals.

While money may pay the bills, it doesn't necessarily buy happiness. The father of the resurgent positive psychology movement and author Martin Seligman writes in *Authentic Happiness*, "Our economy is rapidly changing from a money economy to a satisfaction economy."[8] Americans are looking for more than just another buck. Just like individuals have Hierarchies of Need, so do countries. America is rapidly escalating up the pyramid toward the more intangible benefits that come with recognition and meaning. We'll learn more about that in the next two chapters.

HOW SOLID IS THE BASE OF YOUR PYRAMID?

What does it take to ensure that the foundation of the Employee Pyramid, compensation, is solid and that employees' base needs are met? Money is a tangible measuring stick that any employee can use to compare your company with a competitor. But there are numerous ways to create value. What's curious is why more employers don't look beyond the basic wage and salary they pay their employees when considering the compensation package.

Joie de Vivre conducts an annual work climate survey that helps us understand how we measure up versus the industry average in everything from compensation to recognition. We measure not just salary but a whole range of things that we value as an organization and that we believe contribute to overall employee satisfaction. Vigorously focusing on these results has allowed us to get to the point that, in one of our last surveys, 90 percent of our hotels were above the industry average with respect to overall employee satisfaction, 7 percent were at the average, and only 3 percent were below the average.

The cleverest bang-for-the-buck benchmarking tool we use is *Fortune* magazine's annual "100 Best Companies to Work For" survey that was conceived and is administered by the Great Places to Work Institute. Each year, we survey our employees and answer the detailed questions associated with our compensation practices, work environment, and culture. While we have yet to make it to the top 100, we do receive back a free set of results that shows our employees' "Trust Index" in the five broad areas of credibility, respect, fairness, pride, and camaraderie as well as 56 specific line items. We can compare ourselves with the "100 Best Benchmarks" on measures as diverse as whether our employees consider the company a "fun place to work" or whether our "people are paid fairly here for the work they do." These results are also broken down by job type, gender, age, years of service to the organization, racial or ethnic identity, and part-time versus full-time work status so that we can understand whether there are subgroups within the company that need more attention.

While the private statistics that we receive are interesting, reading the annual article (which usually appears early in the year) is a must for any executive who wants to understand best practices with respect to creative compensation. In reading this article, you'll learn that Timberland employees are offered a $3,000 subsidy to buy a hybrid automobile, that Eli Lilly gives its pregnant employees a month off before their due date, or that J. M. Smucker provides a 100 percent tuition reimbursement with no limit to the dollar amount.

Given that Genentech was rated number one on *Fortune* magazine's "100 Best Companies to Work For" list in 2006, and they're based in the Bay Area, I decided to study them from top to bottom to learn what it is that makes them the best company to work for in America. While it might appear that a multibillion-dollar multinational biotech firm may have little in common with a regional hotel company, we've learned it has a lot. A former Genentech senior human resources exec told me that the company's founders were so inspired with the history of the generous culture of Hewlett-Packard that they endeavored to create the "Rolls Royce of benefits" when they started the company. Most of these benefits were a little rich for Joie de Vivre's budget, but what impressed me most is that some of the benefits Genentech offers its employees are more Volkswagen than Rolls—like the Friday afternoon "ho-ho" (beer kegs in a courtyard) that's been a tradition for decades.

The biggest story in some of the most recent "100 Best Companies" results has been the trend toward compensation benefits that address work/life balance. Back in 1999, only 18 companies on the list allowed telecommuting; now 79 do. That number is now trending toward 90 percent as more and more companies offer compressed workweeks, such as four 10-hour days with Fridays off. From personal concierge services to take-home meals, companies are focusing on anything to make their employees' lives a little easier. And right they should.

In our time-compressed world, maybe the greatest compensation gift an employer can give its employees is time off. For this reason, for years, Joie de Vivre has offered its salaried (and some of its hourly) employees a one-month paid sabbatical every three years of continuous employment. The logic was simple. Our primary business, hotels, never shuts down, so our employees who don't have fixed eight-hour schedules have a great risk for burnout. Plus, we're in the business of housing people from all over the world and building friendships with these far-flung folks on a daily basis. Our staff gets to know these guests, hear about the stories of their exotic homeland, and even build pen-pal relationships with these visitors, many of whom get four to eight weeks of vacation per year (especially those from Europe). So, although it's unorthodox, a month-long sabbatical lets our employees take advantage of the international relationships they've built at the hotel as they get an extended opportunity to travel overseas, which is much less convenient if you have only two weeks off each year.

You can imagine the pressure we were under to terminate this perk when the Bay Area hospitality business fell off the cliff. Few hotel companies offer paid sabbaticals, and frankly, I'm not aware of *any* company that offers a month off every three years. So, sticking to our guns about the importance of this unique perk was a conversation we had regularly with some of our hotel investors and owners. Fortunately, we were persuasive enough that this perk made it through the downturn. To me, it was simple: Joie de Vivre's sabbatical policy was part of our company's DNA.

Fringe benefits are no longer considered fringe by many employees who see them as a pivotal part of their compensation package. At Joie de Vivre, we look for creative ways to compensate our employees beyond their base pay. We bought the largest day spa in San Francisco, the venerable Kabuki Springs and Spa, during the dot-com boom—not just because we thought it was

Time Share

a wise hospitality investment but also because we consciously decided that owning this property would enable us to provide employees with the additional benefit of half-price massages and free use of the exotic Japanese baths.

Similarly, because we operate more hotels in the region than anyone else, why not offer free hotel rooms for our cash-strapped employees who can't afford to travel very far? Based on the story I recounted in Chapter Two, you are aware that some of our hotels are popular with traveling musicians. So why not offer free concert tickets to our employees for those shows that aren't sold out (through the relationship we have with the various concert venues in town)? What perishable asset can your company make available to your employees that would boost their perception of their compensation package? For example, AstraZeneca, a pharmaceutical company, offers its employees free prescription drugs.

Perhaps the king of creative compensation is Ricardo Semlar, CEO of Semco in Brazil. In his book *The Seven-Day Weekend,* he outlines all kinds of interesting perks like customized health plans, but two in particular are worth noting:

1. Rush Hour MBA: A group assembles every Monday at 6 P.M. as a productive way for people to use the time they would otherwise spend sitting in Sao Paulo's rush-hour traffic; instead of wasting two hours commuting, people can attend lectures and classes in the headquarters.
2. Retire-a-Little: This program addresses the fact that when you're most adventurous and fit (at a younger age), you lack the finances to explore, but when you have the finances (at an older age), you often lack the stamina. With this program, employees can acquire from the company as much early retirement as they wish. You can reduce your pay and hours today and redeem them at a later time in your life with the company.[9]

Maybe a Brazilian company feels a little removed for you? Then, consider Ernst & Young, the global professional services firm with more than 100,000 employees worldwide, which has created a People First culture. Ernst & Young introduced a whole collection of new lifestyle-driven benefits, including permanent four-day holiday weekends around Memorial Day, Fourth of July, and Labor Day. This is a brilliant idea because it's a bit idiotic that we all jump on the highway and on airplanes at exactly the same time to celebrate these long weekends, thereby snarling the roads, airports, and train stations. This perk allows Ernst & Young employees to truly sink into a long weekend without having to deal with the traveling hassles of being on the road at the same time as everyone else.

Not to be outdone by their competitor Ernst & Young, PricewaterhouseCoopers (PwC) created a firmwide shut-down twice a year to ensure that people get a true break from their work. For about 10 days over Christmas and four or five days over the Fourth of July, PwC gives its employees the peace of mind that taking some time off doesn't mean they will miss an important meeting or be barraged with thousands of e-mails from coworkers when they return to work. Isn't it encouraging to see that competitors, like Ernst & Young and PwC, are also competing to see which can be the more benevolent employer?

Gary Erickson, founder and former CEO of Clif Bar, writes in *Raising the Bar* about unique perks from an on-site free washer and dryer for employees' personal use to the on-site hairstylist who makes the employees look good to the auto detailer who picks up cars and delivers them back to the employee lot. Who has time for all these off-hours chores? Clif Bar is smart to recognize that its employees' stress is reduced when the company helps support the little details of life that inevitably stack up.

Peak Prescriptions

How can your company better address the compensation needs of its employees? Are you confident these base needs are met? Which other companies can you emulate? Ask yourself—or your supervisor or your colleagues—to consider the following *Peak* Prescriptions:

1. Determine your employees' current state of mind with respect to your company's compensation package. If your company is not doing work climate surveys already, start doing them immediately, and don't assume that once per year is often enough. Do you survey your customers only once per year? Make sure you also do annual wage surveys versus your competitors.

2. Ask employees, "What one thing could we do as your employer to improve your package of benefits or your job

(*continued*)

(*continued*)

security?" Quite often, you can't give a large wage or salary increase, but you can consider unique perks that would meaningfully recognize the needs of your employees. The more you can do this in a customized way for each employee, the happier they'll be. The one-size-fits-all mentality doesn't work for customers or employees any more.

3. Ask departing employees what attracted them to their new job. Participate in *Fortune* magazine's annual 100 Best Companies competition. Acting like a "Best Company" may be good for your bottom line as these top 100 have had three to four times the stock market gain as the Standard & Poor's 500 during the past decade.

4. Do an internal audit of how well you internally publicize your compensation package to your employees. The results of your compensation survey with your competitors may show that you pay 10 percent better than they do, but your employees don't necessarily know that. Determine a way to educate your employees about that fact without sounding too self-congratulatory. Many companies distribute an annual "Total Compensation Statement" with a pie chart that outlines the direct base pay, incentive pay, benefit plans, retirement plans and social security, and other benefits like a car allowance. Making this visual could help your employees recognize that as much as 20 to 25 percent of their total compensation package comes from components that are beyond their base pay. You may offer a variety of unique perks deeply hidden in your employee manual. Rather than publicize the perks, give attention to those employees who have taken advantage of the perks with photos and stories in your company newsletter.

5. Search for perishable assets that would make a difference for your employees. These assets could be things your company produces or gifts you receive from suppliers, but often they could also be assets of your senior executive team. Your chief financial officer may have a ski chalet in the mountains or your vice president of marketing may have season tickets to your local minor or major league baseball team's games. Why not offer these as free perks to your employees, especially those who've surpassed certain goals? The chalet or stadium seats might just sit

empty on many days. This is also a great way to connect your senior execs with your line-level employees.

6. Form a senior executive team (that includes your highest-level human resources exec) and engage in a deep discussion regarding what unique strategy your company uses to address the Money level of the pyramid. Talk about some star performers who left the company, and ask whether it had anything to do with the Money level of the pyramid. Brainstorm some ways your company can become the best-practices leader with respect to providing a signature array of base pay, incentive pay, and unique perks. Consider whether the incentives you're offering your employees are well aligned with your key strategic goals.

But, as we next make our way up to the second level of the Employee Pyramid, let's realize that companies that get preoccupied at the Money level never transcend being an also-ran. Consider Zappos, the online retailer of shoes and apparel that was purchased by Amazon for nearly $1 billion. This peak performer decided to "bribe" their new employees to leave. All new employees, upon completing six days of training with the company, were offered $2,000 (has grown to $4,000) plus all they've earned so far to leave the company, and this offer stands for the balance of their four-week training and for the first three weeks past "graduation." Why does Zappos do this? CEO Tony Hsieh says it's because this offer assures that the company retains only those employees who are truly motivated by something higher on the Employee Pyramid than just money.

Money issues are particularly relevant for companies with hourly workers. Costco's employee turnover is reportedly one-fifth that of Wal-Mart largely because it offers a compensation package that is far superior to Wal-Mart's. The compensation package provided to Costco's employees—versus that at Wal-Mart—includes higher hourly wages, broader access to health care, and dramatically lower employee health care premiums. Approximately 80 percent of Costco's employees receive company-sponsored health care, for which the employee contributes just 8 percent of the cost.

Is it any wonder Costco's employee theft ratio is one-tenth of the industry average, a fact that saves the company millions of dollars each year?

While money is clearly necessary to meet the base needs of employees (and salary-deprived CEOs), it steadily recedes as the exclusive motivation when one progresses up the corporate ladder. Additional motivators come with affluence. Even when money seems to be a prime motivator for a big exec, it is often just a symbol of things found higher up the pyramid. We've all witnessed how some use money to try to buy esteem, a sense of belonging, and sadly, even love. This leads us to examine the second level of this pyramid: the recognition that creates employee loyalty.

RECOMMENDED READING

Authentic Happiness by Martin E. P. Seligman

"Extreme Jobs: The Dangerous Allure of the 70-Hour Workweek" by Sylvia Ann Hewlett and Carolyn Buck Luce, *Harvard Business Review* (December 2006)

"One More Time: How Do You Motivate Employees?" by Frederick Herzberg, *Harvard Business Review* (1968)

Raising the Bar by Gary Erickson and Lois Lorentzen

Search Inside Yourself by Chade-Meng Tan

The Motivation to Work by Frederick Herzberg et al.

"The 100 Best Companies to Work for 2006," *Fortune Magazine* (January 11, 2006)

"The High Cost of Low Wages" by Wayne F. Cascio, *Harvard Business Review* (December 2006)

The Seven-Day Weekend by Ricardo Semlar

CHAPTER FIVE

CREATING LOYALTY

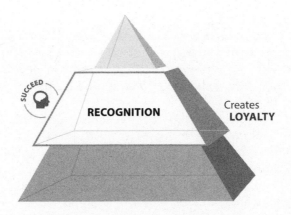

Compensation is a right; recognition is a gift.

ROSABETH MOSS KANTER, HARVARD PROFESSOR AND AUTHOR[1]

In the last half of the 1990s, there was a popular TV series full of philosophical witticisms that became the talk of corporate lunch-rooms, if not boardrooms. Young Boston attorney Ally McBeal, the anxious waif in a miniskirt, had a way of turning a phrase, such as "men are like gum; after you chew, they lose their flavor" or "we're women; we have a double standard to live up to."

If you were a fan of the show, you may recall that Ally (played by Calista Flockhart) had a therapist (played by Tracey Ullman) who told her, "You need a theme song. Something you can play in your head to make you feel better." So Ally and her therapist set about to finding the perfect theme song (with a Motown beat) to help Ally get through her days as a high-pressured attorney and her nights as a romantically challenged single gal. At Joie de Vivre, we figured, if it works for Ally, maybe it can work for us. We didn't create a theme song or some rah-rah cheer that we expected all employees to sing, but we did come up with a theme book that helps define our Joie de Vivre spirit. I've given away dozens and dozens of copies of the children's book *The Little Engine That Could* to our employees to show them my appreciation for their can-do attitude. This was prompted in part by what we learned from Market Metrix, the company that provides our employee and customer satisfaction reports. They discovered that the number one perception that correlates with the likelihood our guests will return is whether they believe our employees showed a can-do attitude with respect to providing them service.

As you may remember, *The Little Engine That Could* is about an overachieving train that is pressed into service to try to get children's toys over a mountain. Against everyone's expectations, the little blue engine is able to accomplish this by constantly reminding herself, "I think I can . . . I think I can . . . I think I can." Although simple and somewhat sentimental, this optimistic and resourceful message resonates well with Joie de Vivre's history and reputation as a David struggling among the Goliaths of the hospitality industry. But this resilient underdog message could also sum up the nature of much of our employee base of immigrant and not highly educated workers. Many of them arrive in this country against all odds and scratch out a living in one of the most expensive areas of the world. The fact that a room attendant is given this book personally by the company's CEO, with a customized inscription inside, makes the recognition all the sweeter. Plus, this employee can go home and share the story with his or her family. We believe that this is much more meaningful than some stale and obligatory plaque on the wall.

I'll never forget a thank-you note I received from Jill Plemons, one of our senior directors of sales at a couple of our hotels. She had been presented with the book in front of all of the Joie de Vivre salespeople to recognize her tenacity in sales during a time when her hotel's renovation project was constantly getting delayed. In Jill's note to me, she wrote, "Thank you so much for the book and recognition at our sales meeting. I cannot tell you how appreciative I am of this gesture. My grandfather was a railroad engineer, and this was an all-time favorite growing up." I'll bet that book was worth more than any random cash bonus we could have given her.

Maslow admired psychologist and philosopher William James, who died about the time Maslow was born. James once wrote, "The deepest principle in human nature is the craving to be appreciated."[2] Hunger is associated with craving. And, as physical hunger needs are met, the kind of hunger people feel most acutely is the hunger for recognition, which addresses the social and esteem needs on Maslow's hierarchy.

Jill's note reminded me that giving recognition could be just as rewarding as receiving it, especially when you realize how meaningful it is to the recipient. Every CEO should be issued a T-shirt with James' quote on it when they start their new job leading their company. Most organizations get so caught up with the tangibility of compensation issues that they forget that giving authentic recognition to peers is one of the greatest ways to ensure low turnover and high productivity. The irony is that compensation costs big dollars yet truly only satisfies base needs whereas recognition is an inexpensive gift that provides a huge bang for the buck in satisfying employees' higher needs. Then why do most companies spend the vast majority of their time focused on the bottom of the Employee Pyramid?

Although Mary Kay Ash, founder of the multibillion-dollar Mary Kay Cosmetics, is best known for recognizing her top salespeople with signature pink Cadillacs, the reality is this Texan's rise to the top was founded on her approach to "praising people to success." She advised her managers to "pretend that every single person you meet has a sign around his or her neck that says, 'make me feel important.' Not only will you succeed in sales, you will succeed in life."[3]

I wish Mary Kay had mentored my first boss, Mac, the guy I answered to when I worked at McDonald's for six weeks at age 14. Mac taught me something about employee loyalty (or lack thereof) that I later learned when reading the book *First, Break All the Rules: What the World's Greatest Managers Do Differently*. Authors and Gallup Organization execs Marcus Buckingham and Curt Coffman surveyed 80,000 managers in over 400 companies and discovered a truism: *"Employees join companies, but they leave their managers."*[4] I joined McDonald's, but I left Mac.

The Gallup folks found that the single most important variable in employee productivity and loyalty is not the pay, perks, benefits, or workplace environment. It's the quality of the relationship between employees and their direct supervisors. As Buckingham and Coffman described in *Fast Company* magazine, "What people want most from their supervisors is the same thing that kids want most from their parents: someone who sets clear and consistent expectations, cares for them, values their unique qualities, and encourages and supports their growth and development."[5] In fact, they found there were twelve key determinants that define a strong workplace. The six most powerful ones all have something to do with an employee and their boss, such as "Has the employee received recognition in the past week?" Or "Does his or her supervisor seem to care about the employee as a person?"

One of my favorite pastimes is to walk into an unfamiliar hotel, plant myself in the lobby, and just feel the vibe of the staff. I can usually get a sense of whether this hotel has a good employer (or more specifically, a good general manager) by the invisible report card the employees are wearing on their foreheads and in the actions I witness between employees and guests and among employees. Sometimes it's just noticing that the ubiquitous Employee of the Month plaque on the lobby wall hasn't been updated for months. If you are keen, you don't have to wait for your annual or twice-annual work climate or employee satisfaction surveys to determine whether you've got an engaged staff.

I welcome you to do this with one of Joie de Vivre's businesses. While we're not perfect, what you're likely to experience is the result of our culture of recognition. During the downturn, we were faced with an unrelenting torrent of bad news. In response, our chief people officer Jane Howard and the rest of our executive committee searched for ways we could create some good news or at least a good vibe among our employees. Some of the steps we took were simple and became habitual, like our former president Jack Kenny calling eight to ten employees per week to wish them happy birthday or to congratulate them on their anniversary of working for the company.

During the downturn, each of our hotels was encouraged to create its own unique approaches to recognition. We educated our managers that recognition was the gift that kept on giving in how it created positive goodwill during a time when the poor economy was instilling a lot of fear. As an example, our budget-priced Hotel Carlton has created some of the highest employee and customer satisfaction scores of all Bay Area hotels and was featured for this fact in the *Wall Street Journal.* The general manager did little things like asking new employees at their orientation to fill out a form entitled "My Personal Favorites" (favorite candy or style of music or book, etc.). Doing this allows our Carlton management team to provide customized rewards to that employee when we want to provide recognition for something they've done.

But our executive team realized that the companies that truly live and breathe a culture of recognition make sure it starts from the top. We take this issue seriously enough that we changed the way we end each of our weekly corporate executive committee (EC) meetings with the top 15 department heads in the company. As a ritual, at the end of each meeting, every EC member is given the opportunity to talk for a minute about someone in the company who deserves a little extra recognition and why. It could be a bellman who climbed six flights of stairs with dozens of bags for a German tour group when the elevator broke down or the front-desk host who, after her shift, sprinted to the airport to return a bag that a guest had forgotten (we even have a story of an employee, about to leave for a vacation in China, who offered to return a personal item to a recent guest of ours in Hong Kong). The stories are usually succinct yet nonetheless poignant. At the end of each story, an EC member from a different department volunteers to call, e-mail, or visit the employee in person to tell them what a great job they're doing.

This little institutionalized program could be enacted in any size company, but it's particularly relevant to Joie de Vivre because we've grown beyond 3,500 employees. Not only does it remind the senior execs in the company about who's in the trenches, but it also helps us feel good about what we're doing. And we had a real thirst for good news during the downturn. In addition, any fast-growing company will find that regularly exercising this recognition muscle will help break down the silos that start to develop between departments. When the director of technology calls a relatively new hotel salesperson to congratulate them on signing up their first corporate account, it sends the message that we're all in this together. The fact that the word has spread beyond their own department head gives that salesperson a sense that this is big news among the company's top execs.

WHY RECOGNITION RULES

What are the best practices of companies that have become strategic in their approach to recognition? First off, they follow best-selling author Bob Nelson's advice that "you get what you reward." If you want to understand what a company truly values, don't just read their mission statement on the wall; ask to see their institutionalized recognition programs and how these connect with the company's financial and strategic goals. Great companies establish a clear link between what people are rewarded for and the organization's priorities.

There are lots of statistics that reinforce how important recognition is in the workplace. In his book *Liberating the Corporate Soul*, Richard Barrett cites a study that shows that about 40 percent of the variability in corporate financial performance comes down to something as simple as employees' sense of fulfillment in the workplace. Further, nearly 70 percent of the variability in employee satisfaction is attributable to the quality of the employees' relationship with their manager. According to a study cited in Adrian Gostick and Chester Elton's *Managing with Carrots,* companies that have an employee recognition strategy show double the return to shareholders compared with those companies that don't have such a strategy.

DaVita is a multi-billion-dollar company dedicated to operating the best kidney dialysis centers in the world. With thousands of dialysis centers nationwide, CEO Kent Thiry knows it's essential that employees clearly understand the company's goals because there's a great risk that what matters at headquarters isn't translating to its tens of thousands of teammates in the field. When Thiry joined the company in 1999, DaVita was in financial default and didn't have a set of core values that defined its operation. Thiry engaged his employees to help create seven core values. Since then, every six to eight weeks, Thiry and his other senior execs call the entire group of 800 leaders who helped create the core values and ask them the question "What evidence is there that we are living and sustaining our core values?" And at the company's annual awards ceremony, Thiry presents awards to the dialysis centers that best exemplify each of those seven values, with the team from each being flown across the country to accept the awards (and receive a video of their speeches that they can share with their coworkers back home).

DaVita's operation has a lot of parallels to Joie de Vivre. In general, the employee base is not highly educated. Ninety percent of its staff is giving hands-on service to customers, so employee attendance is a critical component of the success of a dialysis center because there is very little slack in operational staffing. To align employee recognition with a company goal of minimal absenteeism, DaVita created a We Are Here award that recognizes companywide those employees each year who have perfect attendance. Each of these reliable teammates, who showed up on time every day that year, has their name placed in a hat. Every six months, 50 with perfect attendance records are randomly recognized with a $1,000 bonus, which is given to them at their dialysis center by a senior executive of the company (vice president level or up). DaVita has given away millions of dollars to thousands of employees since starting this recognition program, and the company now has, by far, the lowest absenteeism in their competitive subset. In addition, turnover has dropped in half at the company since it instituted this unique variety of recognition programs.

What recognition program can you put in place in your company that will align your employees' actions with the company's objectives?

CREATING A CULTURE OF RECOGNITION

Best recognition practices aren't limited to just formal companywide initiatives. Great companies educate and obligate their managers to provide one-on-one informal and formal feedback mechanisms to their subordinates to reinforce business objectives.

Informal recognition, which tends to be most prevalent in the workplace, includes actions like positive in-person or e-mail feedback or spontaneously giving someone a small gift as a token of appreciation. This can be powerful because it's in the moment, customized, frequent, and doesn't have to be limited to boss to employee; it can also be peer to peer. Formal recognition includes programs like the annual awards ceremony, the employee-of-the-month club, or the performance review supervisors give their subordinates. Formal recognition executed properly helps to publicly define the company's values and goals and can provide widespread acknowledgment to those receiving the recognition.

Companies that have created a culture of recognition tend to emphasize both informal and formal mechanisms whereas companies that are strong in the formal recognition but weaker in the informal represent a more *traditional recognition culture*. Often these traditional recognition cultures can be a little paternalistic and disconnected from their line-level employees.

On the opposite extreme is the *loose recognition culture*, which describes companies that have strong informal recognition but weak formalized mechanisms. These companies may offer a more collegial environment for employees, but often there's a bit of a disconnect between the company goals and the employees' actions. In fact, because formal recognition programs like employee reviews and companywide goals and rewards are not a high priority, this type of company runs the risk of creating a happy culture while experiencing poor execution of its business strategy.

The grid below shows all three of these recognition cultures, along with the *culture of neglect*, which is a place you certainly don't want to be.

COMPANIES THAT USE INFORMAL VERSUS FORMAL RECOGNITION

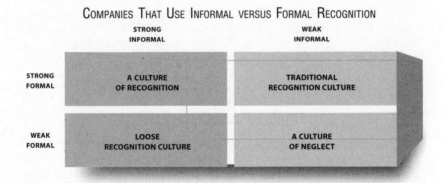

Let's look a bit deeper to understand what you can do to improve your informal and formal approaches to recognition.

One of the benefits of using the Employee Pyramid as a guide is that your leaders can have an internal dialogue about how your organization is addressing money, recognition, and meaning. Companies that consistently exhibit impressive amounts of informal recognition usually have a high emotional intelligence factor among their managers and employees. There's a friendliness and an openness to acknowledging the whole person in these types of company cultures.

For informal recognition to be effective, it must be (1) sincere and deserved, (2) specific and individualized, and (3) offered on a timely basis. Much of informal recognition is about creating a deeper connection with your employees. Providing positive feedback is a bit of an intimate act so many managers can sort of gloss over it or provide it in an abstract way. They say "great job" to someone as they're rushing out the door. No eye contact. No clarity on what "great job" they're referring to. No explanation of how the employee's actions made a specific difference. If the manager thought about it for a moment, he or she might realize that being specific about the recognition could help the employee understand how they can repeat that behavior.

Great recognition cultures have profound ways of training their managers about this stuff. In the book *The Southwest Airlines Way,* author Jody Hoffer Gittell outlines one method Southwest has used with an example involving three groups of supervisors-in-training:

> One member of each team was blindfolded and asked to throw a ball into a trashcan. Unknown to the throwers, one team could say nothing, the second was instructed to say only "good job" or "keep trying," and the third could give detailed information about where the bucket was. Not surprisingly, the third group had the most success. The person who had received the best instructions said, "I couldn't wait for it to be my turn again." "Wow!" said facilitator Chris Robbins. "How does that relate to work? How many agents do you think we have out there who are told nothing or just 'good job' instead of people really listening to them?"[6]

So the more specific and direct you can be, the more likely you'll see improvement in the members of your team.

How should you give feedback or recognition? Bob Nelson, author of *1001 Ways to Reward Employees,* is an expert on the subject and has surveyed thousands of employees. He's found that nearly 90 percent of employees feel that in-person praise is extremely or very important to them (as opposed to only partly important or not important at all). Compared on those same metrics, written praise scores only a little higher than 60 percent, e-mail praise was just under 50 percent, and voice-mail praise was only extremely or very important to 26 percent of the participants in this survey. So the mantra in your company should be "Whenever possible, connect with your people in person."

Not every recognition has to have a reward attached, but if you are going to provide some reward, it's best if it's (1) customized to the tastes or needs of the recipient, (2) publicly offered so that the honoree is held in higher esteem and others can be encouraged to follow suit, and (3) immediately available to the recipient so that there's some instant gratification.

The list of what you can do to promote informal recognition is endless. At Joie de Vivre, on occasion we do all of the following and more:

- Send a flower arrangement to the home of an employee who has been working extra-long hours on an assignment—to thank both the employee and his or her family.
- Give employees a surprise check as they leave on vacation to say thanks for their hard work.
- Take a junior employee along on a visit to see some dignitary just to acknowledge the employee's efforts.
- Make it a practice to create a list of two employees daily who deserve some extra credit; keep that list handy so that when you are commuting, you can use this time wisely by calling the employees (or leaving a voice mail if that's the only choice) and saying thanks for some specific accomplishment.

As for formal recognition, the key is to make sure things don't get stale. Has your annual awards dinner become a little too predictable? Are your awards truly addressing the key goals of the organization? Do you have the same collection of people organizing your same old collection of recognition events? Is your company newsletter dead on arrival from the perspective of your employees' interest in it? You may need some fresh blood with new ideas.

Formal recognition doesn't necessarily mean just some big annual awards dinner. Intuit spends 1.5 percent of its annual compensation budget recognizing employees. They have a formalized approach to something that sounds very informal. The human resources department has created a bag of tricks or rewards like all-expenses-paid weekend getaways that managers can access on a regular basis to thank their star employees. Similarly, Autodesk employees get to surprise coworkers with on-the-spot bonuses of $1,000. Programs like Autodesk's peer-to-peer bonuses and Intuit's bag of rewards have some of the flavor of the informal recognition programs I just described, but the cost and scope of these rewards require a more formal, systematic approach from the organization.

Often, best practice in formal recognition just means taking some vehicle you already have and making it better. I was fortunate to review Southwest Airlines' companywide employee newsletter, "Luv Lines," which came out soon after the Hurricane Katrina disaster in New Orleans. It was hard to read this newsletter without a lump in my throat, as the breadth and depth of the stories of heroism by Southwest employees in New Orleans was truly impressive. One whole section of the newsletter was dedicated to outlining every single job category, from maintenance and engineering employees to the crew schedulers, with an explanation of what extra steps these employees took in the wake of the disaster to not just help speed the recovery of the airline in that region but also in giving back to the community. It's one thing to say a generalized thanks to the employees. It's quite another to offer all Southwest employees this level of detail regarding each job classification.

At Joie de Vivre, we create a peak experience every year with our holiday party, an event that can often be formal and predictable at other companies. This event is so fun and heartwarming that we get dozens of former Joie de Vivre employees showing up each year to reconnect with the thousand or more members of our family who celebrate at this event. One of the most inspiring elements of this party is when we recognize our top performers of the year in seven different categories. We pay careful attention to recognizing all of the nominees (more than 100 people) with their names on a big screen. The finalists come to the stage, and the big winner of the evening (the Extraordinary Service award winner) wins a paid trip for two to some exotic place like Bali, plus an extra week of vacation. There's something magical about employees seeing one of their own, whether it be Horst the night auditor or Vivian the executive housekeeper or Marcel the spa bath attendant, win the award that will take them on a trip halfway around the world. In the downturn, we came painfully close to having to cancel this important tradition. In fact, many of our competitive Bay Area hotel companies cancelled their holiday parties to save money. But my belief is that in difficult times, these events strengthen the bond between our employees and us. In fact, it's even more important to create recognition and culture-producing events during the tough times.

We've found this awards party to be such a culture booster at Joie de Vivre that our company created San Francisco's first Hotel Hero awards for the entire local hospitality industry. At this annual event, the mayor and other dignitaries give out awards to the city's most deserving line-level employees from all San Francisco hotels in front of hundreds of their hospitality peers dressed in black tie and gowns. I came up with this idea in 2003 when it was becoming evident that the San Francisco hotel market's precipitous decline was creating a malaise for managers and line-level workers in our city's biggest industry. In addition, many of the city's hotels were distracted by, and distraught with, the prospect of upcoming adversarial union negotiations. The downward spiral that can affect any business felt like it was affecting our whole regional industry. As difficult as it was to create this new tradition from scratch, and with no start-up budget to work with, our chief development officer, Christian Strobel—who led the Hotel Heroes planning process—used our successful holiday party model as a means of creating a new citywide tradition. This event is one of my personal peak experiences each year because I get to feel the love bubble that's created when deserving doormen, bartenders, and room attendants are the stars for the night.

Another formal means of recognition that most companies can spice up is their corporate-wide goal of the year. Clearly, it's a best practice to have something that all employees can shoot for and, of course, there's often some financial incentive that comes with achieving that goal. At Joie de Vivre, we believe there's even greater mileage if we add some theatricality to meeting the goal. A few years ago, our former president, Jack Kenny, and I volunteered to have our heads shaved live onstage at our holiday party if the company met our can-do attitude goal of the year. While my receding hairline no longer makes this much of a stunt, I can tell you our employees appreciated this wacky payoff for our communal goal. More recently, when the company once again hit its can-do attitude score, Jack, our chief operating officer Fred DeStefano, and I dressed up like Diana Ross and the Supremes and performed "Ain't No Mountain High Enough" at our summer barbecue.

From Virgin's Richard Branson dressing in a wedding gown to Southwest Airlines' Herb Kelleher dressing like Elvis, CEOs have a long history of taking one for the team to celebrate and recognize some companywide goal. In the early 1980s, Sam Walton (Wal-Mart) challenged his employees to exceed an 8 percent pretax profit goal for the year. He said he would do the hula in a grass skirt on Wall Street if the employees in the company helped reach this goal. True to his word, that good ol' boy from Arkansas—accompanied by real hula dancers, ukulele players, and a bunch of Wal-Mart employees—sported a hula skirt for the mass media in the financial district canyons of the Big Apple when his company met its performance goals.

PEAK PRESCRIPTIONS

What can you do to create a culture of recognition in your company?

1. Develop a recognition training program for your midlevel managers. Whether it's creating a weekly recognition inventory that they do each Friday or helping them understand the grab bag of informal recognition methods they have at their disposal, it is essential that this training is deeply embedded in your organization. For example, our hotel general managers have made it a habit to share at least one positive guest correspondence during the course of their monthly staff meetings. Go to http://www.nelson-motivation .com and review Bob Nelson's Organizational Recognition Assessment for Managers, which is a tool to measure your managers' beliefs and opinions about recognition in your organization, helping you create a baseline for where you are now. My number one question I taught my managers to ask their direct reports was "How can I support you to do the best work of your life here at Joie de Vivre?" This simple question, which I carried over to my leadership time at Airbnb, is a profound way of showing recognition.

2. Create a signature method for your managers to understand the importance of really *seeing* your employees. As mentioned earlier in the chapter, Southwest Airlines uses its blindfolded game with the trash cans. In the past, Joie de Vivre has used a sort of musical chairs exercise called "Pass the Photo," in which we have our managers pass photos around at a management meeting, one at a time, until the music stops playing. The manager has to then look at the photo in his or her hand and tell the group something about the personal life of this employee, the employee's greatest strengths and weaknesses at work, as well as frustrations and aspirations. This accelerated course in employee recognition is perfect for hotel general managers who may have dozens or hundreds of employees. What would be the perfect signature training ritual for your company? And is there a

(continued)

(*continued*)

perfect theme book or song that can be used to unite and recognize your people?

3. Use diversity or affinity programs to create both recognition and a sense of belonging. My colleague Sue Funkhouser is a master at teaching *Peak* seminars. She's found that employers who invest in developing internal affinity clubs for under-populated groups (women, LGBTQ, racial minorities, disabled, older employees, etc.) create a better sense of belonging, as it gives these employees a unified voice in a place that often feels primarily populated by people that don't look like them. Most organizations have those that feel part of the *in* group and those who feel left *out*. Beyond the political correctness of helping everyone feel recognized and like they belong, a company is well served by amplifying minority voices, as this is a powerful antidote to the group-think that can exist in a homogenous organization. At Airbnb, we call this "Airfinity" and have tribes of parents, veterans, and foreigners—beyond the normal inclusion groups you see in a company.

4. Use employee reviews as a formalized time to show recognition. Many managers and employees dread performance reviews, but they truly do provide an opportunity to *encourage*. The best reviews (assuming you want to keep the employee) provide employees with the *courage* to step up their game, and feel seen and inspired by their supervisor. Count up the number of direct reports you have, estimate the number of hours you need to prepare for each review (over the course of a few weeks preparing, this may be five to ten hours for a single review), and then sum up the total time you spend reviewing your direct reports each year. You're likely to find that you are spending between 2 and 5 percent of your annual work hours on one of the most important activities that will secure your success and your employees' effectiveness. Promega, the life sciences company, thinks of the review process in three conversations, with each focusing on a specific area throughout the year that helps foster meaningful communication and transparency:

   • 360—conversation will focus on self-awareness, self-actu-alization, and openness to feedback

- Individual Development Plan—conversation will focus on job performance and development, a look back and view forward
- Stay Interview—conversation will focus on employee engagement, connection, and the relationship between employee/manager

5. Don't be stingy about recognizing your best performers. I'll admit it, I'm so much better at giving praise to line-level employees than those closest around me. It seems like the closer one gets to me in terms of their title, the higher my expectations, and the more I treat them with some of the disregard I can apply to myself. Does that sound familiar? Assume that your biggest competitor stole three employees from your company at any level of the organizations. Which employees would be the greatest loss? Do they know that? It's easy to get preoccupied with managing some of your most challenged employees and to assume that your best performers are perfectly happy and well compensated. But just remember, studies have shown that the average salary people accept for new jobs is only about 5 percent more than they're making currently. The key differentiator—even for many of your star employees—is that they feel appreciated and seen for all of their talents and successes.

Creating a culture of recognition at your company will mean you will have happier employees, less turnover, and more productivity. Psychologist John Gottman's landmark study on marriage found that successful relationships averaged a five-to-one ratio of positive to negative interactions. Other studies in the business world have put this ratio at three to one with respect to what drives productivity in employees. If your workplace is more focused on giving feedback only when something is going wrong, as opposed to celebrating what's going right, you may end up with a high divorce rate in your company.

Compensation and recognition are the foundation of the Employee Pyramid. But truly inspired employees, whose work life is transforming into a kind of self-actualized experience, need to have a real sense of meaning in what they and their company do. In the next chapter, we will explore how you can infuse meaning into the workplace.

RECOMMENDED READING

First, Break All the Rules by Marcus Buckingham and Curt Coffman
How Full Is Your Bucket? by Tom Rath and Donald O. Clifton
Liberating the Corporate Soul by Richard Barrett
Managing with Carrots by Adrian Gostick and Chester Elton
1001 Ways to Reward Employees by Bob Nelson
Reclaiming Higher Ground by Lance H. K. Secretan
The Art and Science of 360 Degree Feedback by Richard Lepsinger and
     Antoinette Lucia
The Carrot Principle by Adrian Gostick and Chester Elton
The 8th Habit: From Effectiveness to Greatness by Stephen R. Covey
Why Should Anyone Be Led by You? by Rob Goffee and Gareth Jones

CHAPTER SIX

CREATING INSPIRATION

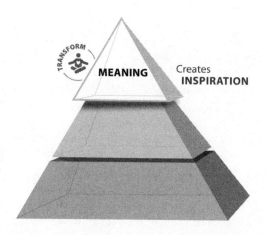

In the end, it is impossible to have a great life unless it is a meaningful life. And it is very difficult to have a meaningful life without meaningful work. Perhaps, then you might gain that rare tranquility that comes from knowing that you've had a hand in creating something of intrinsic excellence that makes a contribution. Indeed, you might even gain that deepest of all satisfactions: knowing that your short time here on this earth has been well spent, and that it mattered.

JIM COLLINS, *Good to Great*[1]

Are you fortunate enough to have found your calling? Was there a moment that spoke to you, saying, "Wake up, this is why you're here on Earth!"? I found my calling by observing someone else live out hers.

I spent a few months of college studying in the English country-side. During one particular break from school, I traveled over to Germany and spent a few days hitchhiking. While in the Black Forest region, I contracted a digestive bug that hit me like a ton of bricks. Fortunately, I flagged down a driver (not easy on the autobahn) who took me to the nearest town and deposited me into a three-room bed-and-breakfast down a secluded alleyway. I knew absolutely no German. Maria, the innkeeper, knew very little English, but she easily recognized my international signal of distress: cold sweats and a need to rush to the nearest bathroom.

Without receiving my credit card or seeing any form of identification, she immediately settled me into a comfortable bed and motioned for me to just rest. I must have slept 12 hours. Miraculously, when I awoke there was a fresh, warm bowl of homemade chicken soup next to my bed. How did she know when I was going to wake up? For the next two days, my life was confined to that bed and bathroom, but each time I woke up Maria had placed something new on my bedside table: seltzer water to settle my stomach, a small bouquet of flowers, an English-language newspaper.

Finally, I was strong enough to take a walk around this small inn and to have a broken-English conversation with Maria. She took me on a proud little tour of her picturesque village, and when I left the next day, nearly fully recovered, I felt like I was leaving family. In fact, on leaving, we both had forgotten that I owed her some German marks for her hospitality. This was so much more than a lodging, or even an infirmary, experience. It was a testament to the spirit of goodwill that is embedded in the basic premise of the hospitality industry. It was clear from Maria's gentle smile, her thoughtful little deeds, and her overall persona that she experienced great satisfaction from taking care of vulnerable people who were far away from home.

I've shared this story with hundreds of my employees and with thousands of hospitality students around the world. It helps to illustrate my belief that there is something very noble about this industry. And while it took five years from that fateful stay with Maria for me to consciously develop a business plan to start my own hotel company, there is no doubt that the experience left an indelible impression on me.

Finding meaning in one's work—both in what you do daily and in the company's sense of mission—is one of the rarest but most valuable qualities anyone can have in their job. C. William Pollard, who grew ServiceMaster into a worldwide company, says in his book *The Soul of the Firm*, "People want to work for a cause, not just for a living."[2]

Author Lance Secretan writes in *Inspirational Leadership*, "What caused followers to dedicate themselves with such passion to the visions of Christ, Buddha, Gandhi, Confucius, Martin Luther King, Mother Teresa, and Nelson Mandela? They were inspired, not motivated." He continues, "We have been confusing *motivation* with *inspiration*. The dictionary tells us that to motivate is 'to provide a motive; to induce, incite, impel'—something we *do* to people. . . . Inspiration is strikingly different from motivation. The word is derived from the Latin root *spirare*, meaning 'spirit,' to breathe, to give life, the breath of God. The dictionary defines inspiration as 'breathing in, as in air to the lungs; to infuse with an encouraging or exalting influence; to animate; stimulation by a divinity, a genius, an idea or a passion; a divine influence on human beings.'"[3] Sign me up for that!

While Abraham Maslow primarily focused on the motivations of humanity with his Hierarchy of Needs, he came to realize that the deepest motivations were at the top of the pyramid and took on an inspirational quality. At one point in his research on people's relationship with their work, he interviewed dozens of nurses and asked the question "Why did you go into nursing?" Although the initial answers were rather superficial, as he dug deeper, asking questions like "What are the greatest moments of reward, or tell me a moment so wonderful it made you weep or gave you cold shivers of ecstasy," he found the nurses expressing peak experiences that were virtually life altering. And those nurses who were most able to express a peak experience seemed most *called* by their work.

Maslow suggested people are more energized in the long-term by work that is not small-minded or self-centered. Collaboration toward a big, common purpose supersedes a competitive mindset based upon zero-sum principles. Why should leaders be surprised when employees respond with apathy or disgust and slowly disengage or withdraw energies from endeavors that are petty and not personally inspiring? *Peak* leaders look for the audacious, legacy-creating vision that miraculously connects diverse people toward a common mission.

A Swinging Company

While I will explore this subject in more depth in the last chapter of the book, I'll say here that there are three kinds of relationships one can have with work: you either have a job, a career, or a calling. Interestingly, each of those perspectives on work corresponds to a different level of the Employee Pyramid. Someone who sees his or her work as just a job tends to be stuck at the money or *survival* level of the pyramid. Those who are on a career path (there's no such thing as a job path) find great motivation on the *success* level in the way they are recognized at work. Yet, outside rewards and recognition can wear out as motivators over the course of a long career because there's a certain level of compliance required. More and more people are finding that they need something that feels more internally generated as their infuser of energy. For those of us lucky souls who experience our work as a calling, there is a natural *transformative* effect when we find great meaning in what we do, what our company does, or both. The rest of this chapter will be devoted to helping you understand how to mix aspiration and inspiration in order to help your employees see their work as more of a calling.

The miracle of inspiration can move mountains. When I was studying in England, I had the pleasure of spending some time in the town of Henley, which holds an annual rowing Royal Regatta that is known around the world. In watching the rowers' synchronized strokes, I would marvel at how an inspired team that was truly connecting with each other could virtually lift the boat out of the water so that it appeared weightless as it glided. Maybe that's why we call rowing *crew*. There's magic in how they can take a heavy boat and, through working in unison as a crew toward a common mission, make it glide effortlessly along the water. This fluidity or flow of rising above the water is known as *swing* in rowing circles. Leaders that develop swing in their companies will create more self-actualized employees and will glide seamlessly past their competitors.

Okay, I know you may be thinking, "Chip, this meaning stuff is only relevant to a small collection of high-minded businesses or nonprofits." I promise you, within all this woo-woo meaning speak, there is a Stanford MBA moment here. Nearly one-third of Joie de Vivre's more than 3,500 employees clean toilets for a living. Another group—the night auditors—spends most of their waking life doing financial audits while the rest of us are sleeping through the night.

Carrying heavy bags, dealing with guests' emotional baggage at the front desk, doing endless laundry—this is a significant part of what my crew does on a daily basis. How do we create a sense of nobility and inspiration in what these bellmen, front-desk hosts, and house-keeping staff do every day? Matthew Fox, an Episcopal priest and author of *The Reinvention of Work,* suggests that all work contains drudgery; yet, the difference between one job and the next is whether employees have a sense of meaning in what they do. In fact, in China, the oldest symbol for business means "life's meaning" or "life's work."

WHY MEANING HAS BECOME MORE MEANINGFUL

Before I start prescribing how you can create more meaning in your workplace, let's look briefly at why meaning has become a bigger issue for many of us. I believe there are three primary reasons why meaning is a germane and essential topic in the workplace today versus a generation ago:

1. Corporate transformation follows personal transformation. And we find that Gen X and Millennial generation employees are particularly seeking purpose in their work more so than past generations.
2. Work is a more dominant part of our lives than ever before and has replaced some of the social structures that previously created connection and meaning in our lives.
3. Over and over again, we see that companies that create lasting success have a deep sense of mission and meaning in what they do.

The human potential movement of the 1970s can take some credit for the fact that our twenty-first-century workplaces are less status *quo* and more status *go*. During the upheaval of the 1960s and 1970s, youth dissented, women joined the workforce, racial minorities strived for equality, and millions headed for therapy or a hot tub to discover who they were and where they were going. *Personal transformation* and *empowerment* were the buzzwords of the era. It shouldn't come as a surprise that a few years later, these same people who were looking for transformation in their personal life would be expecting more from their work.

More and more, people wanted an opportunity to realize their full potential as whole human beings at work. They wanted to work for socially responsible organizations. They wanted to do interesting work. They wanted to be surrounded by a sense of community. Today, many people see their workplace as a playground for who they are and what they can become. And in this post–9/11, post–credit meltdown era, people are even more focused on finding meaning and inspiration in the here and now. This brings us to my second point. It's not surprising that work has become the touchstone for life's meaning when it dominates so much of our lives. We work 25 percent more hours per week than we did a generation ago (and that doesn't even include the e-mails at home and the text messages on vacation). While organized religion has made an American comeback in the past decade, the reality is that many of the social underpinnings that traditionally gave meaning to our lives—our neighborhoods, our social clubs, our extended families—have diminished in importance due to today's more transient and digital culture. Peter Katz, author of *The New Urbanism,* says, "We're a society awash in networks, yet starved for community."[4] And a well-publicized 2006 Duke University study showed that (despite all the new devices supposedly intended to help us connect) we are significantly more socially isolated than we were a decade ago.

If more people are working and commuting longer hours and have less time for external social activities that create deeper relationships, it's not surprising that they thirst for this sense of social connection from work. Actually, I think it's ironic that one of Joie de Vivre's favorite annual employee gatherings for the past decade has been our Bowl-a-rama night when we take over a bowling alley, each hotel's employees come dressed in their own homemade costumes based on a central theme, and we drink, bowl, eat pizza, and share stories. If Harvard's Robert Putnam is correct in his "Bowling Alone" (an essay and book) theory of social isolation, then it's up to the corporate world to help fill that vacuum.

As for my third point, great companies have great causes. Apple was initially founded on the premise of the "democratization of the desktop" and has morphed that cause into being the world's leader in mixing aesthetics and music with technology. Southwest Airlines is about the freedom to fly and connect with loved ones through the low fares they offer. Companies like Genentech and Medtronic are all about making better lives for their customers through scientific breakthroughs of new medical products. As Bill George of Medtronic says, "People must be motivated by a deeper cause. . . . People don't come to work to earn money for themselves and the company. They come to work because the product does something worthwhile, and this is what gets people inspired."[5]

Maslow believed employees could become self-actualized through "becoming heroes by participating in heroic enterprises." Few companies have infused the sense of meaning in what they do and created "employees as heroes" along the way better than Medtronic.

In 1962, five years after the company's visionary founder Earl Bakken invented the pacemaker, the company was on the verge of bankruptcy. Bakken and his board of directors wrote a simple mission statement—"to restore people to full life and health"—that became infused into every component of each employee's life at Medtronic. When employees join the company, they go to the "Mission and Medallion" ceremony where they receive a mission card and a book describing the company's history and mission. They get to meet the CEO and hear anecdotal stories about how Medtronic has changed the lives of both patients and employees. Each new employee is given a medallion with a depiction of a sick person rising. When Bill George was CEO, he would say to new employees, "I ask in accepting this that you accept the mission of Medtronic and look at it and display it to remind you that the purpose of your being here is to restore people to full life and health. If you get frustrated, note that there is a higher calling."

This sense of meaning is reinforced at the annual holiday party in which six patients tell their life stories and explain how Medtronic's products have saved their lives. With two thousand employees and their families gathered, and thousands more Medtronic employees watching by videoconference around the world, these patients' stories help create a peak experience for Medtronic's crew. George describes this annual event as the "defining moment" for expressing the meaning that Medtronic creates in the workplace. He has told me, "One story tells a lot more than the number of patients served."

THE TWO COMPONENTS OF MEANING IN THE WORKPLACE

If you've never read Viktor Frankl's well-known book *Man's Search for Meaning*, I recommend you buy it today. His story—a psychiatrist imprisoned in a Nazi death camp trying to understand the meaning of life—is captivating, intellectually stimulating, and profoundly inspiring. From this experience, he came to believe people have a "will to meaning," as he found that those who survived in the camp were more likely to have a sense of meaning in their life and a need to express themselves through that meaning once they were out of the camp.

He writes, "The more one forgets himself—by giving himself to a cause to serve or another person to love—the more human he is and the more he actualizes himself." This eloquent man lamented, "People have enough to live by but nothing to live for; they have the means but no meaning."[6] Once he reestablished himself after the war, he looked for ways to create meaning in people's lives, including in the workplace. He wrote about how people who were jobless were assumed to be useless and that uselessness meant they felt meaningless. But when Frankl convinced unemployed people to volunteer philanthropically, their "unemployment neurosis" disappeared, and they were more likely to become employed faster. Frankl, who survived the concentration camp, was fond of quoting Nietzsche to his unemployed patients: "He who has a *why* to live can bear with almost any *how*."[7]

It would be interesting if we could refer to a Meaning Index like we do the Dow Jones Stock Index so that we could quickly scan who is playing at the top of the pyramid and who isn't. In reading Frankl's book and in studying dozens of meaning-driven companies, I've come to realize that workplace meaning can be dissected into meaning *at* work and meaning *in* work. Meaning *at* work relates to how an employee feels about the company, their work environment, and the company's mission. Meaning *in* work relates to how an employee feels about their specific job task. Pollard captures the potential synergy of this dichotomy with the following passage from his book, *The Soul of the Firm,* "As a person sees a reason for the task that is personally satisfying and rewarding and has the confidence that the mission of the firm is in alignment with his or her own personal growth and development, a powerful force is unleashed that results in creativity, productivity, service quality, growth, profit, and value."[8]

I believe that meaning *at* work is even more important than meaning *in* work. When employees believe in the work of the company, the whole Hierarchy of Needs is satisfied. Those employees clearly have their base needs met because they have confidence in the financial viability of the company, which means they have a secure job. Believing in the company's mission also typically creates deeper alliances among employees because that sense of being part of a crew gliding above the water, and the pride that comes from that success, satisfies our social or esteem needs. Finally, our self-actualization needs can be met by feeling that we are part of an organization making a difference in the world; plus, "meaningful-ness-at-work practices may indirectly render the work itself more meaningful."

When someone finds meaning *in* their work (they like what they do each day) without meaning *at* work (they aren't enthused by the company's mission), it is much less likely that there is a halo effect or indirect payoff in helping to improve their engagement with the organization. In fact, the larger the gap between a positive *in*-work feeling and a negative *at*-work feeling, the faster that employee is likely to depart the company.

The following figure will help you understand how to evaluate any employee's sense of workplace meaning.

MEANING IN VERSUS AT WORK

Meaning **IN** Work

		LOW	HIGH
Meaning **AT** Work	**HIGH**	Employee loves the company but isn't as inspired by what they do each day; typical of some non-profits	The completely inspired employee; loves the company and what they do personally; use this employee as a mentor as much as possible
	LOW	The completely uninspired employee; try to pair them with a completely inspired employee in the same area	Employee enjoys their functional tasks but isn't engaged by the company mission; beware, this employee may be leaving soon

What does Joie de Vivre do to foster a sense of meaning both *at* work and *in* work? With respect to connecting our employees with the company and its mission, we have found that the simpler and more succinct our mission, the more powerfully it engages our employees. Years ago, I wrote a nine-sentence vision statement that defined my sense of *who* Joie de Vivre was in the world. It never resonated with most of our employees. So later we created a team of managers and employees to write a short mission statement, which became "creating opportunities to celebrate the joy of life."

I came to realize that virtually every company has a conscious or unconscious two-word mantra that describes who they are and what they do in the world. Sometimes these mantras are publicly known, like Apple's "Think Different." Sometimes these mantras may be unconscious but nevertheless describe the behaviors of the company and its people. Nike's would be "Kick Ass" if they claimed a shorter, more amped-up version of their "Just Do It" philosophy. Airbnb's is "Belong Anywhere."

Joie de Vivre's mantra is "Create Joy," and since the time that lovingly crafted two-word truth revealed itself in 2006, it has become a rallying cry for everything we do. Employees took it upon themselves to create colorful rubber bracelets with "Create Joy" emblazoned on them to remind us throughout the day that this is what we're here to do. Our president Jack Kenny has a sign outside his door asking each of us, "What did you do to Create Joy today?" Another employee took it upon herself to add the phrase to all of the T-shirts we wear at the annual AIDS Walk fundraiser in San Francisco's Golden Gate Park. The two-word statement was so compelling that during the walk, our team started chanting it, and hundreds of other walkers started chanting it, too.

Danny Meyer, arguably the most admired restaurateur in the country, calls this "naming it." This means defining who your company is and making sure people who are interviewing with your company completely understand that vibe. Danny and his Union Square Hospitality Group, who operate the most impressive collection of restaurants in Manhattan, named their approach to business *enlightened hospitality*, and this strategy has helped them attract the right kind of people who fit their organization.

I had the opportunity to have breakfast with David Cragg, who spent five years with Genentech in a variety of roles, including the vice president of human resources. He says that part of the reason Genentech has been considered one of the country's best employers is the "purity of purpose" of the organization. Early in its history, Genentech made a commitment to both basic science and translational science (how science is used to help people). While most biotech companies focus on the translational science—because it's where the profits are—Genentech has made a commitment to *science for the sake of science* and has 150 postdoctoral scientists at the company, both to bolster their research and development and as almost a community service to bolster basic science research. That purity of purpose helps

Genentech attract the best and the brightest in the field of biotechnology.

When *Fortune* magazine crowned Genentech "America's Best Company to Work For in 2006," they opened their profile of Genentech in the following manner: "Domagoj Vucic didn't come to Genentech for the rich stock options or the free cappuccino or the made-to-order sushi or the parties every Friday night. He came from the University of Georgia seven years ago because he believed Genentech could help him answer a burning question: What is it that keeps caterpillars infected with baculovirus alive for an entire seven days before they explode into a gooey puddle? Figuring that out could, believe it or not, be a big step toward curing cancer."[9]

I'm not sure what Genentech's two-word mantra is, but their four-word motto is "In Business for Life." If you go to their website, you will see just how they've made the link from all this esoteric science to the patients who have been the recipients of their trailblazing cures and drugs. Specific patients are profiled in ways that remind both the consumer and the Genentech employee just how meaningful that motto is.

Joie de Vivre creates a sense of meaning at work by engaging our employees in a wide variety of key initiatives:

- Philanthropy: While our company has a great history of being actively involved in the communities in which we're located, we had never officially tabulated our impact until 2006, when we came to realize that we raise more than $1 million annually (in cash and in-kind donations) for various nonprofit organizations. Not bad for a small regional company. But this internal philanthropy audit also showed us how disparate our efforts were, so we organized a Philanthropy Task Force with people throughout the company to help us develop a more strategic approach to how we give back. Now, Joie de Vivre's corporate entity supports four particular types of causes that really define the California experience. Our Cultural Ambassadors—one representative from each hotel in the company who together act almost like a city council with respect to cultural issues in the company—help create one companywide philanthropic event per quarter to support each of these four causes. Yet, we didn't want our individual hotels to lose track of their grassroots connection to community, and we didn't want the staff of those hotels to lose their autonomy of choosing which local organizations to support no matter what the cause. After the task force discussed this with each hotel, it was determined that we would define a modest annual goal for each hotel (to provide cash and in-kind donations to the organizations of their choice) of $200 per room or $20,000 for a 100-room hotel. This democratic approach to philanthropy has allowed our rapidly growing company to involve its line-level employees in not just the execution of our community service but also the strategy behind the decisions of who we support. Or you could take Microsoft's approach and offer a dollar-for-dollar match of employee charitable contributions.

- Company Strategy: Most companies, including ours, do off-site retreats with the top managers or leaders in the company, but rarely are line-level employees included in such an important and team-building activity. One of the things we've learned from Market Metrix, the company that surveys our employees' satisfaction twice a year, is that a positive score associated with the phrase "I feel powerful at work" has a significant impact on employees' sense of esteem and engagement. Years ago, we realized that if we truly wanted to empower our employees as entrepreneurs, we needed to include our front-desk staff, bartenders, and bellmen in an annual off-site retreat for each hotel so that they could have a voice in where their hotel was going in the next year with respect to customer service initiatives, capital improvement projects, and enhancements to the employee work environment. Is it difficult creating service retreats for a business that's open 24 hours a day every day of the year? Of course it is. We need to bring in employees from other hotels to run the business while our team is off-site, but the results are dramatic because it means our employees feel a strong connection to the strategic direction of the hotel, and our guests recognize that the vast majority of our employees act like entrepreneurs.

- Joie de Vivre University: Virtually every company has a training program, and most do a pretty good job of engaging their employees in suggestions for the curriculum of their corporate university. We've found that some of our most meaningful programs or classes have bubbled up from our employees. Our Silicon Valley hotels decided to create a Spanish-speaking Inspired Speakers Series because more than half of our employees in that region speak English as a second language. Their first class was called "Life

Enhancement" and included 54 Spanish-speaking employees listening to four Spanish-speaking managers—who had moved up through the company—express how they navigated their rise to leadership in an English-speaking country. This inspiring class led to a second one that was focused on how to raise kids (since a vast majority of our Spanish-speaking employees have children, and 77 percent of their kids were under the age of 12) in America and what kinds of community programs were available to their families. Our Silicon Valley Employee Work Climate Survey scores skyrocketed soon after we started this bilingual Inspired Speakers Series.

CREATING MEANING IN THE DAY-TO-DAY WORK

Up until now, I have focused more on the subject of creating meaning *at* work, but completely inspired employees also feel engaged with their day-to-day work. For the doctors, police officers, and teachers of the world, finding daily meaning probably isn't that difficult. But for the rest of us, sometimes it takes a change in our perspective. Robert Stephens, the founder and chief inspector of the Geek Squad, the tech service company that was purchased by retail giant Best Buy to help service the home technology needs of its customers, says, "The Geek Squad is not going to cure cancer, but we will repair the computers of people who do."

One of the best approaches I've ever seen with respect to making this linkage between what we do daily and what the company does was profiled by Richard Boyatzis and Annie McKee in the book *Resonant Leadership*. Summa Health Systems of Akron, Ohio, spent quite a bit of time interviewing their employees to understand what gives meaning to them before creating the following statement on a wallet-sized card that each employee carries with them:

> You are Summa. You are what people see when they arrive here. Yours are the eyes they look into when they're frightened and lonely. Yours are the voices people hear when they ride the elevators and when they try to sleep and when they try to forget their problems. You are what they hear on their way to appointments that could affect their destinies. And what they hear after they leave those appointments. Yours are the comments people hear when you think they can't. Yours is the intelligence and caring that people hope they find here.

If you're noisy, so is the hospital. If you're rude, so is the hospital. And if you're wonderful, so is the hospital. No visitors, no patients, no physicians or coworkers can ever know the real you, the you that you know is there—unless you let them see it. All they can know is what they see and hear and experience.

And so we have a stake in your attitude and in the collective attitudes of everyone who works at the hospital. We are judged by your performance. We are the care you give, the attention you pay, the courtesies you extend.

Thank you for all you're doing.[10]

If you're a Summa employee, you have a good sense that everything you do touches both the customer (patients) and the reputation of the organization. Summa has done a masterful job of defining its employees' work by its purpose and not by its task. When employees think of their work from the perspective of the ultimate purpose, as opposed to the specific job description, they are able to see their role as more expansive and more linked to the organizational mission. Thus, the organizational success is their success, and a genuine sense of accomplishment can result for the employee. There's no reason why your company can't create a meaningful message for your employees.

New York University Professor Amy Wrzesniewski has built a reputation on her theory of "job crafting" or revisioning employees as active crafters of their work. Job crafting is a means of changing both the tasks and the relational perspective of employees to their work so that they feel more control over their jobs and a deeper connection to the organizational mission. Wrzesniewski cites a number of studies that show how job crafting can create meaning in what an employee does day to day. One particularly interesting study relates to how nurses were moved from a role as a task master to that of patient advocacy, and in doing so, the nurses were both more satisfied in their jobs and more effective in their delivery of care. For those of you who want to understand how job crafting can help you turn your employees' work into a calling, I recommend you do an Internet search to obtain a copy of the article, which is listed at the end of this chapter.

One of the ways that Joie de Vivre tries to expand our employees' perspective on what they do is to ask them to spend the night in one of our other hotels. Each of our employees is invited to stay for free twice a quarter at a Joie de Vivre property.

It's remarkable how fresh one's perspective becomes when we move from being the employee to being the customer. Front-desk hosts realize just how important that moment of truth is when the guest arrives at the front desk for the first time. The housekeeping staff realizes how vacuuming in the hallways before 8 A.M. can disturb guests' sleep. Bellmen come to appreciate how the banter of conversation that goes on with guests on the way to their room allows the bellmen to become a "listening post" for how the hotel staff can address the guests' specific and unique desires during the course of their stay.

It's all about creating fresh eyes and a fresh perspective. Nike's chief of design John R. Hoke III was profiled in *BusinessWeek* magazine about how he created inspiration for his designers. Hoke sends them on design-inspiration trips: to the zoo to observe and sketch animals' feet, to a lecture on Dale Chihuly's fancifully colored glass sculptures, to the Detroit auto show to understand the form and silhouettes of cars, or to an origami class to understand the structural constraints of the ancient Japanese art form.

Creating meaning in the day-to-day work of cleaning toilets or designing shoes may be less about improving the specific work conditions—assuming they are in satisfactory shape—and more about changing the perspective of your people. Meaning is in the eye of the beholder. The more you can create peak experiences—whether it's coming face-to-face with an appreciative customer or building a sense of deep community among your people—the more likely your employees will see the meaning in what they, and the company, do.

PEAK PRESCRIPTIONS

Here are a few ideas for how you can spread a sense of meaning in your workplace:

1. Create an exercise that helps your employees understand just how much they impact the customer experience. At each monthly new-hire orientation, I start my hour with the employees doing an exercise called "Name Your Favorite Shop." This icebreaker asks the employees to think about a service experience that was so great that they told a bunch of friends about it. Employees share experiences of restaurants,

(*continued*)

(*continued*)

dry cleaners, and clothing shops where they received "knock your socks off" service. We talk about how that kind of service makes us feel as a person. Then I ask them to tell us about an experience in which they felt completely neglected or even discriminated against. The employees share the idea that bad service makes them feel either really big and angry or very small and invisible. We all agree that those emotions don't feel good. The purpose of this exercise is to create a point of connection between these new employees. We all share the experience of being a customer every day, and this exercise shows what kind of impact we in the service business can have on someone else's day. Another exercise that some of our general managers use at monthly staff meetings is to read aloud a couple of thank-you letters from hotel guests who had a particularly wonderful experience at the property. Or have a loyal guest who is currently staying in the hotel come to a staff meeting and talk about why she loves this particular hotel.

2. Ask questions that remind your employees about the hidden value of meaning. Like self-actualization, *meaning* is a relatively intangible concept. It isn't something that employers and employees naturally talk about. We have found that the best way to make the issue of meaning tangible is through asking provocative questions of employees in either staff meetings or one-on-one during their employee reviews. Questions like:

   - "What's the best experience you've had in the past month here at work?"
   - "We provide hotel services for travelers. Why is that important?" Gently ask that question five times repeatedly, and you will get down to the fundamental purpose of what you are offering your customers. You could do this for any business. For example, "We are an executive search firm for people looking to change jobs. Why is that important?" Each time you ask the question, it will force the employee to probe a little deeper into why your company makes a difference.
   - "If you did your job badly, how would that affect your coworkers and our customers?" Sometimes pointing out just how valuable an employee's role is helps them have

more of a sense of meaning in what they do. Wong's Supermarkets in Peru took this question a step further and created a video (that's been shown to tens of thousands of employees and their families) depicting how their customers would suffer if there were no well-trained employees at the meat counter or the check-out register: http://bit.ly/MMi7kX.

- "Most of us think of our job in terms of 'What am I getting?' Ask yourself instead, 'What am I becoming as a result of this job?'"

3. Create peak experiences for your employees that build their sense of community with each other. We organize a number of events that help build a sense of affiliation by department in the workplace. Our annual housekeepers' luncheon is one of my favorites because we bring hundreds of housekeepers— speaking seven or eight languages—into a ballroom where managers and senior executives in the company help serve them lunch and tell them just how much they mean to the company. Beyond just creating a cool uniform (the retro short pants, clip-on-tie look), Best Buy's Geek Squad has created many ways for their techies to grow a sense of affiliation even though they are spread across the country. Their agents started getting their driver's license photos taken in their uniforms and then created a Flickr website where they could share photos of themselves with celebrities, in parades, and at play. Founder Robert Stephens says that one of the most effective means of creating meaning for their employees has been giving them the sense of being part of a truly special tribe.

4. Have your managers take our *Peak* Managerial Assessment. Found in the Appendix, this Assessment helps you and your managers to understand which part of the Employee Pyramid they're tending to place their attention. It's a great tool for your managers to use to assess themselves before doing an offsite retreat and better prepare for talking about how to become more of a peak-performing company.

5. Make a list of the 10 reasons people should join your organization. Early on, Google recognized that they needed to attract and retain talent in the very competitive Silicon Valley job market. So they created a top-10 list of why people

(*continued*)

(*continued*)

should join them, with not one of those 10 reasons being related to stock options or compensation. They have reasons like, "Life is beautiful. Being part of something that matters and working on products in which you can believe is remarkably fulfilling." And "Boldly go where no one has gone before. There are hundreds of challenges yet to solve. Your creative ideas matter here and are worth exploring." Our People Services Department was so impressed with Google's list that we created our own, with the focus being on the intangible peak of the pyramid elements that make the Joie de Vivre employment experience different. If you're having difficulty coming up with your list of 10 reasons, you may need to go back and read the last three chapters again.

6. Ask disengaged employees to start a gratitude journal to help them build a sense of connection with the organization and what they do. Maslow wrote, "Gratitude is an extremely important but badly ignored aspect of emotional and organizational health." Studies have shown that those who kept weekly journals of things they feel grateful about felt better about their lives as a whole and were more optimistic about the upcoming week than those who recorded hassles or neutral life events. Your most challenged employees may have some mental obstacles to doing this, but helping them see that there are many things—both in life and at work— that they could be grateful about (including those catastrophic things that *haven't* happened) can increase their job satisfaction and sense of meaning. Paying a gratitude visit to thank someone who's made a difference in our life or in our job has been proven to be one of the best ways to increase our satisfaction with life. If your employees resist all these alternatives, remind them that studies have shown the restaurant bills on which the server writes thank-you produce tips that are 10 percent higher than those without an expression of gratitude. Gratitude doesn't just make you feel better; it has positive economic and career consequences, too.

I know this meaning stuff isn't easy to talk about in most workplaces. But we're all familiar with popular films that show the difference one person can make to others. If one of your employees is feeling apathetic, rent them *Mr. Holland's Opus, Schindler's List,* or *It's a Wonderful Life,* and see whether that sparks some meaningful inspiration in them.

Congratulations. We've made it to the peak of the Employee Pyramid. Hopefully your lungs are acclimating to the high altitude. Most companies don't spend much time in this rarified place because executives have a hard time measuring meaning. Traditional human resources departments worry about the legalities of discussing something that verges on spirituality. Most managers don't contemplate the difference between a job, a career, and a calling. No doubt about it, though, creating employee meaning can be your secret weapon in differentiating yourself from your competition. But remember that *meaning* can mean different things in different parts of the world, so what worked in your American division might not work as well in Japan or India. I was giving a speech in South Africa and was introduced to a book called *Meaning, Inc.,* which does a fabulous job of giving an international perspective to the issue of workplace meaning.

Don't forget that focusing on the top of the pyramid is what you do once you've satisfied the money and recognition needs of your employees. If you have a weak foundation for your Employee Pyramid—as is true in many nonprofit organizations—at some point, even if your mission is full of meaning, your employees will have to leave you in order to pay the rent or feel individually recognized somewhere else.

RECOMMENDED READING

Authentic Leadership by Bill George
Bowling Alone by Robert Putnam
"Crafting a Job: Revisioning Employees as Active Crafters of Their Work" by Amy Wrzesniewski and Jane Dutton, *Academy of Management Review* (April 2001)
"Happiness 101" by D. T. Max, *New York Times Magazine* (January 7, 2007)
Inspirational Leadership by Lance Secretan
Man's Search for Meaning by Viktor Frankl
Meaning, Inc. by Gurnek Bains et al.
Prisoners of Our Thoughts by Alex Pattakos
Religion, Values, and Peak Experiences by Abraham Maslow

(continued)

(*continued*)

Resonant Leadership by Richard Boyatzis and Annie McKee

The Hungry Spirit by Charles Handy

The Reinvention of Work by Matthew Fox

The Right to Be Human: A Biography of Abraham Maslow by Edward Hoffman

The Workplace Revolution by Matthew Gilbert

PART THREE

RELATIONSHIP TRUTH 2: THE CUSTOMER PYRAMID

The new consumer frequently sees the acquisition of authentic products and services as a means of achieving self-actualization, the peak of Maslow's Hierarchy of Needs, signaling the attainment of true potential.

DAVID LEWIS, *The Soul of the New Consumer*[1]

CHAPTER SEVEN

CREATING SATISFACTION

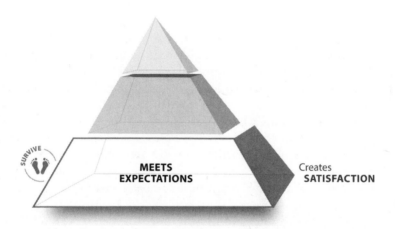

SURVIVE

MEETS EXPECTATIONS

Creates **SATISFACTION**

Every major industry was once a growth industry. But some that are now riding a wave of growth enthusiasm are very much in the shadow of decline. Others that are thought of as seasoned growth industries have actually stopped growing. In every case, the reason growth is threatened, slowed, or stopped is not because the market is saturated. It is because there has been a failure of management. . . . The railroads did not stop growing because the need for passenger and freight transportation declined. That grew. The railroads are in trouble today not because that need was filled by others (cars, trucks, airplanes, and even telephones) but because it was not filled by the railroads themselves. They let others take customers away from them because they assumed themselves to be in the railroad business rather than in the transportation business.

THEODORE LEVITT, HARVARD PROFESSOR AND AUTHOR[1]

Those who have spent any time in the Joie de Vivre orbit know that we like to celebrate. In fact, the first time I walked into the courtyard of what was to become The Phoenix, my initial reaction was, "What an amazing spot to throw a party!" Just four months after I bought the sorry hotel and we'd slapped a bunch of paint and glitter on the place, we welcomed our first guests and celebrated with a fabulous grand opening party.

It was truly an underground event that went late into the night: an eclectic mix of bemused friends, a few local hospitality honchos who were shocked (but intrigued) by The Phoenix's business plan, and some down-on-their-luck media types who were looking for ample quantities of free chardonnay and brie. Fortunately, one of those media types wrote a glowing story about the hotel and its opening party in the *San Francisco Examiner* the next day. The journalist commented on the hotel's unique priorities with respect to what we were offering our guests. He quoted one of our guests that he'd met at the party: "I love a hotel that spends its money on art instead of plumbing." Part Three of this book is dedicated to helping you determine whether art is more important than plumbing to your customers. What are your customers' base needs versus their aspirational needs farther up the pyramid? If there's one talent I think I've honed over the past two decades, it's the ability to deeply understand the psyche of our target customers for each hotel.

The three chapters composing the Customer Pyramid will heighten your talents as an amateur psychologist with respect to how well you know your customers. In this chapter, we'll talk more about companies' conventional approaches to ensuring they are meeting their customers' basic satisfaction needs or, in other words, whether the plumbing is working. But I'll also be critical of the risk that bedevils most companies: getting comfortable with purely satisfying customers rather than delighting the hell out of them. In Chapter Eight we will focus on how to use training and technology to engage in a deeper customer conversation so that you are imagining and addressing your customers' most obvious desires. By the time we finish Chapter Nine, you will have received a crash course in customer mind reading. You'll learn how to know your customers better than they know themselves.

The opening quote for this chapter comes from Theodore Levitt's landmark article "Marketing Myopia," which appeared in the *Harvard Business Review* three months before I was born. In essence, he's saying that when company leadership focuses purely on meeting the expectations of their customers, they can become sitting ducks for a surprise competitor with a new mousetrap. Why didn't Sony, the creator of the Walkman, launch the iPod? Why didn't AT&T create the cell phone? Why didn't Hilton create Airbnb? His observations of how stable companies and industries are upstaged by disruptive innovation and new competition are more relevant today than ever.

Many classic books, from Clayton Christensen's *The Innovator's Dilemma* to Geoffrey Moore's *Crossing the Chasm*, have outlined why customer innovation often happens on the margins by outsiders, instead of by industry leaders, who make the mistake of assuming that their customers are truly satisfied.

There is a parallel between the Customer Pyramid and the Employee Pyramid. It's not that companies don't want to create an inspired employee or a self-actualized customer, which happens at the higher levels; it's just that business leaders become fixated on the bottom of these pyramids—employee compensation and customer satisfaction—because they're easily measurable. Executives can rely on conventional market research or satisfaction surveys to tell them what their customers are thinking. Or, often they can use these surveys to justify decisions they have already made. Unfortunately, as David Ogilvy of the ad agency Ogilvy & Mather once said, most companies use research and surveys "as a drunk uses a lamp post . . . for support, not illumination."[2]

Company executives often aren't looking for illumination. Most companies are stunted by their natural tendency toward the tangible—their perceived need for quarterly evolutionary improvements rather than long-term revolutionary changes. And the conventional corporate fight for scarce resources favors the reliable rather than the unorthodox business strategy. Let's face it: most corporate execs are more timid than they'd like to admit for fear of standing out in a negative way. So instead of imagining what would improve the lives of their customers, companies tinker with their existing products and make incremental product improvements based on the results of conventional customer satisfaction surveys. Most companies are more product-focused than customer-focused.

Harry Beckwith, who wrote a nifty little book called *Selling the Invisible*, believes that every industry has a natural product or service evolution over time. Initially, the companies that launch an industry are just trying to meet the acceptable minimum standards. He calls these "Stage One" companies and suggests that they are focused purely on offering their clients an accepted product. During "Stage Two," new competitors enter the market and differentiation starts to occur, focusing on answering customer needs. The successful companies during this stage of an industry tend to be market-driven.

Finally, Beckwith continues, "Stage Three" dawns, and a new, more innovative competitor emerges that realizes "clients' expectations and expressed needs no longer drive the market. Surveys asking, 'How could we improve?' no longer produce useful data; the customers have run out of ideas."[3] Beckwith suggests that "surprising the customer" becomes the driving force in a Stage Three industry, and the successful companies in this phase are imagination-driven. Stages One through Three profoundly articulate the progression from the bottom to the top of the Customer Pyramid. Peak-performing companies leave the comfortable base camp of purely satisfying customers and explore the further reaches of the higher levels of the pyramid (which we'll explore in the next two chapters).

Using the Hierarchy of Needs to Understand Your Customer

At Joie de Vivre, we've found Maslow's pyramid to be a helpful tool to focus on the needs of our customers. What do you expect from a hotel experience? It probably depends on a variety of influences that helped you choose that particular hotel. If you read a great review of the hotel in *Travel & Leisure* or friends raved about their experience on Facebook, you are likely to have heightened expectations. Similarly, the marketing materials—the website, a blog post, a salesperson—can influence your perception of what you're going to receive. And of course, the price you pay is a big determinant of what value you expect to experience from your purchase.

In my company, we apply the five levels of Maslow's Hierarchy of Needs to the hotel experience (please see the figure on the following page). We believe a guest's physiological needs are met by finding a clean and comfortable room and bed. In fact, in the Stage One era of the proliferation of chain hotels across America, hotel guests were just becoming acquainted with the idea of traveling, as President Eisenhower's construction of a vast interstate highway

HOTEL CUSTOMER HIERARCHY OF NEEDS

MASLOW'S HIERARCHY:

Identity Refreshment — SELF-ACTUALIZATION

Feeling Like a VIP — ESTEEM

Responsive Staff Service — SOCIAL / BELONGING

SAFETY

Well-lit Parking, Electronic Door Locks — PHYSIOLOGICAL

A Comfortable and Clean Bed

system created a red carpet for middle-class Americans to travel like never before. During that era, companies like Holiday Inn addressed their customers' physiological or safety needs by wrapping drinking glasses in paper and covering the toilet seat with those odd sanitized wrappers. There was a time when that form of sanitation was the hallmark of a good hotel. Today, if I walk into a hotel with one of those wrappers on the toilet, I'm a little worried. Times change, but unfortunately, some companies don't. Many companies don't acknowledge that customer expectations naturally evolve. What is your industry's analogy to the wrapper on the toilet? Are you ahead or behind the curve with respect to evolving at a pace that at least keeps up with your customers' needs?

Moving up the pyramid, our customers' safety needs are met by a variety of factors—from whether the parking lot is well lit to whether the hotel provides guests electronic card keys (which are much safer than traditional metal keys) to the nature of the neighborhood where the hotel is located. Social and belonging needs are met by the friendliness of the staff and whether the guests feel some kinship with their fellow guests. Esteem needs are met by a personalized service approach from the staff that helps guests feel truly like VIPs—whether it's the front-desk host remembering their names or perhaps receiving an unexpected upgrade to a suite. Finally, a guest's self-actualization needs are addressed when the hotel creates what I've termed *identity refreshment,* an experience that I'll describe in more detail later in this chapter. Suffice it to say, identity refreshment is a bit like taking an aspirational bubble bath.

The reality is, if we don't get the foundational basics right (like having plumbing that works), most of our customers aren't going to be all that interested in aspirations or the art on the walls. It may be less exciting to focus on the basic blocking and tackling of hotel cleanliness and safety, but our customers' base needs can loom large when they're not properly satisfied. Execution is essential for companies that create baseline customer satisfaction. In some industries, your differentiating strategy may be best served by being the world's leader in meeting the base needs of your customers, although that's rarely the case.

You can create a Hierarchy of Needs pyramid for your company based on the product or service you are offering the marketplace. Just know that, similar to any Maslow-inspired pyramid, what's at the bottom tends to be more tangible or physical (features), what's on the middle level may have more of an emotional or intellectual payoff (benefits), while what's at the top is more transformational or even spiritual in nature.

The Nature of Customer Expectations

At Joie de Vivre, we've found that using this visual approach to describing our guests' Hierarchy of Needs is a powerful way for our employees to understand how to deliver on our customers' expectations. Customers bring with them a preconceived notion of what they're going to experience at our hotel. Unlike the shoes you buy in a store, our guests don't get to sample the product before they essentially buy or rent our product for the night. Often a guest's first experience with our product in the physical realm (as opposed to the process of making the reservation) is when they show up at our doorstep. The moment of truth for that guest comes with the initial impressions they have as they walk into our lobby for the first time and, ultimately, are escorted to their room. Many of your customers have the same experience with your product. They may not buy it "sight unseen" because they have likely gazed at your product on your website. But they are often buying it "sight untouched."

Think of your customers' expectations as a horizontal line. Call it the baseline. If in reality you deliver below the baseline, the variance between that line and what you deliver can be defined as "disappointment." In fact, if you're below that baseline, you don't even make it on the Customer Pyramid because actually meeting expectations is the foundation of this relationship. This chapter focuses on the risks and rewards associated with meeting your customers' basic expectations. Peak-performing companies know that they have to get the basics right at the base of the pyramid, but they won't likely outdistance their competitors by purely providing basic customer satisfaction.

BASELINE MODEL

Sears, Montgomery Ward, General Motors—these faltering stalwarts of twentieth-century capitalism got stuck focusing on the base of the Customer Pyramid. Their unconscious goal seemed to be getting their satisfaction scores high enough so that their customers were just barely over that disappointment baseline. They mistakenly believed that basic satisfaction buys customer loyalty. Clearly, they were wrong.

These companies should have taken note of one of Abe Maslow's most famous quotes: "If the only tool you have is a hammer, everything starts to look like a nail."[4] Companies in decline get too reliant on old tools.

Savvy companies realize that customers are learning to expect more and, due to the Internet, have more access to choices than ever before. Northwestern Professor Ranjay Gulati and Booz Allen Hamilton consultant David Kletter published a detailed study outlining that while 59 percent of companies found meeting customer expectations was a significant challenge in the past, 84 percent now consider it to be a significant challenge today. The combination of more discerning customers and companies' relentless pursuits of cost reduction and commoditization have led to more customers falling into that disappointed category. I'm often heard reciting one of my core beliefs: "*Disappointment is the natural result of badly managed expectations.*" Human beings are wired for disappointment if their expectations are not well managed.

Satisfaction Doesn't Create Loyalty

No company can succeed without addressing its customers' base needs, but too many executives think that simply meeting the basics of satisfaction is a true win for their company. Fred Reichheld and his Bain research teams found that 60 to 80 percent of customer defectors score themselves as "satisfied" or "very satisfied" on surveys preceding their defection. He writes in *The Ultimate Question*, "Satisfaction is simply too low a hurdle if the goal is superior relationships."[5] Reichheld believes that companies should rigorously track customer retention and customer evangelism (how your customers are using word-of-mouth and word-of-*mouse* on the Internet to spread the word about you, your product, or service) rather than just satisfaction.

Patrick Barwise and Sean Meehan suggest in *Simply Better* that "most industries are so set in their ways that they have trained customers to accept something like the existing levels of product and service quality. . . . Sometimes it takes some digging and imagination to unearth important needs that have not been articulated and are not being well met. Note: These are *category* needs. To unearth them, you need to ask customers, and sometimes noncustomers, about what they like and especially what they dislike about the *category*. This feedback will guide you toward the differentiation that matters."[6] This is what Theodore Levitt was suggesting in the quote that opened this chapter. This kind of thinking led Uber and Lyft to disrupt the taxi category.

Barwise and Meehan define a *category* as "a set of competing choices that, as seen by the buyer, share some key characteristics and provide similar benefits." For example, when Southwest Airlines' low fares started proliferating beyond Texas, it wasn't just other airlines that were affected—so were Greyhound and Amtrak. Competition isn't limited to just those companies that are playing by the same rules. In fact, if your whole category is barely meeting customer expectations, you and all of your competitors might be vulnerable.

Think Blockbuster versus Netflix. I bet if we reviewed Blockbuster's customer satisfaction scores in the mid-1990s, we might have found that 75 to 80 percent of their customers were generally happy with their video-store offerings. To use Beckwith's model, the industry was in a Stage One period at that time. In retrospect, it's easy to see the flaws in Blockbuster's business plan. Excessive late fees, poorly trained personnel, long lines, limited choice beyond recently released movies (90 percent of Blockbuster's rentals are new theatrical releases, so many stores didn't have a large stock of older or niche-oriented films), and no sense of personalization or concierge function. But if you asked Blockbuster executives who their biggest competitors were back in the mid-1990s, they probably would have mentioned Hollywood Video or some other national chain, as well as the mom 'n' pop neighborhood video stores.

I had the pleasure of chatting with Netflix founder Reed Hastings about the huge opportunity that faced Netflix when they entered the market in 1997. Reed told me, "Customers are good at telling you on the margins what they're looking for, and maybe Blockbuster was listening to that, but you rarely hear the 'big idea' from a customer as they haven't imagined it yet. We knew that movies are very personal and a Web-based service could deliver a much larger selection of unique films as well as the convenience of not having to jump in the car to pick up your movie."

Reed was quoted in the *New York Times* saying he got the idea for Netflix because of a big late fee. The video "was six weeks late, and I owed the video store $40. I had misplaced the cassette. It was all my fault. I didn't want to tell my wife about it. And I said to myself, 'I'm going to compromise the integrity of my marriage over a late fee?' Later, on my way to the gym, I realized they (the gym) had a much better business model. You could pay $30 or $40 a month and work out as little or as much as you wanted."[7] Thus sprouted the membership idea for Netflix. Netflix created a new expectation line for the customer looking to rent a DVD, and almost overnight, Blockbuster's offering moved from barely acceptable to clearly disappointing. According to Netflix, more than 90 percent of their customers evangelize the service to their friends and family. Any guess what that comparable percentage would have been for Blockbuster back in their heydey? The reasons for the success of companies like Netflix will be explored in the next two chapters. For the sake of this chapter, recognize that you are always vulnerable to a category killer: a new company with an offering that far outpaces the basic satisfaction associated with the status quo.

What kinds of companies are most vulnerable to becoming a victim of the "satisfaction shuffle?" Legacy companies—those that are living on past glory and aren't deeply connected to their customers—have the greatest risk of falling virtually overnight from superior to inferior in the eyes of their customers. McDonald's became a hit more than a half century ago because their product offering—consistent, accessible, inexpensive fast food in a clean environment—became the quality standard by which fast food was judged. Over time, customers' expectations and satisfaction needs grew, while McDonald's became a standardized offering in a commoditized business. Only recently has McDonald's started to evolve its offerings in such a way that it's starting to resonate in the marketplace again. Of course, there are other examples like TWA or Wang that no longer exist because of their inability to see the changes on the horizon.

The larger the organization, the more it tends toward the tangible or it looks to standardize. Bo Burlingham, in his terrific book *Small Giants*, talks about how companies that lose their mojo forget "about the emotional connection with the consumer . . . and concentrate on the process of business."[8] As many companies get larger, they become more disconnected from their customers, more bland and standardized, more focused on managing to the averages, and thus they end up settling in at the bottom of the Customer Pyramid. Plus, the Marriots and Hyatts of the world can be so insulated from innovators that they have no idea what three Millennials, with no experience starting a business, might be cooking up in their apartment. And, they're so wedded to their existing product that these hotel execs have no clue that home sharing might appeal to a broad segment of the traveling marketplace.

Boutique Hotels as Disruptive Innovators

The American hotel industry has followed Beckwith's three stages of evolution. In the 1950s, the Holiday Inns of the world offered consistency and predictability to a middle-class customer who was just learning what it meant to travel frequently. Other chains like

Marriott and Hilton followed suit. With time, the industry evolved to where the big chains started offering a broader product line of choice. Marriott offered its customers a range from the value-driven Fairfield Inn to the Ritz-Carlton (which Marriott purchased in 1998). The focus of the chains was still on predictability, but now they offered a collection of brands targeting various segments of the market. Still, this was merely a replication strategy that didn't allow for much differentiation from location to location.

Prior to hotel chains proliferating in the 1950s, virtually all American hotels were independently owned and operated. By the early 1980s, many travelers were starting to tire of the bland sameness being offered by the chains, and they were once again looking for an independent alternative. It was a ripe time for entrepreneurs like Bill Kimpton and Ian Schrager, both of whom came from outside the hotel industry, to start their boutique hotel companies. (I started Joie de Vivre three to four years after these heroes of mine started their companies.)

Boutique hotels were created based on the premise that just meeting customer expectations wasn't good enough for many hotel guests. Choosing a hotel is a rather intimate product choice. You sleep with the product. You get naked and shower with the product. You experience the product for days at a time and, if it's a memorable experience, for some time afterward. Given the nature of the product, it seems natural that hotels should mirror the aspirations and personalities of their customers. They should also be a reflection of the community in which they're located. So, boutique hotels came on the scene in the early 1980s and immediately started eating away at the market share of the big chains in America's largest cities.

Joie de Vivre's innovation was to create an organizing principle that helped us deliver what *USA Today* called "the most delightfully schizophrenic collection of hotels in America." In creating our first hotel, The Phoenix, I decided that we would use magazines as a touchstone for the hotel's personality. Magazine publishing and boutique hotels have a lot in common. They both develop products that focus on market niches. (Have you ever wondered who reads some of those oddball publications you see on a long magazine rack?) These products are typically somewhat lifestyle-driven. If the publisher or boutique hotelier gets it right, they develop a deep emotional connection between their subscriber or hotel guest and their product. In fact, Condé Nast, America's largest magazine publisher, launched an ad campaign with close-up photos of subscribers passionately embracing their favorite magazines with headlines like, "It's not just a magazine subscription, it's a torrid love affair." That's the kind of relationship that boutique hoteliers seek with their most rabidly loyal customers.

We chose *Rolling Stone* magazine to be the personality of The Phoenix. We also introduced the practice of using five words to define the magazine and the kind of hotel we wanted to create: "irreverent, adventurous, cool, funky, and young at heart." Every decision we made—from the staff we hired to the uniforms they wore to the design of the guest rooms to the unique services we were offering—had to match up with this list of five adjectives. This organizing principle helped ensure that all parties, from our investors or owners to the designer or architect to the general manager or sales team, were on the same page. This is one pivotal reason why Joie de Vivre has won numerous national awards, not just for our design but for the unique experiences we create.

I didn't realize the magic in this approach until I started talking to our regular guests at The Phoenix and found that what attracted them to the hotel was something intangible. Our biggest cheer-leaders for The Phoenix weren't necessarily people who fit the hotel's *demographic* of young, male, Los Angeles–based musicians with tattoos. The hotel's biggest fans were people who fit the *psychographic*: the guests who would have used those five adjectives to describe themselves (Dr. Timothy Leary, mentioned at the start of Chapter Two, was a good example of this). In essence, by staying a few days at The Phoenix, these guests experience an *identity refreshment* when they leave: feeling a little more funky, cool, and irreverent. However, not everyone wants this type of aspirational bubble bath. For example, my mother is not a big fan of The Phoenix. That didn't matter, though, as Joie de Vivre started growing by imagining new niches in the market that were under-served, finding a magazine that defined that segment, creating a unique boutique hotel, and then tapping into this psychographic population and letting them evangelize about the product. A high percentage of repeat customers, big word-of-mouth (and word-of-mouse), and rampant positive press help keep us busier than our competitors for a fraction of the promotional expense.

Over the 24 years I was CEO of Joie de Vivre, we created 52 boutique hotels, each of them based on different magazine person-alities – from *Wired* to *Town and Country* to the *New Yorker*. Some of our most interesting hotels are based on a hybrid of two magazines like our Galleria Park Hotel, where *Business Week* meets *Vanity Fair,* or our Hotel Vitale, which goes after the post-W (Starwood's brand), pre–Four Seasons guest by marrying *Dwell* to *Real Simple,* creating a hip yet holistic and mature ambience for the *bourgeois bohemian* of the world (what the *New York Times* columnist and author David Brooks calls "bobos"). In essence, Joie de Vivre recognized that the modern hotel customer was having their baseline expectations met at the big chains, but this customer was looking for something more. They wanted a hotel experience that spoke to them on a higher level of the Customer Pyramid. Yet, Joie de Vivre had a big challenge. It's one thing to create a rock'n'roll hotel that seeks out adventurous and young-at-heart travelers, but when we upped the ante to create an entire collection of niche-oriented boutique hotels throughout the San Francisco Bay Area, we risked confusing our customers when they came to our website. We could imagine our customer saying, "I like the idea that Joie de Vivre has the perfect hotel for my personality, but how do I choose the right hotel among the collection?" As we grew the number of Joie de Vivre hotels, we grew the risk that our guests would end up in the wrong hotel for them, as happened when the conservative president of the American Medical Association (and his wife), who were friends of my parents, showed up at the funky Phoenix for a room. The fright on their faces will stay with me for a lifetime.

Given that "disappointment is the natural result of badly managed expectations," we needed to figure out a way to better educate our guests about what kind of personality they should expect when booking a stay at each of our hotels. And there were other storm clouds brewing on the horizon that also required a shift in how we educated our guests. While boutique hotels had been the disruptive innovators of the hospitality industry in the 1990s and the early part of the new century, we were about to be disruptively innovated by some new players to the market.

JOIE DE VIVRE ON THE BRINK OF DISASTER

In the late 1990s, Expedia and Travelocity launched their travel websites with a unique value proposition to the traveling public. Their websites created an *efficient* market for what had historically been an *inefficient* one. What I mean is they gave power to the hotel customer by providing travelers an efficient and transparent way of comparing hotel prices and products. This supermarket strategy of plentiful supply at the best prices was being mirrored on the Internet across other industries, but in no other industry was the shift of power from producer to consumer more pronounced than in the travel industry.

The power of Expedia and Travelocity soon multiplied over-night due to the 9/11 tragedy and the ensuing downturn in travel. The traveling public began flocking to the Internet to find the best-priced airfares and hotel rooms. All of a sudden, travel was seen by most as virtually a commodity, and websites like Hotels.com became a traveler's best friend. From Joie de Vivre's perspective, this was a disaster, not just financially but also in terms of our relationship with our customers because we had long enjoyed a direct, personal relationship with our loyal following. Financially, this new commod-itized approach to booking hotel rooms meant that our average room rate was plummeting by 20 percent or more as the power now rested in the hands of the consumer. Furthermore, these travel websites charged us up to a 25 percent commission on every room they booked with us. So our $200 hotel room had to drop to a $160 hotel room because of the newly efficient market. And then, if that room was booked by a company like Expedia, we would receive only $120 net of that $160 rate. Our profit margin was wiped out overnight.

Adding insult to injury, the nature of our guests also started to change. Previously, the guests who discovered our hotels had usually done their homework (or had heard about us through friends) and knew why they wanted to book one of our personality-driven hotels. But with this new influx of travel-website guests, who were choosing hotels primarily for price, we found that our customer satisfaction scores started to plummet. It was the worst of all worlds: we were making less money, and our guests were less happy. In analyzing this situation, we found that the guests who had the lowest satisfaction were those who'd booked on the third-party travel websites. Their dissatisfaction seemed to come from the fact that their expectations didn't match the product. Whereas before the Internet our product differentiation was one of our strengths, the fact that we weren't predictable like the Sheratons or Hilton Gardens of the world was coming back to haunt us.

We needed to solve two problems quickly: (1) improve our margins and (2) make sure the right guest was matched with the right hotel so we could improve customer satisfaction. We needed to figure this out fast because the percentage of our business that was coming from the Internet was doubling each year. Unfortunately, at that point in 2002, only 20 percent of our Web-based reservations was coming from our own website, with the balance coming from the high-commission third-party sites.

Thankfully, I'm surrounded by very talented and resourceful people. In 2003, we came up with a clever yet inexpensive solution that leveraged our company's core values of creativity and quirkiness. This solution has translated into millions of dollars of margin improvement and a big uptick in customer satisfaction. Our marketing team introduced a cartoon character named Yvette, the Hotel Matchmaker, on our home page. Yvette asks you to take a one-minute personality test that helps us understand your psychographic persona. Once you take the test, Yvette immediately delivers back to you five of our hotels that best fit your personality. Yvette also provides some matchmaking with respect to what you should do when you visit the Bay Area. She offers up two local people (out of a few dozen who are profiled on our website) who are most similar to your personality and shares their lists of favorite hidden treasures you shouldn't miss during your stay. Finally, Yvette also gives you six specific recommendations of things to do (from a list of a couple hundred local favorites) that seem perfectly suited to your psychographic. (Joie de Vivre recently retired Yvette's image from our website because her cartoon character didn't fit with the company's new design.)

This creative matchmaking tool became an overnight hit, got lots of press, and ultimately won Joie de Vivre the "E- Marketer of the Year" award worldwide in the hospitality industry two years in a row. Not only did this hotel matchmaking approach drive more guests to our website—so that we didn't have to pay that 25 percent commission to travel websites—it also produced a less commodity-driven customer who had much higher satisfaction because we matched him or her with the hotel that best fit their personality. In essence, we did a better job of managing the expectations of our guests. Guest satisfaction grew, and the percentage of our total revenues coming from the Joie de Vivre website escalated at nearly twice the annual growth rate compared with America's big hotel chains. We were able to dodge the bullet that still plagues many other independent hoteliers who have become reliant on the high-commission third-party websites.

In many ways, Yvette was a lightweight means for us to be way ahead of the game in the world of customer customization for which Netflix, Amazon, and Spotify have become famous. And, the thinking that led Joie de Vivre to create Yvette is alive and well at Airbnb, as we use the wide variety of data signals we get from our customers to deliver personalized suggestions of where to stay and what to do for our guests.

PEAK PRESCRIPTIONS

The foundation of the Customer Pyramid is ensuring that you are delivering on the expectations of your customers. Here are some ideas that will help you succeed at addressing these foundational needs:

1. Use your existing customer satisfaction measuring tools in more effective ways. As flawed as basic customer satisfaction surveys can be, there are many ways to make the most of what you already have. Joie de Vivre is able to address problems in real time because our online guest surveys come into us one at a time throughout the day. So, our general managers and their supervisors (who also receive the data) can jump on a problem immediately after a guest expresses some dis-satisfaction with their experience. Furthermore, any guest survey that comes in from any of our hotels with a score of 100 (along with enthusiastic comments) or below 60 receives a customized e-mail response within a couple of days from me personally, expressing our thanks or our apologies. This kind of unexpected customized responsiveness turns cheer-leaders into even bigger evangelists and helps turn many frustrated customers into new believers. Another responsive organization is Harley-Davidson. They don't just trap valu-able customer service data in some silo of the company where it won't be acted on. They use company retirees (who want to stay close to the company by working part-time) to do follow-up calls with their customers.

2. Reach out to your customers with more direct questions that are relevant to your product or service. Maybe the generic

survey you're using just doesn't capture what you want to learn from your customers. The authors of *Simply Better* suggest your surveys help you answer the following rather basic questions:

- What are the main benefits you deliver for your most important customers?
- Do you deliver these for all your customers?
- Do your competitors also offer these benefits?
- How regularly are you monitoring your performance on these benefits?[9]

Ask questions that will help you see early trends in your business. For example, many hotel companies in the late 1990s were slow in adding high-speed Internet to their guest rooms because generic industry surveys didn't list it as one of the top five items of what a guest is looking for in a hotel. But by the time those surveys were published, it was old information, given the speed that the Internet was being adopted as an essential tool for most business travelers. Consider asking the "Ultimate Question" that Fred Reichheld has so effectively outlined in his book of the same name, which is now labeled *Net Promoter Score* (NPS): "How likely is it that you would recommend us to a friend or colleague?"[10] Some of our hotels have asked the question, "What are the three biggest problems with our hotel?" Then the general manager of the property trains his or her staff in how to address these most frequent problems. Sometimes you can learn more from the drivers of dissatisfaction than from the drivers that create baseline satisfaction.

3. Move beyond looking just at your company's satisfaction surveys and look at the broad category in which you're competing. Look at the potential drivers of dissatisfaction in your category. Ask open-ended questions of your customers that allow them to think beyond the current product offerings in your business. Compare your industry with another one when asking for feedback from your customers. In the mid-1990s, when retailers like Pottery Barn, Target, and Gap were offering a more stylish design to the middle class (that had previously only been available at the high end of the market), I started asking the following question in conversations with our hotel customers and corporate

(continued)

(*continued*)

accounts: "What could the hotel industry learn from these retailers, and what are the best and worst things you can say about the hotel industry's best-known mid-price hotel chains like Holiday Inn and Radisson?" These are not the typical questions you ask your customers. But the answers to these questions helped Joie de Vivre realize that there was a huge market of middle-income Americans who were looking for a moderately priced boutique hotel product that was both stylish and functional. It gave us confidence that, unlike some of our boutique hotel competitors who were developing only high-end hotels, we should continue to create mid-price boutique hotels for the masses.

4. Engage your executives and employees in a brainstorming session about how you would apply Maslow's Hierarchy of Needs to the motivations of your customers. Earlier in the chapter, I showed how Joie de Vivre used this exercise to help our team understand how we can deliver what our customer is looking for. I doubt if Starwood used Maslow's pyramid, but they certainly discovered an insight in 1999, when they launched their luxurious "Heavenly Bed" for their Westin brand. While having a comfortable bed is a base need for every hotel customer, strangely enough, no hotel company had ever truly innovated the bed product to create a brand product differentiation. Don't assume that your competition has gotten the basics right. Be willing to ask foolish questions about whether the base of your Customer Pyramid has truly been satisfied.

Expectations are what drive customer satisfaction or disappointment. The Customer Pyramid can help you better understand the motivations and expectations of your customers. This pyramid will remind your executives that customers are actually collections of people with collective psychological needs and desires. Covering the basics of these customer needs creates baseline customer satisfaction. You can't move up the pyramid without it. But as we've learned, today's customer is rather promiscuous at this base level of the pyramid. Now let's explore what it takes to create a more committed relationship between you and your customer.

RECOMMENDED READING

Crossing the Chasm by Geoffrey A. Moore

"Customer Loyalty and Experience Design in E-Business" by Karl Long, *Design Management Review* (Spring 2004)

Loyalty Rules by Fred Reichheld

"Marketing Myopia" by Theodore Levitt, *Harvard Business Review* (July–August 1960)

Selling the Invisible by Harry Beckwith

Simply Better by Patrick Barwise and Sean Meehan

Small Giants by Bo Burlingham

The Innovator's Dilemma by Clayton M. Christensen

Trading Up by Michael J. Silverstein and Jay Fiske

Treasure Hunt by Michael J. Silverstein and John Butman

CHAPTER EIGHT

CREATING COMMITMENT

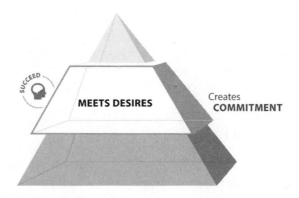

We should be able to institutionalize all the democratic, communicative, respecting, loving, listening customer satisfaction kinds of things in the future by using the advantages of technology. In other words, keeping all the benefits of smallness but also capitalizing on the benefits of bigness.

ABRAHAM MASLOW[1]

The bigger you get as a company, the more you need to create forums for engagement with your customers. Even if you're big, act small. People are more likely to trust you when they can relate to you. And being humble usually means you're a more empathic listener.

One of the unique methods Joie de Vivre employs to learn the longings of our customers is to hold a series of town hall meetings in the community where we're developing our concept for a new hotel. Joie de Vivre's goal is to create individual landmarks that are a reflection of both the aspirations of a certain customer group and the personality of the community in which the hotel is located. For example, in Sacramento, California, we are creating the city's first luxury hotel, called The Citizen, out of a historic high-rise office building across the park from city hall.

After we received our city approvals to move forward with this project, we hosted a series of town hall meetings where locals could help us develop the concept and unique features of this hotel. I even volunteered my personal e-mail address to be printed in a business column of the *Sacramento Bee* to solicit ideas from locals (we got more than 100 interesting e-mails). The city didn't require us to do this. But we knew that if we genuinely engaged the locals, we'd create good buzz and develop a better understanding of what unique services, amenities, personality, and design they would want to see in this boutique hotel and its signature restaurant.

One of my favorite town hall memories happened one night when, after presenting some of the basic facts of what we hoped to do with this Sacramento hotel, we handed out a list of 40 adjectives that we thought might describe the essential nature of Sacramento. We asked the 70 locals who showed up for this exercise in democratic capitalism to each circle five words that best described the city's personality and where it is going. We educated them on our magazine approach to developing concepts for hotels (explained in the last chapter), and then we split them into four groups, gave each an easel, and asked them to arrive at their consensus five words and a list of some unique services and amenities that would be a perfect reflection of the community. Mind you, most of these people had never met each other. They had just responded to an article in the local paper that included my e-mail address. I saw fear in the eyes of some when they realized they were being asked to move from a passive role to actually having a voice. Fortunately, we had one Joie de Vivre manager act as a facilitator in each of the four groups to make sure they got off to a good start.

By the end of the night, we had gathered some very valuable information, including many subtleties we would never have fathomed if we were just brainstorming in the Joie de Vivre corporate offices back in San Francisco. These randomly self-selected locals were able to spark new relationships through the bonding process of talking about their community and how the hotel should reflect Sacramento. I believe they also felt like they had their fingerprints all over our blueprints (the truth is, they did have a big influence on the product we've ultimately created). I'll never forget the comment one beaming fellow gave me as he was leaving the room: "I came here expecting a hearing or a feisty inquisition, and I'm leaving feeling like I've been to a personal growth workshop."

Welcome to the social and esteem levels of Maslow's Hierarchy of Needs as applied to the customer. Our town hall meetings address the social and esteem needs of our stakeholders in the community. But the real win for any peak-seeking company is how the company addresses those needs for their rank-and-file customers.

Abe Maslow was a smart man. He made the pro-technology statement that opens this chapter at a time when the average computer was the size of a Buick and Steve Jobs was barely hitting puberty. In Maslow's musings as the shrink-in-residence at Menlo Park's Saga Corporation in the late 1960s, he expressed concern that as companies grow, they naturally get more disconnected from their customers' desires. They don't seek out unique ways to listen to their customers. But he expressed a hope that through the proper investment in technology and training, any company, no matter what its size, could deliver on its customers' desires.

WHAT ARE CUSTOMER DESIRES?

In Chapter Two, I introduced the concept of the Transformation Pyramid, which suggested that employees, customers, and investors have basic *survival* needs that grow into *success* needs that in turn progress into *transformation* needs at the peak of each pyramid. In the previous chapter, we addressed the survival needs of our customers. If we deliver more than the customer expects, that usually translates into a successful customer experience. For our hotel guests, that means they aren't just impressed with an efficient check-in, a clean and comfortable room, or what feels like a safe and secure atmosphere. Hotel guests who've had their desires met may have experienced one of the following customer successes:

• They had their social needs met by having an engaged conversation with the front-desk staff, concierge, or room attendant.

- They had their belonging needs met by connecting with other friendly hotel guests at a complimentary wine hour where guests informally talked about their experiences as tourists in the town that day.
- Their affiliation needs were met just by staying in a hotel that caters to other guests who look like they do (for example, families are reassured when they check into a resort that has other families).
- Their esteem needs were met by being surprised with an upgrade to a room with a better view, or maybe they received a small bottle of wine, their favorite snacks, and a personal note from the general manager on arriving in their guest room.

It may be as simple as having all the hotel staff recognize them and use their name when greeting them throughout their stay. These are the kinds of desires that hotel guests wish they could count on every time they visited a hotel. When a hotel truly delivers on these desires, the guest is much more likely to become committed to the organization as a loyal, long-term customer. So, meeting desires is about understanding the unique preferences of a customer. In today's lingo, we call this mass customization or the ability for a company to cater to a market of one and to do so over and over again. To do this well, it requires that a company take Maslow's advice and invest in both systems and service.

In their book *Priceless,* Diana LaSalle and Terry Britton describe the sort of mass customization experience at Paris Miki that Maslow might have dreamed of:

> Upon entering one of its stores, the customer is greeted by an associate who takes a digital picture of the customer; the computer then measures the distance between her eyes and the length of her nose. The customer then chooses from a list of sixty image words such as "glamorous," "intelligent," "sporty," "sexy," "distinctive," and "professional" to describe the look she desires. Based on the customer's facial shape and the selected adjectives, the artificial intelligence system recommends frames and lenses. The results are displayed onscreen over the digital image of the customer's face, allowing her to "try on" several pairs without leaving her seat. The customer can even customize the eyewear if the look is close but not exactly right. The whole process takes between fifteen and twenty minutes and custom glasses are delivered within two weeks.[2]

We've moved from a one-size-fits-all culture to what author and Maslow expert Deborah Stephens calls a *one-size-fits-one* customer. Being normal doesn't carry the currency it once did. We all want to feel special, a little different, and companies that indulge this yearning will be richly rewarded. Ironically, the two common elements that define companies that deliver on this level of the pyramid seem diametrically opposed to each other: technology (hard) and people (soft). Companies that know how to harness their technology *and* empower their people have the potential to deliver customized service that will translate into committed customers.

USING TECHNOLOGY TO MEET DESIRES

Surveys show that only one in five customers is committed to the extent that they're truly loyal. There are all kinds of ways to create loyalty. AOL created pseudo-loyalty by making it difficult to disconnect their service after the free trial period (they got sued in 2003 because of it). The airlines do it with their mileage points, which are more bribery than loyalty programs. They're just retention tactics based on trying to influence behaviors. True loyalty comes from influencing a customer's attitude by having keen insight into their desires or preferences. Historically, companies have relied on long-term employees to remember the preferences of their customers. Today, technology answers that call.

So how does a company really come to understand its customers' desires? Don Peppers and Martha Rogers suggest in *Return on Customer* that there are three insightful ways to anticipate your customer's preferences: memory, editorial inference, and comparisons with other customers. You'll see that technology can play a pivotal role in each of these.

Memory refers to repeat customers who have already expressed their preference for their profile—the kind of car they like to rent, whether they want to take the insurance offered by the rental car company, and what kind of credit card they might use. Investing in customer relations software that allows you to store these preferences creates a great return on investment and one that, I'm embarrassed to admit, my company waited way too long to implement. Your customers' esteem needs are met when they realize that you remembered their favorite guest room or what kind of pillow they want in their room so they don't have to ask for it. At Joie de Vivre, we relied too heavily for too long on our staffs' memories of our repeat customers' desires. Finally, we realized we needed to invest in technology to help us remember that each time a particular guest stays in one of our hotels, we know to deliver a *New York Times* instead of a *San Francisco Chronicle* in the morning.

Peppers and Rogers suggest that the second method of understanding customer desires relates to using that memory and applying it to an *editorial* categorization. They write, "The fact that a customer celebrates her mother's birthday with flowers means she might want to celebrate Mother's Day, too, or perhaps some of her relatives' birthdays. Because a customer buys music CDs, she might be interested in CD-cleaning solutions or CD players."[3] Clearly, there's more guesswork in this approach, but it's almost like having an angel on the shoulders of your customer asking, "Have you thought of this or that?"

Finally, the third shortcut to understanding customer desires allows you to harness data to *compare* this customer's buying patterns with those of other similar customers in order to make recommendations. Most large Web-based retailers now use software that connects you as a customer to the desires of other affiliated customers. Netflix does this by explicitly showing you recommendations of your friends. Clearly, this is a means of applying Maslow's social level of the Hierarchy of Needs Pyramid, as it allows you to share your experiences and preferences with your friends.

With technology in an enabling role, companies can create *learning relationships* with their customers such that the more the company interacts with the customer, the better the company understands the customer's desires. Peppers and Rogers suggest, "The more you can get a customer to 'teach' you about his needs—provided you can actually meet them with an increasing degree of customization or an increasing amount of service—the more loyal that customer will become, because he won't want to have to expend the time or take the risk to re-teach some other firm what he's already taught you."[4]

Amazon deserves the crown for harnessing technology to develop learning relationships. It's been a trailblazer in using technology to anticipate its customers' desires. It's religious about letting me know when a new book is coming out that fits my typical buying preferences. You can bet that if there's a book with a Maslow focus about to hit the shelves, Amazon will tell me about it before I even know the book exists. Clearly, the company knows I have pyramid envy!

Still, my customer commitment to Amazon was hard-won. I'm a big fan of independent bookstores, and there are still a few in San Francisco that I love to frequent. But as my tastes in books became more eclectic, I found these books harder to find in my local bookstores. Yet, because I bought a few books with Amazon, they had a technologically driven intuition about which new books I might enjoy. Frankly, founder Jeff Bezos finally won me over when he sent me (and probably millions of other customers) the following letter a few years ago with 10 one-cent stamps enclosed:

> *Dear Friend,*
>
> *From the start, one of our primary goals at Amazon has been to make the lives of our customers easier. For over five years, this sensibility has guided our growth, site design, and the addition of new features and services.*
>
> *But recently, it struck me that despite all our hard work there are still many inconveniences we haven't yet addressed. We can't wash your dishes. We can't pick up your dry cleaning. We can't change the little light bulb in your refrigerator. We can't make your tuna salad just the way you like it. Then I realized there was one thing we could do that we've never done before—spare you the hassle of an extra trip to the post office! First-class postal rates went up a penny to 34 cents on January 7, so enclosed you'll find ten one-cent stamps— a necessity for using up your old 33-centers. Sure, we're only talking ten cents in value, but hopefully the time you'll save will be worth much more.*
>
> *Sincerely,*
> *Jeff Bezos*

I still have those 10 stamps, and I occasionally show them and Jeff's letter to people when I give customer service speeches. For a cutting-edge, high-tech company, this was a perfect execution of *high touch*. Some might consider this a gimmick, but no one can doubt Amazon's service quality, as their representatives are first class. Both their technology and their service are a big part of the reason that Amazon is arguably the most highly respected e-commerce site in the world.

In 2016, 43 percent of all U.S. online retail sales were through Amazon. Amazon is a great example of a high-tech, high-touch company that's mastered its approach to mass customization. It represents the wave of the future as companies move from selling one standardized product to many people to focusing on selling many products to one person over the course of his or her lifetime. That's the nature of a committed relationship with your customer.

High-Tech, High-Touch Cultures

Validate me. That's what customers are looking for on this middle level of the Customer Pyramid. Sophisticated technology alone can't do it. Today's market leaders realize that *touch* is possibly more important than *tech*.

FedEx revolutionized the way we send packages, and they also use technology to address our desire of knowing just where our package is at any particular point in time. But if you ask the senior execs at FedEx who the most valuable employees in the company are, they will tell you it's the couriers who pick up and deliver packages and have the most direct contact with customers. FedEx is a master at hiring and training line-level staff people and empowering them to create solutions for their customers.

Enterprise Rent-a-Car revolutionized its industry by focusing on a different market segment (people who need a replacement car— usually involving an insurance company—because their primary car is in the shop). It is a pioneer with respect to how it uses technology to satisfy its customer base and connect with insurance companies in innovative ways. Enterprise's well-known, high-touch brand promise revolves around its willingness to come pick you up wherever you are. In addition, as a customer, I am constantly amazed at the quality of people it hires and their can-do attitude as compared with the *can't-do* staff I meet at many of the other rental car companies. It makes a difference that one Enterprise employee takes care of all my needs from the time I am at the counter to when that person escorts me to my car.

Similarly, Best Buy uses technology to constantly do in-depth evaluations of its customer profiles. Over the last few years, based on analyzing these data, it has determined that there are five types of highly valued customers who represent the greatest upside potential to the company, from younger men who want the latest in technology and entertainment to busy suburban moms who come to Best Buy to enrich their children's lives. The company trains its store personnel to be more proactive in sizing up each customer who walks in the door. The sales staff determines whether the person fits one of these five niches so that they can suggest customer-centric solutions that fit this particular niche. For Best Buy, high tech fosters high touch.

Introduced in Chapter Six, Danny Meyer's Union Square Hospitality Group is probably the most respected restaurant organization in the country. Its Manhattan restaurants, from Union Square Cafe to Gramercy Tavern, are consistently rated the best restaurants in the competitive New York City marketplace. In talking with Danny and in reading his book *Setting the Table*, it is clear that his restaurants use technology as a means of tracking the preferences of their customers. Their OpenTable reservations system allows them to make customer notes on where in the dining room a guest likes to sit, whether they're allergic to shellfish, or if they prefer to have their coffee served after dessert. But Danny readily acknowledges that in the restaurant business (and in the service industry in general), technology *enables* great service, it doesn't *create* great service.

For Danny, great service comes from finding the right people and creating a culture that is devoted to meeting the desires of their customers. In interviewing prospects, he asks his managers if they believe the candidate has the capacity to become one of the top three performers on their team in his or her job category. He's particularly concerned about the natural tendency for businesses to hire middle-of-the-road performers.

He writes,

> It's pretty easy to spot an overwhelmingly strong candidate or even an underwhelmingly weak candidate. It's the *"whelming"* candidate you must avoid at all costs, because that's the one who can and will do your organization the most long-lasting harm. Overwhelmers earn you raves. Underwhelmers either leave of their own volition or are terminated. Whelmers, sadly, are like a stubborn stain you can't get out of the carpet. They infuse an organization and its staff with mediocrity; they're comfortable, and so they never leave; and, frustratingly, they never do anything that rises to the level of getting them promoted or sinks to the level of getting them fired. And because you either can't or don't fire them, you and they conspire to send a dangerous message to your staff and guests that "average" is acceptable.[5]

In many ways, I agree with Danny, but I think he doesn't acknowledge that the *whelmers* may be the most moldable depending on what other kinds of employees surround them. Peter Drucker believed that the distance between the star performer and the average always remains the same. As the bar moves up because of a few new star performers, those employees at the bottom must shift their game up. The problem with most service businesses, though, is they let the whelmers create an inertia rut of being purely satisfied with the status quo. If you let that happen, it's almost certain that your service culture will have a hard time rising to the level of consistently meeting your customers' desires.

CREATING A GREAT SERVICE CULTURE

One of my greatest lessons about how to create a bar-raising service culture goes back to the weeks before we launched our flagship Hotel Vitale in the winter of 2005. Seven years in the making, Hotel Vitale was going to be San Francisco's first luxury waterfront hotel, which is sort of surprising considering the city is surrounded by water on three sides. On many levels, this project was a defining moment for the company.

We shocked the local hospitality industry when we beat our bigger rival across town, Kimpton, in the request-for-proposals process with the city in 1997 to 1998 (the hotel is located on city-owned land). Given that this hotel site had some controversy attached to it, and there was a heavy antigrowth sentiment during this dot-com boom period, we survived votes from seven different city commissions or boards, winning approval each time. After four years, we had our green light from the city to move forward with the project, but those development entitlements were gained just as the hotel market started its year 2001 swoon. So, we sat there, paying the city rent for the land while we tried to scrounge up the financing to build the 200-room hotel. We had raised $43 million of the $51 million we needed to start construction, but that last piece of mezzanine financing (a high-cost second mortgage in addition to our first mortgage) was elusive, especially because lenders aren't fond of providing construction loans on leased land. I had provided a multimillion-dollar personal financial guaranty with the city that was in danger of being called, and not having taken a salary in a few years, I had run out of cash.

Two years into this waiting game, after hearing *no* from more than 50 different lenders, we secured our mezzanine financing and built the hotel in record time at a cost that was probably $10 million less than it would have cost us just one year later when construction prices skyrocketed. During the 17-month construction process, I was virtually tethered to the hotel, as we had little room for error given how much cost cutting we'd performed to meet the lenders' requirements. Stress became my middle name. I knew my company had a lot riding on our first luxury hotel launch.

Danny Meyer and I have something in common. We both get a little queasy as the construction nears its completion for one of our new projects. So about six weeks before we were to open the Hotel Vitale, I took a sales trip to New Zealand and Australia with the San Francisco Convention and Visitors Bureau. I came back from my down-under trip rested and relaxed. I was really ready to meet the 150 newly hired members of the Vitale service team. But after a couple of orientations with the group, I had a vague sense of being troubled that I couldn't put my finger on. I sensed that there were a number of superstars in the bunch, but I could also see there were more weak links in the group than I expected. After a couple of sleepless nights, I sat down with the Vitale management team, who had been hired long before I left on my trip, and asked them about the group that had been hired. Without prompting, they admitted they weren't perfectly satisfied with the group, although they believed that the training process would help to polish some of the weak links. A couple of days later, I checked back with the managers and found that their doubts about some of the staff remained, but of course, they had their hands full with the hotel opening in a month, so it was hard for them to see the troubling big picture that was emerging.

Finally, the puzzle pieces came together for me. I was able to articulate a truism that has defined Joie de Vivre's successful approach to delivering a people-empowered service culture ever since. The reality is there are typically three kinds of employees: the superstars, the silent majority, and the weak links. To successfully launch a new hotel, especially one competing in the luxury category, you want to make sure you have twice as many superstars as weak links because the silent majority will gravitate to what's dominant. This isn't just relevant to hotels; it's important for any business that's trying to improve service or any business where employees are influenced by each other's performance. Employees are constantly looking for clues about how high they're supposed to jump. The superstars set the bar, but if they're in the minority compared with the weak links, the whole service infrastructure will slump. Even the superstars will lower the bar in that situation. The result for the customer might be service levels that may meet the basic levels of satisfaction but never aspire to that next level of meeting customer desires.

Once I figured this out, I realized that we had to change the alchemy. We immediately moved some of our Joie de Vivre service superstars from other hotels to the Vitale, and we had frank conversations with a number of the weak links in this new staff, clarifying that they had to improve or else they might lose their jobs. Fortunately, we have an amazing training department staff and a committed collection of Vitale managers, so by the time we opened, we had moved from a ratio of maybe one superstar for every weak link to a preferred alchemy of 2:1. And the process of getting to this preferred alchemy had sent a message to the silent majority in between: this hotel expects a high standard and looks for you to step up to the highest levels of service you are capable of offering.

What an amazing experience it was preparing for our opening and living in the hotel the first 10 days we were open. It was evident to me that the whole Vitale team had turned into superstars and that they really cared about exceeding the guests' expectations. I built some incredibly close relationships with this remarkable team during that time. The Hotel Vitale has turned out to be one of Joie de Vivre's biggest success stories. Extremely high customer loyalty and world-class customer satisfaction scores have led the hotel to posting the highest occupancy in its competitive set, which includes worldwide luxury giants like Four Seasons, Ritz-Carlton, Mandarin, St. Regis, and W. It is a testament to the talent and determination of our managers and employees of the Vitale that this little independent hotel that could climbed to the top of this class in its occupancy percentage so quickly after it opened. It also made me realize we'd come a long way from the days when our biggest competition for the funky Phoenix was the Travelodge one block away.

PEAK PRESCRIPTIONS

Will it be tech or touch that builds your expertise of understanding your customers' desires? If you're a leader in your industry, it will probably be a combination of the two.

1. Engage intimately with your customers so you can truly understand their desires. Nearly 80 percent of companies say they are moving to customized value-added solutions as opposed to selling just standard products or services to their customers. General Electric's CEO Jeff Immelt has instigated *dreaming sessions* with key customers to understand just what they're looking for from his products as well as to understand where their needs may be in the future. Meg Whitman, former CEO at eBay and now CEO at Hewlett-Packard, instituted a bi-monthly *voice of the customer* program in which 12 to 18 customers are flown to eBay's headquarters for a full day of discussions and brainstorming. I know lots of senior executives who spend a few hours each year on the front lines listening to their customers. What are you doing to institutionalize a conversation starter with your customers? Think of this as a marketing investment for your existing customers—as opposed to a marketing cost for new customers—that has an enormous return on investment. You can't rely exclusively on customer satisfaction surveys to understand your customers' specific desires. There's a distinct correlation between profitability and a company's ability to create customized solutions for its core customers. Ask yourself, "How many of our top 10 customers have been the beneficiary of a customized solution from our company?" If you don't create that solution, someone else will.

2. Use technology to test your concept with your customers even before you launch it. Before the first guest had the opportunity to stay in Starwood's new "aloft" brand, a couple hundred thousand potential guests got to experience a cyber-conceptual version of this hip, mid-price offering on the site Second Life (www.secondlife.com). Second Life is a virtual world where community inhabitants or avatars (computerized representations of the web users themselves) roam around virtual locales, meeting other avatars, and basically explore a three-dimensional game of life. Starwood joins an elite cast of companies who've established a presence on Linden Lab's Second Life website. Starwood gets the benefit of tapping into these avatars' desires and receiving a wealth of feedback on everything from the hotel restaurant concept

(continued)

(*continued*)

to how the bathroom should be laid out. Starwood has even been able to track which lobby magazines are most popular. It's also given Starwood the ability to create buzz about its product even before the first aloft opens. The company created a launch concert with singer-songwriter Ben Folds that was standing-room only in a virtual kind of way. Virtual worlds like Second Life give companies the ability to create a participative relationship with prospective customers so that these customers' desires are understood even before a product is launched.

3. Consider how you can build a learning relationship with your customers. Depending on your business, you could take the Amazon or Netflix mass customization approach by using technology to support deeper knowledge of your customers. Or you could take Best Buy's approach of defining its most important customer niches and training its staff on exactly what those customers are looking for (after, of course, first spending time engaging with those customers to really know their desires). At the heart of this prescription is the need to segment your customers so that one size does not fit all. Your competition may be stroking its customers' esteem needs. Are you doing the same for your customers?

4. Address your customers' social and belonging needs by making them feel a part of something bigger than themselves. Harley-Davidson is a master at this with its Harley Owner Group (H.O.G.) affiliation clubs. The former headline of the H.O.G. website says it all: "Express Yourself in the Company of Others . . . The Harley Owners Group is much more than just a motorcycle organization. It's one million people around the world united by a common passion: making the Harley-Davidson dream a way of life." The Internet gives you ample opportunities to create customer networks or communities, especially through social media sites like Facebook, YouTube, and Twitter. Many companies mistakenly think that these sites are just another means of creating a transaction, but they can also be used as a means of creating a deeper relationship. Whether it's through viral videos that feature key employees, a CEO blog or Twitter site that humanizes the leaders of the organization, or through

customer forums, you can build on the affiliation needs of your customers using this new technology. Using behavioral science, Lithium Technologies has become the leading provider of social customer-relationship management solutions to power high-tech companies' customer networks. Check out their website (www.lithium.com) and you'll see that they identify, engage, and leverage the SuperUser (those who most actively use the product), the 1 percent that represents your strongest brand advocates, which will drive 40 to 50 percent of your user-generated content associated with what customers are saying about your product and how they can improve their experience with your product or service. Given how engaged we are with technology today, why not use your customers as a free and compelling sales force for your product?

5. Whether you're in the service business or not, inventory your staff to determine whether you have at least a 2:1 ratio of superstars to weak links. Change will not happen if the equilibrium of your staff is equally weighted with people on the extremes. Your silent majority won't shift without a change in this chemistry. Have your managers confidentially assign a designation of *superstar*, *silent majority*, or *weak link* to your team to determine the current state of affairs. How do you determine which category to put an employee in? I suggest to our managers, "How comfortable would you feel if this front-desk host was on their own and responsible for checking in one of our most prized but challenging guests?" If you feel perfectly fine, that employee is a superstar. If you're scared as hell, they're a weak link. Anything in between, that employee is part of the silent majority. Once you've done this inventory, determine how you can add to your superstars (maybe because there's a few silent majority folks who could step it up) or subtract your weak links (either through moving up one level or moving out). Sometimes it's a matter of role modeling. Danny Meyer encourages each of his managers to take 10 minutes a day to make three gestures that exceed expectations and address the special interests of a particular guest. This institutionalized managerial habit helps set the bar for the rest of the staff.

We're scaling this Customer Pyramid very well and are just about to reach the peak of the customer experience. The path from meeting expectations to meeting desires to meeting unrecognized needs is a subtle one because the line of demarcation between these three levels isn't as clearly distinguishable as what we've highlighted on the Employee Pyramid (money, recognition, and meaning). But when a customer feels the sense of self-actualization that a peak-performing company can deliver, you will know you've created a peak experience for that person, and you've immediately expanded your sales force with truly committed customers. On we go to creating evangelists.

RECOMMENDED READING

Exceeding Customer Expectations by Kark Kazanjian
Let Them Eat Cake: Marketing Luxury to the Masses—as Well as the Classes by
    Pamela N. Danziger
More Than a Motorcycle by Rich Teerlink and Lee Ozley
One Size Fits One by Gary Heil, Tom Parker, and Deborah C. Stephens
Priceless by Diana LaSalle and Terry A. Britton
Return on Customer by Don Peppers and Martha Rogers
Setting the Table by Danny Meyer

CHAPTER NINE

CREATING EVANGELISTS

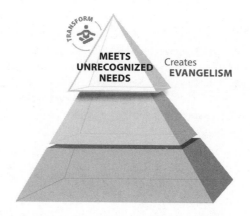

If I had asked my customers what they wanted, they would have said a faster horse.

HENRY FORD (ATTRIBUTED)[1]

I remember the first time I heard boutique hotelier Bill Kimpton say he was in the business of "selling sleep." Bill was a bit of an idol of mine. In 1981, in his mid-40s, he departed from his stuffed-shirt investment banking life and started what was originally called Kimco, then the Kimpton Group, and ultimately just Kimpton. Kimpton has been a worthy competitor for us to benchmark ourselves against, especially since they're the only hotelier in the world that operates more boutique hotels than we do. Ironically, our home office is just four blocks from their headquarters (although they're now owned by InterContinental Hotel Group).

While I admired much of what Bill did and said (he passed away in 2001), I was always puzzled by his favorite phrase about being in the business of selling sleep. I guess I imagined that would be a base need on the hotel guest pyramid. Certainly, it's foundational for any guest because without that physiological need met, everything else up the pyramid isn't very relevant. But boutique hotels stand out versus the chains not because we sell sleep but because we deliver dreams. We create experiences that allow our guests to get out of their linear, by-the-book lives and live it up a little. At Joie de Vivre, we've even created a Dreammaker program to meet the higher needs of our guests (which I talk about in the *Peak* Prescriptions for this chapter). If we get it right at our boutique hotels, we don't just satisfy our guests' physiological, safety, social, and esteem needs: we bring them to an awareness of self-actualization, what I called *identity refreshment* in Chapter Seven. Somehow, by staying in one of our hotels, you feel renewed and refreshed as though the hotel helped reconnect you with who you are (or who you aspire to be).

If you're staying at the Hotel Rex, that means you may feel a little more clever and worldly because as well as providing a unique literary environment in its decor, the hotel regularly hosts author book signings in the lobby's library bar. At our Hotel Avante, it might mean you feel smart and visionary because of the avant-garde art or the miniature mind-twisting game collection (like Rubik's cubes) embedded in the guest room desk. At our Hotel Vitale, it could mean you're feeling modern and refreshed while soaking up the natural style of the interior design or after you've indulged in a complimentary yoga class, followed by an outdoor bath in the rooftop bamboo grove. Or at The Phoenix, you may feel funky and irreverent because you're surrounded by oddball art and even more oddball guests in a really offbeat neighborhood.

Remember that what's at the top of each pyramid is transformative. If you get it right, it can have a profound impact on the customer's life or how they see themselves. My premise is, all other factors being equal (location, size of room, etc.), one boutique hotel will succeed over another based on its ability to address the unrecognized need of its loyal customers: the need to have their identity refreshed. Ian Schrager, the man behind Studio 54 in the 1970s, created the world's most stylish and edgy boutique hotels in the 1980s and 1990s, and he was able to charge a premium because his followers felt stylish, edgy, hip, and in-the-know when they stayed in one of his hotels. Not all boutique hotels have to create this kind of slightly narcissistic identity refreshment, but the key lesson here is that boutique hoteliers ventured outside the box of just meeting the expectations or expressed desires of Mr. and Ms. Customer.

In the epigraph at the beginning of Chapter Seven, we read Theodore Levitt's quotation about how most companies become myopic about their business strategy over time. While focus is an effective, time-tested approach to operating a business, if you are limited in terms of how you see your relationship with your customers in today's constantly changing world, you are likely to become irrelevant (the most frightening word any company can imagine in an increasingly competitive world).

Today's peak-performing companies are opportunistic and agile. Nokia morphed from manufacturing boots for the military to becoming the world's leading telecommunications equipment manufacturer and then it got disrupted. Apple transitioned from being an also-ran in the computer hardware wars to being at the front of the pack for how the world purchases and listens to music in the twenty-first century. Neither one of these companies shifted its business model because of extensive focus groups with its customers. They rethought what business they were in by doing an introspective inquiry into who they were as a company. They also did a bit of mind reading with respect to what their customers (or potential customers) would truly love but didn't know could be available to them.

This reminds me of one of Peter Drucker's most famous and wise questions for executives, "What business are you in?" That question is more relevant today than when he asked it more than 50 years ago. What business is Joie de Vivre in? We're in the business of refreshing our guests' identities and creating priceless memories for them. We want to wow our guests by delivering them experiences they hadn't even imagined. We know that if we accomplish that, our guests will be more loyal. These loyal customers may even become evangelists (defined by Webster's as "an enthusiastic advocate") for our hotel as an unpaid sales force spreading the gospel. And clearly, these evangelists will think of our product as more than just a commodity, which means we can charge a premium. It's one thing to offer a comfortable place to sleep; it's quite another to create an environment where a customer feels at one with themselves and truly in their ideal habitat.

PEAK'S APPLE AND HARLEY-DAVIDSON CUSTOMER PYRAMIDS

Peak companies are a rare breed. In the last two chapters, I suggested that moving up this pyramid has a lot to do with increasing the intimacy of your customer relationships. The level of intimacy is directly correlated with the quality of the listening or empathy you're offering your customer. One thing we know from studying the Hierarchy of Needs is that what's at the peak is often intangible and priceless; yet, few companies *seek the peak.*

The first step in rising to the peak of the Customer Pyramid is to be willing to ask the simple yet penetrating question "What business are we in?" It may sound rhetorical, and it may elicit blank stares from your colleagues, but don't be intimidated by the stunned silence. Know that this question has helped some legendary companies climb to the peak of their customers' pyramid. But make sure to follow this question up with "What are the unrecognized needs of our customers?" Let's explore two companies that have transcended their base-line industries—computers and transportation—to rethink their business and address the unrecognized needs of their customers.

Ron Johnson was senior vice president at Apple in charge of retail stores worldwide. Before being with Apple, he was the guy who helped reposition Target into a fashionable big-box retailer by introducing designer Michael Graves' $40 teapots (previously, the most expensive Target teapot was $10). During Ron's time with Target, the company moved up the Customer Pyramid such that shopping at Target became a bit of a status symbol for those who wanted to think of themselves as smart, hip, *and* thrifty.

I had the pleasure of spending a morning with Ron on Apple's campus, talking about how the company used Maslow in conceptualizing the launch of its retail stores. The question Ron asked his colleagues was "What if the store is more about the higher needs of the ownership experience than the base needs of a sales transaction?" He summarized this higher need in the following way: "We will help you get more out of your Mac so you can get more out of yourself."

There is a historical context within Apple for seeking to create higher potential for its customers. Steve Jobs' original contention was that the personal computer was a "bicycle for the mind," giving people the ability to "explore like never before." So, the store could meet the base expectations of a customer with the opportunity to purchase an Apple product in a nicely designed store. The customers' desires (social and esteem needs) could be met by creating a sort of clubhouse for Apple users to connect. And their unrecognized needs might be satisfied by giving Apple users the sense that they can do just about anything with their Apple product. I would also suggest that Apple provides its customers with an identity refreshment because being an Apple user means you're connected to a hip brand.

Of course, Apple's *think different* approach to going retail wasn't widely supported back in 2001 when it launched its first store, as many stock analysts questioned Apple's contrarian logic at a time when the tech biz was weakening. In fact, Apple decided to go retail just as Gateway was starting to close its stores and Dell was winning the personal computer war with its direct approach that had nothing to do with retail stores.

Typically, retailers who sell you the products you buy infrequently (like cars, appliances, and computers) choose low-rent locations, but Apple chose to be in highly centralized locations with expensive rent. The company designed expensive and stylish showrooms (a far cry from Radio Shack), hired noncommissioned salespeople, and provided free Internet access to anyone who entered the store. Excuse the silly pun, but Apple was going way out on a limb.

Ron told me that Apple took its cues from the hotel industry. He brought 18 friends and associates (whom he considered *thought leaders*) together and asked them about their ultimate service experience. Sixteen of the 18 mentioned a hotel experience, so Ron and his team patterned the Apple stores after how a hotel operates. There's a greeter at the door of the Apple stores, just like a hotel doorman. There's a Genius Bar, sort of like the old hotel bar, but instead of dispensing alcohol, these geniuses dispense practical advice about how an Apple user can get the most from their Mac or how other Apple products can be successfully integrated. Ron even had his first 10 employees spend some time observing service at Ritz-Carltons in Washington, D.C., and New Orleans because he wanted to create a "culture of service" that was unheard of in consumer technology stores.

Ron and his team launched Procare to satisfy the peak needs of Apple's customers. This program offers Apple's "most self-actualized customers" the ability to pay $99 per year for unlimited access to

PEAK'S APPLE CUSTOMER PYRAMID

everything in the store, including one free hour of personal training each week. These customers end up being the company's biggest individual spenders and most avid word-of-mouth evangelists.

Given this contrarian strategy, Apple became the fastest retailer in history to reach $1 billion in sales, and it has some of the highest per-square-foot retail sales of any retailer in the world. Its price per square foot of sales is five times more productive than Best Buy. In a way, Ron Johnson likes to feel that these are "like a gift to the community while, at the same time, providing Apple a great platform for our brand."

So, if we were to summarize the Apple Customer Pyramid, it would look something like the figure above.

How about Harley-Davidson? What does its Customer Pyramid look like? At the base of the Harley customer experience is the Rider's Edge program (now called the Riding Academy), which introduces new potential customers who don't have a motorcycle license to the bike experience. Working with its independent dealers and collaborating with each state's motor-vehicle department, Harley created an educational safety course for people to learn how to ride a motorcycle. Once you've completed your course, the dealer schedules you for a road test and lends you a bike to take the test. The total cost is low and is credited toward your purchase of a Harley motorcycle.

The social and esteem needs of the Harley enthusiast are met by the opportunity to join one of more than 1,000 Harley Owner Groups (the world's largest motorcycle club) that are perfectly suited to Harley owners' specific identity or affiliation needs. At the peak of the Harley Customer Pyramid is being able to "express yourself in the company of others," Harley's version of identity refreshment. Self-actualized Harley customers like their bikes and enjoy the social connection, but they are truly at their peak when they're experiencing freedom of expression. That expression can manifest itself in the route a rider chooses to use, whether it be the back roads or coast side or in the way they choose to customize their bike because Harley owners regularly embellish their vehicles with grassroots folk art. This self-actualization also manifests itself in the message Harley riders send themselves by just knowing that Harley stands for being a rebel or individualist. If you want to see this Harley self-actualization on full display, go to Sturgis, South Dakota, each summer for the motorcycle rally.

Jeffrey Bleustein, the former CEO, says, "We want to fulfill the dreams of our customers through their motorcycle experience."[2] Harley-Davidson is a self-actualizing (and evangelical) tribe, not just a motorcycle company. How do we know that? What other company has hundreds of its customers tattooing its logo somewhere on their body? Harley's Customer Pyramid might look like this:

PEAK'S HARLEY-DAVIDSON CUSTOMER PYRAMID

CREATING YOUR OWN CUSTOMER PYRAMID

Virtually any well-known company that has created an evangelistic customer base could draw its own pyramid. If you are struggling with how your company could draw a powerful pyramid, let me give you two more examples.

Consider Whole Foods Market, the world's leading natural and organic foods supermarket. Whole Foods has created a food fervor among its customers based on providing a great product at the base of the pyramid, engaged and personalized service and a real sense of community at the middle level, and a commitment to environmental stewardship and sustainability at the peak. Whole Foods is a great example of how customers can feel self-actualized by supporting a company that is committed to a cause. The figure below depicts my interpretation of what their Customer Pyramid might look like.

But Whole Foods' former co-CEO Walter Robb suggested to me that this model needs to acknowledge that what's at the top of the pyramid may vary depending on which set of customers you're talking about. Whole Foods stores are serving three primary customers: (1) those who live a natural or organic lifestyle, (2) those who might consider themselves foodies, and (3) those who are mission-driven and choose the companies they buy from that match their worldview. Robb believes that the peak of their Customer Pyramid is being "a place to help you become what you want to be,"

PEAK'S WHOLE FOODS CUSTOMER PYRAMID

which is very Maslovian. So, if you're a foodie, the peak would be feeling that Whole Foods helps you become even more knowledgeable and proficient as a food connoisseur. On the other hand, the fact that the company has an environmentally sustainable mission might satisfy the other two market segments. Robb's point is a good one. Your customers aren't monolithic; therefore, your pyramid needs to be adaptable depending on which customers you're talking about and their changing tastes.

Come to think of it, Joie de Vivre's brand and its individual hotels don't have the same customer pyramid. The base of JdV's brand pyramid would be California flavor at good value. The middle would be a unique, localized experience, maybe with a socially popular restaurant or bar on site. At the peak would be delivering identity refreshment. But, for an individual hotel like the small, 26-room Petite Auberge, the details would be more specific. The base is an affordable, safe, and quiet Union Square location. The middle is an opportunity to meet other guests at the plentiful breakfast or evening wine hour, both free to guests. And the top of the pyramid would be the specific adjectives that define this hotel's identity refreshment (as well as some services, amenities, or décor that deliver this): *European, cultured, sensible, calm,* and *coquettish.*

Let me show you one more customer pyramid based upon conversations I've had with WeWork vice-chair Michael Gross. Founded in 2010, WeWork is the leading global shared work-space company that provides collaborative office space, community, and services for entrepreneurs, freelancers, startups, small businesses, and now Fortune 500 enterprises. Some observers might suggest they're a real estate company but their pyramid suggests differently. They've done such an impressive job of both creating a quality experience for their members and putting dots on the map (roughly 200 locations globally by year-end 2017) that their private market valuation is now more than $18 billion. The *meet expectations* base would be defined by *work*: the quality of the spaces that their members use, the flexibility of not having to sign a long-term lease, and the affordability of paying for things like group meeting spaces only when you need them.

WeWork's *meet desires* middle would be defined by a combination of ambience, services, and *network*. WeWork is well known for the quality of services they provide as well as the collegial nature of the design of their spaces. This design fosters connecting with locals who might be able to provide you with graphic design, legal, or branding services, and access to major metropolitan markets globally to tap into their local WeWork locations and networks. This is particularly appealing to the growing number of global nomads who need just a good WiFi connection, their laptop, and a smartphone to do business anywhere. Plus, like Holiday Inn offered in the early days of the hotel chains, a member—who may be new to coworking spaces—can appreciate the familiarity and predictability that WeWork offers in their spaces globally.

Finally, at the "meet unrecognized needs" peak of the pyramid is "thrive" or the sense that WeWork helps you to create your life's work, not just make a living. Part of the way WeWork accomplishes this self-actualizing differentiation is fostering community and interpersonal camaraderie by being the largest events company in the world (more than 19,000 events in their spaces in 2016). Whether through their trademark "Lunch and Learn" or wellness classes or social events, there is a strong sense of community connected by common values of passion, open-mindedness, and ambition. So, the WeWork pyramid would look like the one shown below.

Think of just about any company that's at the top of its game, and you'll find that it's scaled the peak of its own Customer Pyramid. Nordstrom, Zappos, In-N-Out Burger, Amazon, Google, Airbnb, Trader Joe's, Dyson—these companies follow business plans that have deviated from the norm. But they haven't done this just to be different. Whether it's been a conscious part of their

PEAK'S WEWORK CUSTOMER PYRAMID

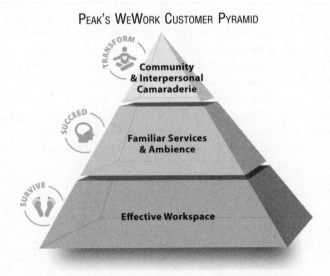

business strategy or not, these companies have moved up the Customer Pyramid by addressing the unrecognized higher needs of their customers. Companies that create self-actualized customers inspire true devotion and evangelism.

UNDERSTANDING THE UNRECOGNIZED NEEDS OF YOUR CUSTOMER

New York–based supermarket chain Wegmans has built a loyal following and was named *Fortune's* number one "Best Company to Work For" in 2005. Company CEO Danny Wegman recognizes that the company's success is due to its "near-telepathic sense of customer service." He says, "Focus groups will tell you what they want to shop for, but that isn't enough anymore. Today, it is a retailer's job not only to deliver what the customers want, but also what they'd never think to ask for."[3]

So how do you get inside the head of your customer? Go out and buy Harvard professor Gerald Zaltman's insightful book *How Customers Think: Essential Insights into the Mind of the Market.* Zaltman believes that most companies think their customers make consumer decisions in a linear or hierarchical way, but he writes, "Figuratively speaking, they [the customers] don't experience a cake by sampling a sequence of raw ingredients. They experience fully baked cakes." He goes on to say that consumers' buying behavior is driven more by unconscious (or unrecognized) thoughts because 95 percent of thought, emotion, and learning happen without our conscious awareness. Zaltman says, "The more skilled companies are at listening to customers, the more effective their marketing strategies will be in establishing the value of the firm's offerings."[4] But his idea of *listening* is at a subconscious level.

This book helped me to understand there are metaphors or mantras that underpin the purchase decision our guests make when they choose our boutique hotels. Essentially, in making a purchase decision, our Hotel Vitale customer is sending a message to herself like "I'm not getting older, I'm getting better." This is because Vitale reaches out to the guest who has outgrown the hipper boutique hotels but is not yet ready for the more formal and stodgy luxury hotels (what we call our "post-W, pre–Four Seasons" guest). It isn't just that they're getting their identities refreshed; these guests are also creating a story about themselves based on the purchases they make. Apple and Harley customers clearly also have subconscious mantras.

After your crash course in mind reading from Professor Zaltman, you need to channel a little Margaret Mead. Cultural anthropologist Mead did her groundbreaking research studying the behaviors of people on the distant corners of the planet. My sister was an anthropology major in college, and I was always intrigued with the subject but felt it wasn't practical enough for the business world. Boy, was I wrong!

Consider Richard Hayne, cofounder and CEO of Urban Outfitters, a company that has demonstrated a remarkable knack of completely understanding the nature of its 18-to-30-year-old "upscale homeless," whose purchasing behavior is driven less by their home lives and more by their social lives. Hayne was educated and trained as an anthropologist. Maybe that explains why he named his next retail chain Anthropologie, which became a hit, with more than 100 stores perfectly suited for the sophisticated 30-to-45-year-old woman who has a "natural curiosity about the world." William C. Taylor and Polly LaBarre write in *Mavericks at Work* that Hayne went on a "cultural odyssey" for two years with architect Ron Pompei to understand the nature of this customer. The result of their research "translated into a retail concept that was as much about human behavior as about purchasing behavior."[5]

We have a modern word to describe anthropology as applied to your customer: *ethnography*. This practice has become very popular: many of America's largest companies have hired a fleet of ethnographers in-house to study the behavior and minds of their customers.

Ethnographers closely observe people where they live and work, which allows companies to zero in on their customers' unarticulated desires. Intuit, the dominant retail software company for tax preparation and small-business accounting, is well known for its sleuthing skills, and they even have a cute name for this ethnography practice: a "follow me home." Intuit's follow-me-home team looks for "pain points" or surprises that arise from customers using their products. In *Fortune* magazine, founder Scott Cook said he discounted initial research showing that its Quicken software for individuals was being used by small businesses. But once he dispatched employees to visit users at home or work, he came to savor the surprise that Intuit's new QuickBooks product could be customized for small businesses. Cook is such a believer in this sort of ethnography that in 2003, Intuit's QuickBooks division sent more than 500 employees on follow-me-home assignments for three days.

In the book *Priceless*, Diana LaSalle and Terry Britton cite an example of how ethnographers from Kimberly-Clark spent time in their customers' homes and "discovered that parents didn't consider diapers a disposable product as the company thought, but an article of clothing. This discovery gave the product a whole new dimension in terms of looks as well as pricing, but more important, it uncovered hidden value. By observing and then talking to parents, the company learned that the adults saw pull-on diapers as a positive step toward more mature behavior and very useful in the potty-training process."[6] Kimberly-Clark came to realize its product was part of an unrecognized rite of passage for both children and parents, which led it to launch the successful Huggies Pull-Ups with an "I'm a big kid now" theme.

Can't afford an ethnographer on staff? Neither can we. Consider other ways to get inside the heads of your customer. I know a hotel company that gave its guests disposable cameras and asked them to photograph things they considered "magical" or "dreary" at its property. Then, at the end of the guest's stay, a hotel manager would meet with the guests to hear their vivid stories and observations about what worked at the hotel—and what didn't. Or the example from marketing professor Barry Bayus, who cites a study that Konica did with its customers in his fascinating paper "Understanding Customer Needs." Konica found that its customers asked for only minor improvements to their existing camera models, but Konica's team went to commercial photo-processing labs to investigate the actual prints taken by customers. They found blurry images, under- and overexposure, and blank film rolls, which suggested that the customers had latent needs they weren't expressing to Konica's researchers. This led to Konica making a series of product improvements from auto focus to built-in flashes to automatic film rewinding.

In sum, my job requires that I not just be an amateur psychologist but also a budding sociologist. I love that Eureka! moment when I feel like I've truly understood the zeitgeist of a certain niche of the population. The last hotel I created, my fifty-second one, was in downtown Palo Alto, surrounded by tech start-ups and innovation labs. It was clear that many of the guests who would be coming to stay at this new hotel were looking for a moment of serendipity that could help them channel a breakthrough creative idea. We called the hotel The Epiphany (now rebranded as a Nobu) and designed the décor and collection of services to create the conditions for people to feel they could have mulitiple *aha* moments. The Epiphany became so successful that Oracle founder Larry Ellison bought the hotel just a little over a year after it launched.

FOUR THEMES AT THE TOP OF THE CUSTOMER PYRAMID

How do you create a self-actualized customer? Once you've plumbed the depths of your customers' unrecognized needs, it's time to consider which of four themes you will pursue to help create self-actualization. Some companies, like Apple, are able to engage with their customers using all four of these themes, but most companies are lucky if they can connect on just one.

1. Help your customers meet their highest goals. Apple does this with its Procare service. Nike hints at this with its "Just Do It" motto, as does Home Depot with its "You can do it. We can help." Lululemon Athletica offers a free tool, aptly named "goaltender" for setting and tracking one-, five, and ten-year goals for your career, personal life, and health. When a company can comprehensively assist customers to reach their highest goals, it has built a deeply engaged relationship.

   Google is a splendid example of this theme. In a *New York Times* article, "Planet Google Wants You," Donna Hoffman, a University of California researcher who studies online consumer behavior, says Google "literally augments your brain. I don't have to remember quite a few things now because Google can remember them for me. Google is an additional memory chip."[7] But Google's success is also a function of the vast array of products—from Gmail to Google Calendar to Google Earth—it is creating to assist you in your life without adding complication. One Web designer was quoted in the *Times* article as saying that Google's elegant simplicity allows her to impose her own personality on the site while most other websites are full of clutter and blinking ads. This designer, Toni Carreiro, says that other sites have all this animation going on, but "I just want my stuff. That's what Google gives you—'me.'" When a customer defines the product or service as a positive extension of herself, you've got to believe there's a little self-actualization going on in the relationship.

Bank of America's "Keep the Change" savings program is another example of how a company can create a self-actualizing program for its customers by helping them reach their goals. In 2004, the company hired a firm to do ethnographic research on boomer-age women with children to understand how to get this consumer segment to open new checking and savings accounts. It learned two key insights: first, these women regularly round up their transactions because it makes the math easier in their checkbook; and second, the women were having a difficult time saving money. Keep the Change was the successful outgrowth of these findings. Here's how the program works: the amount consumers spend on each transaction of their Bank of America debit cards is rounded up to the nearest whole dollar, and the difference is transferred from their checking account into an interest-earning savings account each evening. The bank will match a portion of the amount saved with an annual limit. This program, which really was a form of customer mind reading, has created more than billions in savings for its old and new customers because it's easy to understand (sort of like an electronic change jar) and didn't require any dramatic change in the customers' behaviors. And Bank of America looks like a star, as it becomes an enabler of its customers' dreams rather than a barrier to their achievements, which is the way that many customers feel about their bankers.

2. Give your customers the ability to truly express themselves. The Apple iconoclastic halo effect makes its users feel special and unique. Harley-Davidson helps small-town middle-aged accountants feel like rebels. Joie de Vivre helps our customers express themselves with our approach to creating identity refreshment. If buying your product helps your customers to get in touch with a higher vision of themselves, you are helping to facilitate a peak experience.Peter van Stolk started Jones Soda Company (originally called Urban Juice and Soda) the same year I started Joie de Vivre in 1987. On his company's website (www.jonessoda.com) van Stolk previously wrote, "Jones was developed with the mindset that the world does not need another soda, so it is imperative that consumers feel that Jones is theirs." This little company has grown its sales primarily because of the unorthodox ways it connects with its youthful customers. Jones invites its customers to create home-designed advertisements for its products, and it

places thousands of expressive customer photos on the labels of its soft drinks. Van Stolk explained, "The photo labeling is important to Jones because it allows our consumers to be involved in the brand, thus giving everyone a sense of ownership. This is critical for Jones because it truly allows us to differentiate ourselves from our competitors and create an emotional connection that in my opinion is the essence of the brand."

Visitors to the Jones website can rate customer label submissions on a one-to-five scale, and the company selects about 50 winning photos each week. These winners get to see their photo on labels in stores across North America. Jones has received millions of photos from customers with a fraction of these appearing on its website.

While Jones has created a way for its young customers to express themselves, Starbucks has taken on a curator role for its slightly affluent, middle-aged customer base. The company has morphed from being the creator of America's luxury coffee experience to becoming the purveyor of a premium-blend culture based on the music, books, and films it is recommending in its stores. Thomas Hay, a 48-year-old contractor from Hartsdale, New York, says Starbucks helps him by editing down his cultural choices. He's quoted in the *New York Times* saying that the entertainment purchases he makes at Starbucks give him the impression that "some people of caring hearts and minds have looked at this and felt it was worthwhile and beneficial and would create a good vibe in the world."[8]

Howard Schultz, the founder and executive chair of Starbucks, believes that curating a lifestyle for his core customers "adds to the emotional connection with the customer" and keeps the Starbucks experience from feeling "antiseptic." The *Times* article goes on to say that Starbucks executives describe the goal of the company's cultural extensions to be creating a sense of discovery for its customers. "Customers say one of the reasons they come is because they can discover new things—a new coffee from Rwanda, a new food item. So extending that sense of discovery into entertainment is very natural for us," says Anne Saunders, senior vice president of global brand strategy and communications for Starbucks.

So, if Starbucks created a Customer Pyramid, it would probably have *premium product* at the base level, *providing a "third place" to connect with community* or *being recognized by my barista* on the middle level, and *creating a sense of discovery* at the peak of its pyramid. Starbucks is acting as the curator for customers to express themselves through their beverage and lifestyle purchases.

3. Make your customers feel like they're part of a bigger cause. Guy Kawasaki, former senior Apple exec and author of *Rules for Revolutionaries: The Capitalist Manifesto for Creating and Marketing New Products and Services,* says, "Macintosh started as a vision; then it became a product supported by a cult; finally, it became a cause—propagated by thousands of Macintosh evangelists."[9] TOMS "One for One" business model means when you're buying shoes, sunglasses, or apparel from them, they are reciprocating with similar goods to someone in need somewhere else in the world. In his later years, Maslow expanded his Hierarchy of Needs Pyramid from five to eight levels, with the highest level being *self-transcendence,* the almost spiritual sense of being on this planet for something beyond your own personal needs.

Running their company like a community has created enthusiasm for socially responsible brands like Ben & Jerry's, The Body Shop, Clif Bar, Benetton, Kenneth Cole, and Timberland. But few companies do it better than Patagonia. Since 1985, Patagonia has pledged 1 percent of its annual sales to organizations that are helping to preserve and restore the natural environment. More recently, Patagonia helped create "1% for the Planet," an alliance of hundreds of businesses that are following Patagonia's lead in donating 1 percent of their revenues to environmental causes. Check out Patagonia's website (www.patagonia.org), and you'll see how this company engages its customers ("Patagoniacs") to be part of the solution rather than part of the problem. This sense of being committed to a cause greater than themselves—even in the pursuit of consumerism—helps Patagonia customers feel more fulfilled. And it gives them motivation to evangelize about the company.

Do you have to be perceived as a do-gooder brand to be able to connect your customers to a greater cause? No. Macy's flagship store in New York has held unique product presentations as a means of giving back. Instead of the typical demonstrations from suppliers hawking their wares, Macy's has brought in stately African widows to weave baskets that customers line up to buy. Hundreds of these African women are escaping poverty by selling baskets in this business partnership with Macy's. This is no charity. It is a win-win-win relationship that creates goodwill for Macy's, a good life for the women, and a good vibe (and entertainment) for the shoppers, especially once they learn each woman's unique story.

4. Offer your customers something of real value that they hadn't even imagined. Apple launched the iPod, which gave people a choice they didn't even know would ever exist. The Geek Squad offers a theatrical experience that punctuates a typical day's monotony and a frustrating day's tech woes.

   Jet Blue created a disruptive innovation with its launch of DirecTV service on all its flights. This brilliant offering allowed Jet Blue customers the ability to customize their in-flight entertainment and to have a bit of control in an environment in which they're completely out of control (being strapped down in tight quarters for hours at a time). Jet Blue created a peak experience for its customers, and this created nightmares for its competitors. On an Air Canada flight, the woman in the seat next to me asked the flight attendant about the choices of movies during a long flight. When the flight attendant mentioned the innocuous movie that was to be played (and then went to fetch the tape so we could read a little bit about it), my neighbor threw a fit and screamed, "Why are you treating us like cattle and forcing us to watch a single movie all at the same time? . . . Don't you know that Jet Blue got this whole thing figured out years ago?!" A bit of an overreaction, but perhaps my seatmate was irritated because some brilliant exec at Air Canada made the decision to start charging for pillows and blankets (yes, that's right) on their flights, yet flight attendants were giving headsets away for free (so we could listen to the movie we didn't want to watch). Who came up with that set of priorities for a long flight? Air Canada could use a Customer Pyramid to clarify the base and higher needs of its customers.

   Or how about Progressive Insurance, one of the fastest-growing auto insurers in the nation? It's delivered on a couple of unrecognized needs for its customers. Think of what happens when you're in a car crash with another driver. You're disoriented, maybe a little upset, and possibly it's not even clear whose fault it was. Progressive was the first insurer to promise it would have one of its adjusters on site within two hours of being notified. The adjuster is able to evaluate your damage and give you a check on the spot to save you all the hassles associated with the bureaucracy of dealing with your insurance company. Furthermore, Progressive's approach to quoting auto insurance rates for potential customers is completely unconventional but very convenient for the consumer. Progressive will quote its rates right next to the rates of the top three other insurers in that local market, even if Progressive's rates aren't the lowest. This idea sprouted within Progressive not because its customers were asking for it but because Progressive's CEO Peter Lewis was a college classmate of consumer advocate Ralph Nader—and Ralph suggested it.

Sometimes the companies that will surprise you may be right in your own neighborhood. There's a healthy raw-foods chain of restaurants in California that I frequent called Cafe Gratitude. You probably won't find a place like this in Wichita, but we can all learn something from how this restaurant has trained its staff in a truly unconventional manner. When a server shares the special of the day with customers, he or she also asks a provocative question of the day (which changes daily) intended to awaken the customers' awareness of why they should be grateful. Owners Matthew and Tercis Engelhart shared a story with me about when two women customers were asked the question of the day "Who would you like to acknowledge in your life today?" Both women's eyes filled with tears as one of the women said to the other, "I would like to acknowledge her for performing open heart surgery on me!" Most customers don't have quite that moment of synchronicity, but a question of the day can offer an unexpected, deep conversation starter between the partners in a meal on a subject that may allow them to experience a little *joie de vivre*. Any restaurant that can help foster that kind of dining experience is at the top of my pyramid.

PEAK PRESCRIPTIONS

Here are a few suggestions for how you and your company can focus more on your customers' unrecognized needs at the peak of the Customer Pyramid:

1. Do an off-site retreat focused on creating your own Customer Pyramid. Ask Drucker's famous question, "What business are you in?" or adapt it to "What business do your customers (or your future customers) wish you were in?" Based on some of
(continued)

(*continued*)

the examples I've used in this chapter, Bank of America reached the peak by creating an easy-to-use piggy bank, and Jet Blue created personalized entertainment for a captive audience. That wasn't necessarily their core business, but it tapped into the unrecognized needs of what their customers were looking for. Make sure that whatever is at the peak of your Customer Pyramid is an achievement that truly touches your customers' highest needs, and don't forget the Whole Foods exec's suggestion that you may want to create different pyramids for different sizable market segments of your business. Once you've created this pyramid, use it throughout your organization to stay focused on how you're delivering these intangible qualities to your customer.

2. Focus on the four themes that help you address the peak aspirations of your customers. Companies that create self-actualized customers usually do it through satisfying one or more of four themes: (1) helping customers meet higher goals, (2) allowing customers to express themselves more fully through using this product or service, (3) connecting the customer with a larger cause, or (4) offering something completely different that the customer never imagined you're offering your customer. Ask yourself whether your product or service truly differentiates itself on any of these themes. The key is differentiation. If all of your competitors are already connected to a cause, and you're just doing it for *me, too* purposes, you won't get any traction. But if your competitors haven't quite understood what specific cause or what method of connecting with that cause would make your target customer feel more fulfilled, you may have the opportunity to create a point of differentiation.

3. When in doubt, be a *Dreammaker.* As I mentioned earlier in the chapter, Joie de Vivre is in the business of creating dreams, not selling sleep. A decade ago, we created an extraordinary service initiative, the Dreammaker program, that empowers our line-level employees to try to understand the unrecognized needs of our guests and deliver on those needs in a surprising or delightful manner. Whether it's using "listening posts" like our reservations staff or our bellmen, who may overhear that a guest is celebrating a birthday or

bringing their high school teen to visit a local university, we've trained our staff to be super-sleuths. Sometimes our staff will even make a few investigative calls to the executive secretary of a businessperson planning to stay in our hotel to find out what special snacks or drinks this guest might appreciate. When a guest is welcomed with a bouquet of birthday roses, a collection of college pennants decorating the walls, or with an abundant basket of their favorite comfort foods in their hotel room and they realize it was the hotel staff that masterminded this surprise, we've created a new evangelist.

4. Measure and communicate about the mood of your customers. The Inn at Little Washington in Virginia's Shenandoah Valley is consistently rated one of the top 10 restaurants in America, even though it's not located in an urban gourmet mecca like New York, San Francisco, Chicago, or New Orleans. I know people who've dined there, and uniformly they tell me it is a transformative experience. Much has been written about the Inn's unique approach to customizing service and its intense focus on observing the individual quirks or preferences of its customers, especially based on body language. While there are numerous elements to co-owner and chef Patrick O'Connell's signature approach to service, one method the restaurant uses could be applied to any business. After the guests are seated and the waiter has had a chance to assess the party's collective mood, the waiter then ranks the table on a 1-to-10 scoring system and logs this into the restaurant computer system, which appears at each workstation throughout the restaurant. The goal is that no party will leave the restaurant with less than a score of 9, and all staff—both in the dining room and in the kitchen—do everything in their power to help that waiter constantly upgrade the score throughout the meal. This could mean a few extra smiles from other waiters or bussers, a surprise dish from the kitchen between courses, or a visit from a manager just to make sure everyone at the table is feeling good. How does your team communicate about the mood of your customers, and how is your team empowered to make a difference when it is clear that one of your customers is having troubling experience using your product or service?

An interesting study entitled "To Do or to Have? That Is the Question" was highlighted in the book *Let Them Eat Cake* (which is recommended at the end of Chapter Eight). The researchers conducted three different kinds of experiments and found that nearly 60 percent of the consumers they interviewed believed intangible experiences make them happier than tangible material possessions. The researchers wrote, "A person's life is quite literally the sum of his or her experiences. The accumulation of rich experiences thus creates a richer life. The same cannot be said of material possessions. As important and gratifying as they some-times are, they usually remain 'out there,' separate from the individual who attained them."[10] Interestingly, the more wealthy the household, the higher the ratings for experiential happiness, which seems to suggest that customers, once they've had their base needs satisfied, look for more intangible and unrecognized benefits farther up the pyramid. If you can deliver on those higher needs, you may very well create a customer evangelist for life. This is part of the reason why Airbnb expanded in 2016 from being just an accommodations company to offering travelers the opportunity to connect with locals through bespoke experiences.

RECOMMENDED READING

Brand Hijack by Alex Wipperfurth
Creating Customer Evangelists by Jackie Huba and Ben McConnell
Ethnography for Marketers by Hy Mariampolski
How Customers Think by Gerald Zaltman
Lovemarks by Kevin Roberts
Marketing That Matters by Chip Conley and Eric Friedenwald Fishman
Mavericks at Work by William C. Taylor and Polly LaBarre
The Experience Economy by Joseph Pine II and James Gilmore
The Myth of Excellence by Fred Crawford and Ryan Mathews
"To Do or to Have? That Is the Question" by Leaf Van Boven and Thomas Gilovich, *Journal of Personality and Psychology* (volume 85, number 6, 2003)
"Toward Meaningful Brand Experiences" by David W. North, *Design Management Journal* (Winter 2003)
"Understanding Customer Needs" by Barry Bayus, Kenan-Flagler Business School at the University of North Carolina (January 2005)

PART FOUR

RELATIONSHIP TRUTH 3: THE INVESTOR PYRAMID

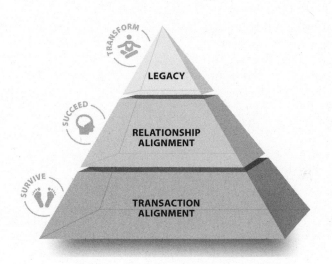

The difference between the great and good societies and the regressing, deteriorating societies is largely in terms of the entrepreneurial opportunity and the number of such people in the society. I think everyone would agree that the most valuable 100 people to bring into a deteriorating society would be not 100 chemists, or politicians, or professors, or engineers, but rather 100 entrepreneurs.

ABRAHAM MASLOW[1]

CHAPTER TEN

CREATING TRUST

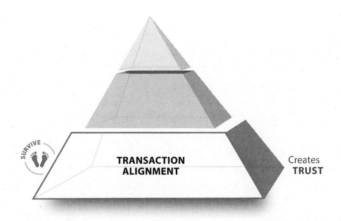

TRANSACTION
ALIGNMENT

SURVIVE

Creates
TRUST

Always get to know the character of those whose approval you wish to earn, and the nature of their guiding principles. Look into the sources of their opinions and their motives and then you will not blame any of their involuntary offenses or feel the want of their approbation.

MARCUS AURELIUS, ROMAN EMPEROR[1]

Rarely am I asked, "What are the most painful lessons you've learned over the course of your career?" If you want to engage in a deep conversation with a business leader, throw this zinger question at them. For me, one of my greatest lessons had to do with the subject we're now going to address: aligning goals with investors.

In the mid-to-late 1990s, we were approached by a sophisticated local real estate developer and investor who was acquiring 400 acres of California coastland just a short walk away from the beach and one hour south of San Francisco. This land, which is surrounded by some of the most pristine beaches and wilderness on the Pacific Coast, was partially entitled by the county and the California Coastal Commission to be a motor lodge and campground. The original developers had run out of money and hit a wall in their entitlements process. Therefore, my associate, who is a shrewd real estate investor, was able to acquire this remarkable site relatively inexpensively.

Personally, I was very excited by this out of the box project because I'd spent quite a bit of time hanging out on this part of the coast during college and graduate school and knew it was some of California's most untouched coastland. Joie de Vivre was brought in as a small investor and the hotel management company in this proposed development with the responsibility of creating a more compelling concept than a basic motel and campground but still working within the restrictive development entitlements. It was one of the first *glamping* developments ever pursued before the trend of glamorous camping went mainstream. We were also responsible for building alliances with skeptical locals who had created roadblocks to this development. At the same time, the real estate investor was responsible for going out and raising the additional equity necessary to fund this project.

We spent a lot of time working with locals and environmentalists to come up with a one-of-a-kind concept (using some of the town hall techniques I talked about at the start of Chapter Eight) that would still work within the stringent entitlements. Our whole executive team was thoroughly engaged in this visioning process. I don't think we've ever expended as much time and creativity to develop such a unique and unorthodox concept. What evolved out of this laborious process was Costanoa, an upscale coastal property featuring a 40-room lodge, 12 private cabins, and more than 120 tent bungalows that were completely decked out with first-class mattresses, designer down comforters, heated bed pads, and all kinds of other creature comforts from caffè lattes in the general store to outdoor fireplaces, saunas, and heated floors in the camp bathrooms. To use my magazine analogy from Chapter Seven, Costanoa was *Outside* magazine meets *Vanity Fair*. In other words, we were creating a business strategy focused on an oxymoron: luxury camping.

Within the first couple of months of our opening, *USA Today* printed a front-page feature on Costanoa, suggesting that this was the start of a new national trend of cushy camping or "connecting with nature without getting your hands dirty." While Costanoa got lots of press and was very busy on weekends, it struggled to attract weekday business. Fortunately, during the first couple of years, we were able to attract many weekday corporate retreats even though we had limited conference facilities. Costanoa was the alternative to a golf course resort for the dot-com companies that were looking for a hipper retreat spot where their Gen Xers could mountain bike or ride horses in between meetings. So, while Costanoa had its challenges, we were seeing progress, especially recognizing that a groundbreaking concept in a remote location, where there was historically no lodging demand, meant it would take a little longer for the facility to hit financial stabilization.

Then the dot-com bust hit, and 75 percent of our weekday business dried up as those high-tech companies that survived the downturn were limiting their expenditures on corporate retreats. Although we did our best to reduce expenses and market to other types of groups, it was clear in the 2001 to 2003 period that we had to have a long-term perspective on this irreplaceable asset. Joie de Vivre was caught in a difficult position. Do we adhere to our original concept of Costanoa but face financial losses, or do we just do what we have to do to satisfy our investors' short-term financial minimum standards? While we had a cordial relationship with the investors and they were very understanding, we could see the potential for a difference of opinion with respect to long-term versus short-term priorities. Even so, we did our best to streamline the operation to meet our investors' wishes. But this took its toll on our Costanoa employees.

Part of the challenge stemmed from the fact that the real estate developer-investor had chosen an investment hedge fund as Costanoa's lead equity partner. I don't fault him for making this choice as it was easier to tap into this "hot money" than trying to privately raise more than $20 million from lots of smaller investors. But the hedge fund's goals in this project weren't completely aligned with ours even though we had a respectful relationship. Their primary goal was return on investment as quickly as possible, a requirement that was increasingly seen as futile by all investors, including Joie de Vivre.

In the end, our partners chose to sell Costanoa for cents on the dollar (we would have loved to buy the place, but as I told you earlier in the book, I was flat broke during the post-9/11 down-turn). This was a painful experience because Joie de Vivre had invested a huge amount of heart, soul, time, and energy into this innovative development. We could see things starting to turn, as we'd found new market segments including rustic wedding recep-tions, that were proving to be profitable. We truly believed that Costanoa had a great long-term future ahead of it. It's just that we had a different definition of success than our investors. And this lack of transactional alignment was starting to affect our mutual trust in each other.

If early in the concept development of Costanoa I had heeded Marcus Aurelius's advice and learned the investment time horizon goals of the project's biggest equity partner, I might have saved our company the agony of seeing Costanoa slip through our fingers. Lesson learned. After that experience, each time we engaged in a potential new hotel project, we had a series of key questions we asked the primary investor group (if we weren't raising the money our-selves) to ensure that we had alignment regarding the transaction.

THE INVESTOR PYRAMID IS RELEVANT TO ALL EMPLOYEES

This is the point in the book when you might say, "Thanks, but no thanks; this investor stuff doesn't apply to me because I never engage with our company's investors." I would posit that everyone in a business is affected by the relationship a company has with its investors. For example, all of our employees at Costanoa had to suffer through the consequences of a misaligned relationship. Similarly, the principles you will learn in the next three chapters are relevant to whomever in the workplace you are accountable. Many of these themes about alignment and legacy are just as transferable to the relationship between you and your boss as they are between a company and its investor. An employee can think of his or her boss as an investor of sorts: the boss invests time and money in hopes that the return on investment will be a productive employee. These principles are also relevant in a non-profit with the donors or Board being in the role of investors.

Many people think that entrepreneurs or CEOs enjoy life without a boss. That's an illusion. Almost all of us answer to someone in the workplace. An entrepreneur or business leader is accountable to his or her investor or capital source, just like an employee needs to make sure that his or her boss is happy with their performance.

This Investor Pyramid focuses on how you create a strong foundation for this relationship with the person to whom you report. At the base, it is essential that you have what I call *transaction alignment.* You can't meet investors' expectations if you don't understand their goals. Get this right, and you've created trust, the foundational bricks and mortar that any successful relationship needs. Without trust, the structure of your business relationship may start looking a bit like the Leaning Tower of Pisa. It's amazing how many young tech entrepreneurs wanting to become the next unicorn (private tech start-ups with valuations over $1 billion) don't get this right.

Clearly, based on his quote that opens Part Four of this book, Maslow recognized the importance of entrepreneurs to society. He also acknowledged that entrepreneurs wouldn't be in business without their capital source. So, although we've already explored in detail the first two key constituencies in any business, the employee and the customer, it's now time to turn our attention to the last part of this essential trinity, the investor.

ARE INVESTORS HUMAN?

When I speak to business leaders about the Relationship Truths Pyramid, I get a very positive reception when I'm applying the Hierarchy of Needs to the employee or customer relationship. But somehow, when the subject turns to the Investor Pyramid, many businesspeople conveniently forget that investors are human beings with needs, too. The prevailing comment I hear is "Investors don't act like humans. They're purely focused on how to get the highest return on investment (ROI) possible."

So, are all investors ROI robots? This part of the book will help you understand that you can provide your investors with a high ROI and do it in a way that creates a deep human connection. In fact, I would argue that creating a deep relationship is a helpful step toward achieving a strong ROI because having a poor relationship with your investor distracts you from the proper running of your business. We've all seen companies that went down the tubes because the CEO and executive team were preoccupied by a challenging relationship with their investors.

If you recall the Transformation Pyramid from Chapter Two, you'll recognize that the *survival* need for investors has similarities to those you'd find for an employee. Employee compensation is a tangible metric, just as investor return is at the base of the Investor Pyramid. The fundamental need for any investor—unless they're purely thinking like a philanthropist—is making sure their transaction goals are being met. The *bottom line* is the bottom level of the Investor Pyramid. During the next two chapters, we will explore the *success* and *transformation* needs of investors. These two levels will make it even clearer that investors are human because many of their decisions are driven by emotional, not utilitarian, needs. For the time being, let's explore what an investor is looking for at the base of this pyramid.

Hundreds of articles and books have been written about the psychology of these particular human beings we call investors. There's even a whole field known as behavioral finance that attempts to better understand and explain how emotions and cognitive errors influence investors and their decision-making processes. Behavioral finance has shown that these ROI robots aren't as rational as we may think. For example, one theory called the *Fear of Regret* suggests that investors avoid selling stocks that have gone down in order to avoid the pain and regret of having made a bad investment. *Anchoring* is another psychological concept of investors that is based on the idea that an investor assumes current prices are about right. In a bull market, for example, each new high is anchored by its closeness to the last record, and more distant history increasingly becomes irrelevant. People tend to give too much weight to recent experience, extrapolating recent trends that are often at odds with long-run averages. The result is investment market overreaction or underreaction that can lead to bubbles and crashes, two extreme results from investors who are a little too human.

So, let's accept that investors are people, too, and that they have a Hierarchy of Needs just like employees and customers do. What's foundational for an investor is the peace of mind that comes with feeling that his or her investment goals are aligned with the company's goals, such that a strong ROI is being created. When this sort of transactional alignment occurs, trust develops. Or as Warren Bennis and Burt Nanus are quoted as saying in Fred Kofman's *Conscious Business,* trust could be defined as the "lubrication of cooperation" in business.[2]

Stephen M. R. Covey (son of Stephen R. Covey, the well-known author) has written a book called *The Speed of Trust*, in which he suggests that companies experience either a trust tax or a trust dividend with respect to the relationships that are created within their organization or with the outside world. He says, "In a company, high trust materially improves communication, collaboration, execution, innovation, strategy, engagement, partnering, and relationships with all stakeholders."[3] He cites a Watson Wyatt study from 2002, which shows that total return to shareholders in high-trust organizations is almost three times higher than that in low-trust organizations. Clearly there is a friction created (the trust tax) when a foundation of trust doesn't exist in a business relationship with investors. That's why trust is at the base of the Investor Pyramid. Without trust, it's almost like the physiological and safety needs of the investor aren't met, which means it's hard to scale the rest of the pyramid.

How do you create a high-trust investor relationship? In a *Harvard Business Review* article, "The Decision to Trust," Robert F. Hurley suggests that before a person places his or her trust in someone else, that person carefully weighs the question "How likely is this person to serve my interests?"[4] When people's interests are completely aligned and an investor believes in the integrity of those he or she has invested with, trust is the natural response.

ATTRACTING AN ALIGNED INVESTOR

No doubt, creating value and a strong return on investment is an essential part of what an investor is looking for, but to talk about the outcome (ROI) without considering the environment (the inputs) that can enhance that ROI seems shortsighted. You can't get milk from a cow that hasn't been fed. In fact, California cheese makers remind us in their ad campaigns that it's the "happy cows" that make great cheese. If it works for the cows, it works for me.

If American business leaders were asked to name the wisest man in the land of investing, Warren Buffett would probably win hands down. I stumbled upon a rare book called *The Essays of Warren Buffett: Lessons for Corporate America*, which outlines his philosophy of how alignment with investors provides the sustenance for company leaders to create great outcomes. Buffett believes getting that alignment correct on the front end is one of the most important responsibilities of an investor. He writes, "The CEOs at Berkshire's various operating companies enjoy a unique position in corporate America. They are given a simple set of commands: to run their business as if (1) they are its sole owner, (2) it is the only asset they hold, and (3) they can never sell or merge it for a hundred years."[5]

Imposing this unique set of commands helps Berkshire's various company CEOs have the proper blinders on to focus exclusively on the well-being of their business without the distractions that are typical of most companies. It allows these CEOs to focus on creating enduring value in their businesses, and it helps take away the natural friction (the trust tax) that can occur between a company and its investors.

Buffett is such a believer in aligning the goals of his company and his investors that he even asks his shareholders to designate the charities to which the corporation donates so there's not a risk of misaligned goals even in that arena. He is also insistent that Berkshire's compensation policies are directly correlated with the kind of return it gives its shareholders. He wrote in one of his famous letters to shareholders, "I cannot promise you results. But we can guarantee that your financial fortunes will move in lockstep with ours for whatever period of time you elect to be our partner."[6]

Buffett represents a growing set of business leaders who believe that "companies obtain the shareholder constituency that they seek and deserve." He suggests that if companies "focus their thinking and communications on short-term results or short-term stock market consequences they will, in large part, attract shareholders who focus on the same factors."[7] In other words, just understanding your business plan isn't enough for business leaders. You need to also understand the motivations of your investors to ensure they're aligned with your own.

Bill George, who presided as CEO over Medtronic's 10-year meteoric rise in market capitalization from $1 billion to $60 billion, says in *Authentic Leadership* that we should be wary of the "shareholder of the last five minutes." Being loyal to the short-term investor doesn't help you as a company in the long term. George says, "Do your shareholders choose you or do you choose them? Sophisticated CEOs choose their investors by defining their particular business approach and strategy and assuring that their investors are aligned with that program."[8]

Apple's chair Arthur Levinson concurred with George in *Fortune* magazine when talking about his time as CEO of Genentech,

"There is so much pressure to hit your numbers. I've been very clear with Wall Street since 1995 that if we see an opportunity to make better drugs and more money down the road at a short-term cost, we will do that every time. And you need to know that's the kind of company we are."[9]

CREATING TRANSACTIONAL ALIGNMENT

How do you ensure that you are on the same page as your investors? Well, if you're a public company, much of it has to do with what George and Levinson suggested. Most public company CEOs think part of their job is selling their company to Wall Street analysts; yet, more and more are realizing that it's really about attracting the right investors who truly get who you are as a company and where you're going. The era of Sarbanes–Oxley transparency means that investors have a clearer sense of all facets of a company, which suggests that stock market investors will increasingly be able to align themselves with companies that fit their goals.

When it comes to investors in private companies, it's a little like dating. You don't rush into a marriage until you've made certain that you're compatible on some of the key basics. The reason many company–investor relationships don't work out is that the two parties didn't communicate their individual intent to see if they had the same goals. So, let's discuss some of the key utilitarian elements that any private investor is looking for. Ask yourself the questions that are listed under each of the five points, but more importantly, consider the nuances and subtleties that might exist between how you would answer these questions and how your primary investors would:

1. Rate of return: What's the minimum rate of return they are expecting from the investment, how is that being calculated, and what kind of extra incentives do you and the company receive if you hit some of their return thresholds?
2. Liquidity timing and strategy: What is the time horizon for their investment, to whom would they sell their investment, and how does that sale affect your control of the company? (Often, the liquidity plan for a business requires a sale to another entity, which means you and your management team may no longer be involved, as was the case for us with Costanoa.)

3. Definition of the market and the company's approach to differentiation: Do you concur on the size of the market, the composition of your management team, and their fundamental business strategy for maximizing the opportunity? In other words, do you agree on the basic business plan?
4. Cash needs to execute on the business strategy: Based on how you are going to grow the business and what key strategic investments need to be made to allow this scalability, are there expected cash-call requirements from these existing investors, or are you going to bring in another round of financing from other investors, and what's the approach to valuing the new and the old money?
5. A single metric that defines effectiveness: Do you concur on what metric is the leading indicator of whether you are effectively managing the business?

THE DEFINITION OF EFFECTIVE PERFORMANCE

As for that last point, few subjects create more animated discussions between companies and their investors. Quite often, discord on point 5 means there wasn't concurrence on point 3. Every company faces conflicting objectives: Profitability or growth? Short-term perspective or long-term? The benefits of organizational synergy or the analysis of stand-alone unit performance? Dominic Dodd and Ken Favaro have written a terrific book, *The Three Tensions*, which outlines ways for a company and its investors to create a dialogue on how to deal with these potentially conflicting objectives.

Similarly, Jim Collins in *Good to Great* showed that even companies in unspectacular industries could post impressive financial performance if they were able to see clearly what one "economic denominator" drove effective performance in their business. Walgreen's switched from profit per store to profit per customer visit because it found that profit per store inhibited its ability to create the convenience of multiple stores within a particular community, which is what the consumer is looking for from Walgreen's. Collins points out that a company can have multiple economic denominators, but focusing on just one helps provide the insight that can come from that singular metric.

We were faced with an enormous challenge during the Bay Area's sharp hotel downturn in 2001, because the primary metrics that had defined Joie de Vivre's effectiveness in the previous half decade were year-over-year revenue, or net income growth, both of which had shown phenomenal results for our investors and owners. But we began to realize that an annualized growth metric was really a lagging indicator of our efforts in terms of creating a great product or building customer loyalty. In addition, annualized revenue or net income growth didn't give us a relative standard to judge each hotel's performance because it was more of a broad barometer of the success the Bay Area was experiencing during the dot-com boom. We were faced with having to refocus our investors on a new, more meaningful metric.

As I mentioned in Chapter Three, explaining who my boss is complicated: a large patchwork quilt of various investors that we own hotels with and an even larger number of owners whose hotels we manage. Fortunately, I had no boss at Joie de Vivre per se because I owned the management company and brand outright. Yet, because the hotels we operated are owned by others or in partnership with others, I still answered to more than 100 individuals or entities, representing 22 different owner groups, who were all shocked by the 2001 downturn after six consecutive years of record revenue growth.

Actually, I had to start delivering bad news even before the 9/11 tragedies. Bay Area hotel revenues began a quick decline in the winter of 2001, about a year after the stock market started punishing the high-tech industry for the silly bubble that had been created. After years of receiving healthy investor distribution checks from Joie de Vivre, our investors and owners reverted back to the bottom of the Hierarchy of Needs Pyramid, as they were worried whether their base ROI needs were going to be met. In other words, they wondered if they would still be receiving checks or if they were going to have to start writing them to cover the hotels' growing negative cash flows.

It was clear we needed our investors and owners to rethink how they defined Joie de Vivre's effectiveness. I remember the conversation I had with one of our long-term investors who was disgruntled with how far our monthly revenue and net income numbers had fallen in 2001. I asked him whether effectiveness is meant to be a relative term. He acknowledged that it was, so we started brainstorming about the ways Joie de Vivre could show its relative effectiveness to our competition during a time when every hotel in our region was experiencing declining revenues and net income.

While I showed the investor that our employee and customer satisfaction scores continued to be a good bit higher than the hospitality industry averages, he repeated a well-known phrase from the film *Jerry Maguire*: "Show me the money!" He didn't want to be convinced that there was a direct line from happy employees or customers to profitability. Since our hotels are privately owned and we can't compare exact profitability with our directly competitive hotels, we needed to look for another metric that had a profound impact on a hotel's relative success in the marketplace: market share.

Each of our hotels receives competitive market share data on a weekly basis from a third-party source, Smith Travel Research, which the hotel industry uses religiously. This confidential data allows us to review whether we are gaining or losing market share at each hotel, and we can break it down by day of the week and whether the week-to-week variance is due to occupancy or average room rate changes. Fortunately, more than 80 percent of our hotels were growing market share during the downturn versus their competition. So, while the proverbial pie was shrinking in our marketplace, our slice of the pie was growing quickly.

I still had to sell the rest of our investors and owners on why this market share metric should be their primary means of determining whether we were performing effectively. Some investors concurred immediately while others took more time. I was able to give to some of them (especially those who took a little longer to come around) studies that showed the link between market share and profitability. I showed a few of them former Medtronic's CEO Bill George's book *Authentic Leadership*, in which he wrote, "Market share is the best measure of how well a company is serving its customers. . . . Market share gains create higher levels of profitability . . . increases in share are highly motivating to employees, making the best people want to work for you and giving them incentive to reach higher levels of performance . . . market share gains create a positively reinforcing cycle."[10]

Some of these doubting investors were able to see that these small wins in market share were helping our frustrated, yet resilient, hotel general managers and sales staff continue their enthusiastic leadership during a truly depressing time. As I used to say to our management team, "When you're running a marathon in the mud, any small win helps give you that little boost of energy to keep you moving forward." Karlene Holloman, our former vice president of operations, told me that shifting this most-watched metric from something that was unattainable (growing revenues in a market that was seeing 35 to 50 percent revenue declines over a three-year period) to something that was attainable (growing market share) completely changed the mood at the monthly investor meetings she led at each hotel.

Peak Prescriptions

Here are some suggestions for how you can ensure that you've created transactional alignment with your investors:

1. Before they invest, make sure you understand the tangible motivations of your investors. Earlier in this chapter, I outlined some of the most basic questions that you could ask a prospective investor to make sure you're on the same page with respect to your goals (Creating Transactional Alignment). These questions are less relevant if this is a small investor without a controlling interest, but sometimes those small dogs are the biggest yappers, so it wouldn't hurt to explore this with them, also. I wouldn't recommend that you give your investors a questionnaire to fill out, but inserting some of these questions into the varied collection of meetings you may have with these investors will allow you to understand what they're expecting from this investment.

2. Beware of the *wrong-owner syndrome.* George McCown has raised more than $1 billion through various private equity funds he's created with his firm MDC. He introduced me to this term when referring to how he experienced wrong-owner syndrome as a senior executive at Boise Cascade. In the 1970s, McCown was tasked with the responsibility of selling off some of Boise Cascade's real estate development projects in order to clean up the public company's balance sheet. In many cases, he would figure out a way for the divisional chief who was running the development to buy the development with private capital supporting him. Over and over, McCown saw that these developments, which were performing sub-optimally, would start to flourish once they left the Boise Cascade stable. He began to feel like he was on the wrong side of the table as he watched a few of his former

(continued)

(*continued*)

employees-turned-entrepreneurs cash in. He ended up purchasing one of the divisions with venture capital backing, and that started him on his career as a private equity investor (in fact, he bought three additional divisions from Boise Cascade). McCown says that when he invests in a new company, "We attempt to provide a completely focused and congruent set of objectives so that everybody is lined up, everybody is on the same side of the table. . . . What we have tried to do is to create a set of conditions within the companies we acquire where people can self-actualize and create." McCown has found that as many as half of all U.S. companies have owners who are misaligned with the management team or with the ideal business strategy. There are lots of great examples of companies that have flourished once the organization was able to break free from its misaligned investors or owners. Within Joie de Vivre, we look for new opportunities by actually searching for wrong-owner syndromes. We've made some of our best hotel or spa purchases when we bought from an owner who was overseas and not truly in touch with the potential of the property or when the business was merely a small distraction for a huge company but could be a sizeable business for us.

3. Create an investor survey that helps you get inside your investors' heads on a regular basis. In Chapter Seven, we talked about how disappointment results from badly managed expectations. Yet, you can't manage your investors' (or boss's) expectations if you haven't explicitly asked them what those expectations are. Joie de Vivre has a long history of reviewing monthly customer satisfaction surveys and twice-yearly employee work climate surveys, but we'd never applied that same approach to the constituency that paid our fees as the hotel management company: our investors and owners. The reality is, we didn't know any hotel management company that had created an annual owner–investor survey. In the summer of 2002, when it was very apparent that the post-9/11 travel world was far from recovering, we decided to create our first annual owner–investor survey. At the time, when we were likely to receive the worst scores from our investors and owners, given their bad mood regarding the

hotel industry's decline, we asked them to rate us on 35 different measurements, from whether we had parallel goals with them to the effectiveness of our sales and marketing efforts. While execs at other hotel management companies thought we were a little crazy for opening Pandora's box, we received a very positive response from our owners and investors as well as some insightful suggestions for how we could create a more aligned business strategy for certain hotels. Just the fact that we created this forum for communication impressed some of our investors. We conducted this survey annually, and as far as we know, we were the only independent (nonchain) hotel management company in the United States that used this kind of survey on a regular basis.

4. Practice honest, direct, and regular communication with your investors. The irony is that when things get bad, most company executives or entrepreneurs take the exact wrong approach. They communicate less as opposed to communicating more. I know it's hard to have difficult conversations with your investors, but being proactive shows your investors just how important this matter is to you, which will build their trust. Investors get most agitated when they feel that the company or entrepreneur isn't taking a particular business problem or surprise seriously enough. In general, people turn up the volume when they think you aren't hearing them. This is also true of investors. Jim Collins suggests "leading with questions, not answers,"[11] as it shows humility and integrity— and that you don't necessarily have all the answers. By asking some insightful questions that are pertinent to the investor's particular interest (and maybe his or her knowledge base), an entrepreneur or company executive can collaborate with the investor in finding a solution, and in so doing, the investor is more likely to be satisfied with this path because they helped create this solution. Know that integrity and trust grow out of doing what you said you were going to do. It's that simple.

Maximizing profits for investors is a legitimate and essential part of running a business. Assuring that you have transactional alignment in terms of the key elements of the business will create more harmony in your company–investor relationship. But this chapter has focused purely on the transactional nature of this relationship. The deal is the glue that keeps the company and investor together on this level of the pyramid. The investor on a path toward self-actualization realizes that the scarce commodity in the investment world isn't necessarily a good deal but a good partner relationship. The deal is the milk; the relationship is the cow. We will now shift our focus from the tangible elements of transaction alignment to how investors create long-term relationships with companies or entrepreneurs who provide them a lifetime of opportunities and oodles of moolah.

RECOMMENDED READING

Good to Great: Why Some Companies Make the Leap . . . and Others Don't, by Jim Collins

"The Decision to Trust" by Robert F. Hurley, *Harvard Business Review* (September 2006)

The Essays of Warren Buffett: Lessons for Corporate America by Warren E. Buffett with Lawrence A. Cunningham

The Speed of Trust by Stephen M. R. Covey

The Three Tensions: Winning the Struggle to Perform Without Compromise by Dominic Dodd and Ken Favaro

"What Do Investors Want?" by Meir Statman, *Journal of Portfolio Management* (2004)

CHAPTER ELEVEN

CREATING CONFIDENCE

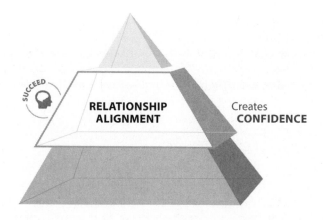

The secret to great investing isn't becoming the ultimate whiz kid at financial models or necessarily being the shrewdest negotiator in the room, it has a lot more to do with building long-term relationships with entrepreneurs and business leaders who deserve your confidence.

BILL PRICE, COFOUNDER, TEXAS PACIFIC GROUP[1]

One of the smartest decisions I ever made in my professional life was to join the Young Presidents Organization (YPO). YPO is a celebrated international organization of youthful senior leaders of small and large companies who meet in local chapters to learn from each other. Sounds good, right? Still, I initially had some reluctance as I thought, "Who has the time to meet once a month for a whole day with a bunch of similarly stressed-out business leaders?" My expectations have been more than surpassed, as I've learned so much from the experience of sharing my company's strategy and my personal path with other entrepreneurs, executives, and investors who are full of wisdom, encouragement, and more often than not, a badly needed sense of humor. I came to one particular meeting with my mind racing a million miles a minute. My body, on the other hand, was ready for a serious pit stop, as I hadn't had much sleep in days. I was in the middle of negotiations on a variety of new hotel deals, most of which were with first-time partners who'd brought us potential opportunities. All of the negotiations were resting on the early Transactional Alignment level of the Investor Pyramid, where the seeds of trust are just beginning to take root. After I shared my story, one of my fellow YPOers took me aside on the break and said, "You have serious 'negotiation fatigue,' as the process of building new relationships with investors takes its toll. It's like finding a new dance partner. You start out stepping on each other's feet until you really understand how the other person moves and you find the rhythm of your relationship. It's time you stopped dancing with everyone at the party."

In essence, what he was saying was that it was time to transcend the bottom of the Investor Pyramid. The focus of transaction alignment is the deal, both the structure of how the investment is made and the cash flows that are generated from the business. The focus of Relationship Alignment is the long-term collaboration that can flourish when a money source and an entrepreneur or company come together. When a relationship with your investor doesn't rise above the bottom level of the pyramid, at the end of a particular deal (for example, when we sell a hotel), the relationship is over. And whether good money was made or not, both parties go their own way. But when this relationship moves to the middle level of the pyramid, the transaction is like a chapter in a book, and there's excitement to move on to the next chapter.

EMOTIONALLY INTELLIGENT INVESTING

Earlier in this book, I talked about Daniel Goleman's successful series of books on emotional intelligence. Hugh Massie, CEO of

Financial DNA Resources, wrote an article about how savvy investors apply emotional intelligence to how they approach their investments. In essence, he suggests that most investors bring a primal fight or flight instinct into their investment relationships, which means that an investor can become overadrenalized with a flood of negative emotional surges due to fears that naturally arise from the unpredictable nature of investing.

Massie refers to an Australian TV show that staged an experiment of two drivers—one a professional and the other not—who were tasked with the responsibility of driving for a half-hour on the freeway during busy afternoon rush-hour traffic. The professional driver was asked to use his skills to dart in and out of traffic, while the other was asked to drive more patiently and stick to one-lane driving at a more moderate speed. The results were enlightening in a tortoise-and-hare kind of way. The professional driver made it to the destination 60 seconds sooner, but he used twice as much fuel and caused 150 percent more wear to his engine than the patient driver. The TV show couldn't measure the wear on the emotions of that professional driver—and possibly, more importantly, the emotions of all the other drivers on the road who had to deal with the guy—but I'm sure there were real costs, too.

Investors who take a short-term perspective on the market and are looking for a "quick killing" on a transaction are more like the aggressive driver: switching lanes whenever something that looks more profitable comes along. They are investing with their adrenal glands. Investors who seek relationship alignment aren't stupid. They won't be satisfied with poor long-term results, but they are more apt to be patient and less likely to be distracted by perhaps a more seductive yet riskier opportunity of the moment. These investors recognize that their vehicle (a metaphor for their relationship with an entrepreneur or company) will wear out more quickly if they drive it too hard or if they're constantly shifting gears.

As Bill Price, one of the cofounders of one of America's largest private equity companies, TPG, suggests, "Relationship investors don't judge the people they invest in on a moment by moment basis. That would be like judging a sailor by each tack he performs as he weaves his way across a windy bay. What these investors are looking for is the overall strategy for how you're crossing the bay."

Too many investors and entrepreneurs fail to comprehend the costs associated with their maniacal journey on the financial freeway. You've probably heard of the ten-year Scottish study (which was confirmed by further results in France and the United States) that shows that the most likely time of the week for heart attacks is on Monday morning when most people are going back to the workplace. Is it possible that Monday "mourning" is the collateral damage that occurs when an organization takes on the stress of a misaligned, transactionally driven company–investor (which translates to employee–employer) relationship? In the past few years, I've come to appreciate the adage *money follows, it doesn't lead.* When money or ROI (return on investment) becomes the only language that glues a company and its investor together, it is likely this will be a short-lived relationship. But just as humans transcend their base needs when they trust they will be fed and sheltered, investors who move beyond the base of this Investor Pyramid start to live a better life where their social and esteem needs start to be addressed as they build confidence in the longer-term relationship they are making with a company or entrepreneur. Goleman has shown that the importance of emotional intelligence increases the higher you go within an organization. So, one could surmise this would apply to the highest reaches of a company: how an investor and the CEO or entrepreneur relate.

In *Plain Talk,* Ken Iverson sums up the importance of relationship alignment when he describes how he helped to turn around the steel company, Nucor, nearly a quarter century ago. He recites a ballsy speech he once made to a group of stock analysts: "Many of you, with your short-term view of corporations, remind me of a guy on drugs. You want that quick fix, that high you get from a big spike in earnings. So you push us to take on more debt, capitalize start-up costs and interest, and slow down depreciation and write-offs. All you're thinking about is the short-term. You don't want to think about the pain and withdrawal that our company will face later on if we do what you want."[2]

Iverson also cites a speech he gave to his managers on the same subject: "We're not dogs on a leash, doing tricks to manage the stock price or maximize dividends quarter-by-quarter. We're eagles. We *soar.* If investors want to soar, too, they'll invest in us. The speculators, we don't need."[3] Now you understand why the name of his book is so appropriate. Iverson recognizes that having aligned investors helps create a healthier company.

FROM TRANSACTION TO COLLABORATION

When I've asked my friends and colleagues who invest for a living about the Investor Pyramid, many of them chuckle and say that the base level should be satisfactory returns, the middle level should be great returns, and the peak should be spectacular returns. While I can see the logic in that progression, it's not really a Maslow-inspired pyramid. It once again suggests that investors are just ROI robots with only one thing on their minds. Part of the challenge here is that there are all kinds of investors. How can you make blanket characterizations that apply to the wide variety of people and entities that range from venture capitalists to your Aunt Millie? Rather than dissect how Maslow applies to each of these investor classifications, let's look at what characteristics describe the investor who has transcended a purely transactional relationship.

Drew Banks is a business author, entrepreneur, and one of my most trusted advisors. He has been involved with a number of Silicon Valley tech firms and believes that what takes an investor from the transactional alignment level to the next level is having *motivational alignment.* Drew shared his views with me, saying,

> First, it behooves the entrepreneur or company to determine the social or esteem drivers for each of their investors. Venture capitalists [VCs] want to find the "new new" thing as they thrive on the ego or esteem benefits of spotting some disruptive innovation before the other VCs discover it. Some invest with a "serial entrepreneur" because they know that it will give them the right to be involved in future deals with this guy who's a success magnet. They may also make a bet on a company because it allows them to collaborate in a particular niche they know well or want to learn more about. Private equity and angel investors (affluent individuals who make early stage investments) will often invest for the "thrill of entrepreneurialism" and the opportunity to get their hands dirty in the nuts and bolts of a start-up. For family and friends who invest, there's clearly a social element as is true for investors in sexy businesses or in businesses where the investors build some kind of relationship with each other. So, there are many varieties of motivation when an investor moves beyond just the ROI focus.

Jack Crawford Jr., general partner of Velocity Venture Capital, suggests that many wealthy investors are looking for community on this middle level of the Investor Pyramid. He says, "It seems the more wealth investors accumulate, the smaller and more elite their social circles become. With that said, they clearly want to remain active in projects, make a contribution and be 'in the know.' My experience is that investments allow them to travel outside of their typical social circles into other 'communities' for collaboration."

Collaborating with your investors such that they truly feel a part of the enterprise is at the heart of what happens on this middle level of the Investor Pyramid. Studies overseen by William McEwen, global practice leader of the Gallup Organization, suggest that confidence is an essential part of what allows a company to transcend the promiscuous base of the pyramid where investors are just seeking out the hottest-looking deal. Gallup has found that both customer and investor relationships are susceptible to the confidence the company inspires. Some of that confidence is rational (based on performance), but much of it is emotional.

Mike Meldman is the founder and CEO of Discovery Land Company, a developer of golf and recreational residential communities. Discovery has developed extremely high-end projects in bucolic locations all over the United States as well as some exotic foreign spots. *Forbes* magazine featured a story on Meldman and talked about how Hall of Fame quarterback Terry Bradshaw and other celebrities have been buying whatever Discovery serves up. The article suggests, "Meldman has attracted a swarm of investment groupies who will buy lots just about anywhere he builds—and Terry Bradshaw is one of his biggest fans. 'I am investing in Mike's projects because he has a proven track record.'"[4]

Meldman told me that when institutions or individual investors initially place money with Discovery, they're likely just focusing on the transaction. But as they build confidence in what his company does, these investors want to create a long- term relationship with him. There's clearly a social element to his repeat investors' rationale because the individual investors in these high-end developments (approximately 375 homes in each project) can ultimately use their investment for their family by building a dream home on the land they've invested in and connecting with a rather utopian recreational community. It also helps that Meldman and his partners are extremely personable. Many of his investors have said not only do they have confidence in Meldman; they also just like spending time with him and his top execs.

To sum up, Warren Buffett has said something that most of us have felt, especially if we've had challenging investors: "We would rather achieve a return of X while associating with people whom we strongly like and admire than realize 110 percent of X by exchanging these relationships for uninteresting or unpleasant ones."[5]

CREATING AN EMOTIONAL CONNECTION WITH INVESTORS

When you name your company Joie de Vivre, you have clearly defined *joy* to be an integral part of the work experience with employees, customers, and investors. Although our mission statement as a company is "creating opportunities to celebrate the joy of life," in the downturn it was really hard to hold onto this mission with our investors and owners. I believe we did a yeoman's job of creating trust and confidence during this time. But frankly, it was a really sobering experience. There were moments during the downturn when I asked myself, "Is this all there is to life?"

Fortunately, our former president Jack Kenny has a wicked sense of humor and an impeccable sense of priorities. Jack's positive spirit was often the icebreaker that would help our regular meetings with owners and investors get off to a harmonious start, even when we had to talk about troubling financial details. Jack helped us ensure that our relationships with our bosses—the owners and investors—were joyfully collaborative, no matter how bleak the economy looked.

In the summer of 2002, when Joie de Vivre introduced our first owner's survey (which I discussed in the previous chapter), we also needed to deliver some unhappy news to our investors (defined as those we were in partnership with in a particular hotel, as opposed to third-party owners whose hotels we only managed). After years of consistently receiving quarterly or annual investor cash distributions, most of our hotels were going to have to do investor capital calls (writing those aforementioned checks) during the upcoming slow winter season. For most investors, this wasn't a big surprise, but it was the kind of thing they wanted to ignore. I figured that I needed a way to deliver this news in a manner that would get their attention. *Warning:* What I'm about to tell you should not be attempted without first developing the trust and confidence of your investors.

With our third-quarter investor report of 2002, we sent out the usual market report from me, as well as the specific details that related to each hotel. We also included a T-shirt. On the front of the T-shirt was a graph showing the San Francisco hotel market's revenue growth from 1980 to 2002. The line showed consistent revenue growth in the first 15 years, with spiked-up growth during the last half of the 1990s. Starting from 1995 to 2002, we also showed a dashed line forecasting where revenue growth would be if the 1980 to 1995 trend had continued into the future. By the summer of 2002, that dashed line, which had been way below the actual revenue line during the late 1990s, was 20 percent higher than where the market had fallen to a year after 9/11. There was a headline on the front of the shirt that read, "San Francisco Hotels 2002. The Sky Is Falling." On the back of the shirt was another headline: "Joie de Vivre Hospitality. Strong Enough to Restore the Sky!" along with a little 1950s-style cartoon businessman with a bubble coming out of his head saying, "I bought a hotel in San Francisco and all I got was this lousy T-shirt?!"

JOIE DE VIVRE HOSPITALITY:
STRONG ENOUGH TO RESTORE THE SKY!

There was a great risk in sending this out to our nearly 150 investors. Would they have a sense of humor about what we were going through? Would this bring us together or tear us apart? Would they mind receiving this at the same time as I was asking them to write checks to cover negative cash flows? Did they truly trust us and have confidence in Joie de Vivre's leadership? I was very nervous when these went out. But I felt it was worth the risk because I wanted something to raise our investors' spirits—and ours, too.

Within a day, I was receiving dozens of phone calls and e-mails from investors who said things like "you did a phenomenal job of sugar-coating this bad news" or "I'm getting lots of capital call memos these days; most of them I try to ignore as it's like reading a funeral announcement, but you have my assurance, when you call me on the phone, I'll take your call because I know, as bad as things are, I'll have an enjoyable and respectful phone call with you, and that's worth something."

One of our investors was so moved that he sent the T-shirt to the *San Francisco Business Times,* which printed a picture of the T-shirt in the newspaper. Ultimately, we gave each of our general managers one of these T-shirts, and it helped lift their spirits, too.

A year later, when the market had tanked even further (but fortunately, we were growing market share), I sent a first anniversary gift of a double-strength Excedrin pill to each of our investors because it was time to do another round of capital calls going into the winter. We had to do more than 20 capital calls during the three-year downturn, but not once did we hit a roadblock in being able to raise the money from our existing pool of investors.

A couple of years later, once it was clear the travel industry recovery was in full swing, one of our investors returned the favor with a surprise T-shirt for me. It read "Joie de Vivre Hospitality . . . No Bankruptcies, No Defaults, No Salary," in tribute to the fact that we survived the downturn unblemished while our two biggest competitors had either bankruptcies or lender deficiencies that plagued them in San Francisco. The CEO (me) not taking a salary for three years helped us to hang in there, and thankfully, by the time this investor expressed his karmic thank you, I began to receive some compensation from Joie de Vivre again.

The moral of this story: our investors were investing in a relationship, not just a specific asset or the timing of the market. While the T-shirt may have given them a chuckle, it reaffirmed their gut feeling about Joie de Vivre as a partner. One investor's phone call summed it up for me. He said, "You've given me even greater confidence, as you're showing me that your company hasn't been beaten down and is still creative—even in how you deliver bad news."

PEAK PRESCRIPTIONS

Here are some suggestions for how you can create relationship alignment with your investors:

1. First and foremost, make sure you have chosen investors who are interested in moving beyond pure transactional

(*continued*)

(*continued*)

alignment, and then explore their deeper motivations. Some investors will never move to a more relationship-driven paradigm because they're just not wired that way. They will always be deal-focused. That's fine. The transaction is a basic need and can provide an investor with the cash to perhaps satisfy higher personal needs in some other part of their life. But there are investors who are more likely to be relationship-oriented. While it can be dangerous to generalize, there's a natural progression from hedge funds to venture capital to private equity to angel investors with respect to their tendency to look at the long term. Because angel investors tend to invest at an early stage before venture capitalists or private equity investors, they often take the greatest risk and expect the biggest reward. But often these investors are former entrepreneurs themselves who get some ego gratification and intellectual stimulation out of being involved with a start-up again. While it's probably unwise to ask an investor exactly what their motivations are, asking a leading question like "What has been your most satisfying investment relationship and why?" may help you uncover some of the hidden reasons they may be interested in funding your business.

2. If your investors have social or belonging needs, take a lesson from Berkshire Hathaway's annual shareholders meeting. Once again, when it comes to the Investor Pyramid, Warren Buffett's company is a wonderful role model. Their shareholder meeting held in Omaha, Nebraska, each May is like an extended family reunion with picnics, cocktail parties, and Warren's signature event, which has been called the "Woodstock of Capitalism." The event is held in the Qwest Convention Center with more than 40,000 shareholders coming together with Warren and president Charlie Munger for five or six hours of questions and answers in an open forum format. For a hilarious yet insightful look at this annual pilgrimage, check out Peter Webb's website (www .peterwebb.co.uk), which is full of British humor and sly observations of the festive, friendly nature of this extreme example of addressing investors' affiliation needs. The true status symbol question of the weekend is "How long have

you been a Berkshire shareholder?" It's an important question because the company has chosen to never split its stock, so that one class A share (which will allow you entrance to the festivities) now costs more than $250,000 (class B shares are far less costly). But there are many proud long-term shareholders who bought shares a decade or two ago for just a few thousand dollars. Some observers have suggested that this is almost a religious revival as shareholders come with their confessions of faith in Warren and his company.

3. Consider some perks that might sweeten the relationship. One of my investors once told me, "Most of us investors have more money than we need. What we're really looking for is access, a little VIP treatment, or something to spice up our life." Discovery's Mike Meldman confirmed this when he told me that his wealthy investors, who had everything money could buy, were just looking for fun or to be part of a really cool development. At Joie de Vivre, we offer our investors and owners the ability to receive a Friends and Family discount at all of our hotels. It's not really the discount they're looking for but the feeling of being part of the inner circle or family. In addition, and more recently, our staff has started creating Dreammakers (profiled in the *Peak* Prescriptions of Chapter Nine) for each of these investors or owners when they stay with us to help deliver on the unrecognized needs of these VIPs. This also helps the investors see one of our proprietary Joie de Vivre programs in action. So, what can you offer to deepen the relationship with your investors? Is it taking your top investor to the Super Bowl or giving them the opportunity to try out your top-secret new product before it hits the market?

In *Good to Great*, Collins writes about how executives in these role model companies found not just mutual respect in their work relationships but also lasting comradeship. He suggests that considering "first who" you want to surround yourself with in a company will truly "be the closest line between a great company and a great life . . . the people we interviewed from good-to-great companies clearly loved what they did, largely because they loved who they did it with."[6] Those sentiments also completely describe the nature of an engaged collaboration with your investors.

So, on we go to the peak of the Investor Pyramid, where an investor has the opportunity to really experience the power of transformation through his or her investment choices.

RECOMMENDED READING

Angel Investing: Matching Start-Up Funds with Start-Up Companies—The Guide for Entrepreneurs, Individual Investors, and Venture Capitalists by Mark Van Osnabrugge and Robert J. Robinson
"Feeling Your Way to Wealth: Emotional Intelligence in Investing" by Hugh Massie, www.raymondjames.com
Plain Talk by Ken Iverson
Working with Emotional Intelligence by Daniel Goleman

CHAPTER TWELVE

CREATING PRIDE OF OWNERSHIP

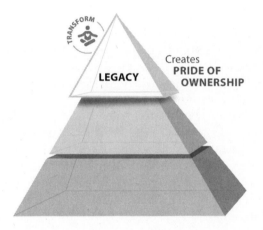

Never doubt that a small group of thoughtful, committed citizens can change the world.® *Indeed, it is the only thing that ever has.*

MARGARET MEAD*

If there's one constant theme in all three pyramids, it's that conventional wisdom is wrong. Conventional wisdom suggests that (1) money is the primary motivator for employees, (2) customers stay loyal when they're satisfied, and (3) investors are exclusively focused on the financial return on investment. As we've seen, these are simply base needs that ignore higher human needs. At the peak of the Investor Pyramid, it's ultimately a legacy, not liquidity, that people seek.

---

* Used with permission of the Mead Trust.

Take a glance at Larry and Ann Wheat, and you might imagine a healthy San Francisco Bay Area version of American Gothic. This attractive couple has been married nearly 60 years and seems appropriately joined at the hip. Despite being retired, you can see in their eyes an industriousness and a stick-to-it ethic that bonds them in their purpose.

I met the Wheats in 1993, when the three of us were considering investing in a small new restaurant that was going to become a tenant in one of my San Francisco hotels. Margarett Malone had helped create a successful upscale vegan restaurant in Marin County and now wanted to launch a larger, urbane version of this establishment. The Wheats, a few others, and I provided Malone the start-up capital for Millennium restaurant. Within the first year, Malone decided to move to Europe and leave the business. So, the Wheats and I took over the operation and marketing of the fledgling venture. That's when I learned why this rather conservative-looking suburban couple had gotten mixed up in this vicarious vegetarian venture.

Larry had been with KPMG, the large international auditing and tax firm, for 30 years, the last 20 as a partner. Ann had been a physical therapist, primarily doing community volunteer work. Frankly, they truly reminded me of my Goldwater-loving parents in that kind of "grew up in the 1950s, had our kids in the 1960s, worked real hard in the 1970s and 1980s" kind of way. The only thing is, my parents didn't choose to go vegan 30 years ago as Larry and Ann did.

When it came to investing, Larry tells me, "Due to the time commitment at KPMG, I didn't have time to have active investments, so I invested in stocks and bonds mostly through mutual funds in a highly disciplined fashion. It wasn't an exciting investment portfolio. I spiced it up with some RJR securities during their leveraged buy-out that made us lots of money, but Ann gave me a lot of flack for investing in a tobacco company. I started thinking that the way we invest could make a difference in the world."[1]

Ann says, "We consider our investment in Millennium to be our contribution to the vegetarian movement and not just a commercial venture. The restaurant has helped to break the stereotype that vegan restaurants have to be austere, downscale, and serve you just bean sprouts. At least half of our customers are not vegetarians, but they're intrigued by the sexy and abundant cuisine we serve in a really beautiful dining room. We attract them with our great product and then help educate them about the benefits of an organic vegetarian diet. It's good for them and the planet. It doesn't hurt that Millennium has been voted the 'Favorite Vegetarian Restaurant' in the U.S. for five years running." Like the Wheats, I have a deep pride of ownership for my financial and emotional investment in Millennium (although the restaurant has now moved to Oakland from San Francisco and the Wheats and I are no longer investors in the new location). While it doesn't fit the rational investor model that many of us grew up with, especially if we went to business school, I believe it's the wave of the future.

More and more investors are putting their money where their heart is. Maslow might suggest that these legacy-driven investors have seen their financial needs topped out, and so they are seeking higher needs such as intellectual satisfaction, or even self-actualization, from the investments they make. Their sense of legacy might come from bankrolling their daughter to become an entrepreneur in the family tradition. Or it could come from investing in a new business that will potentially have a positive impact on the community. Or it could come from investing in a public company with well-publicized socially responsible goals that are making a big difference in the world at large.

Later in his life, Maslow considered that the Hierarchy of Needs could grow to seven or eight levels, with Transcendence at the peak. Legacy investors typically invest the way they do in order to give back in a significant way and transcend their own lives. They seek the psychic returns of making a difference in the world—returns that will outlast their time on the planet. I call this social-actualization, not self-actualization.

How Big Is the Legacy Investor Market?

The nature of a pyramid is that what is at the top is always smaller than what is at the base. Socially responsible investments (SRIs) are estimated to represent approximately 8 to 10 percent of all American investments, or far more than $2 trillion. That's a big number, but it only represents the percentage of funds under professional management by investment firms. It doesn't count the Larry and Ann Wheats of the world. And that $2 trillion probably doesn't include the Omidyar Network, a $400 million mission-based private investment group created by Pierre and Pam Omidyar (who founded eBay) to invest in for-profit (and some nonprofit) ventures that are meant to make a difference in the world.

Baby Boomers control the wealth in America today, and many of these bourgeois bohemians want to make a difference with their investing. Bob Buford, who has written many popular books on the transitions of midlife, including *Halftime,* suggests, "Our first half is about how to make a living, and our second half has the promise of being about how to make a life."[2] Author Ken Blanchard echoes this when he says, "Success is all about *getting*; significance is about *giving back*."[3] Those with the means are looking for a way to create meaning in their lives by how they invest. SRI research shows that the growing prosperity of people younger than 40 is quickly skewing investment activity into more legacy-driven directions, as there's a renewed idealism and sense of choice that these computer-savvy younger investors bring to their investment philosophy. More and more, individual investors are moving up the alignment hierarchy from transactional alignment to relationship alignment to mission alignment (legacy). It should be no surprise that SRIs are a natural extension of a phenomenon that's already well established in consumer markets, especially among Gen Xers and Millennials: the idea that consumers make buying choices aligned with their worldview.

There's a history of legacy investing in this country. Religious investors have long married morals with money. In the American colonies, Quakers and Methodists often refused to make investments that might have benefited the slave trade, and other religious orders chose not to invest in *sin stocks* that had anything to do with alcohol, tobacco, or gambling. Indeed, the first fund to incorporate such sin-stock screening was the Pioneer Fund, which was opened in 1928 and started screening out sinful investments in the 1950s to meet the needs of Christian investors. More recently, Tom Monaghan, a born-again Catholic, grew Domino's Pizza from a single shop to a company he sold for an estimated $1 billion. Since selling Domino's, Monaghan has pursued a number of legacy-driven avenues, including helping to set up the Ave Maria Mutual Funds in 2001, targeted toward clients who want to make sure their investing is aligned with the principles of the Roman Catholic Church.

Changing one little letter makes a world of difference, as Domini Social Investment Funds is to the left what Ave Maria Funds is to the right. In 2005, Amy Domini was featured in *Time* magazine's cover story as one of the "most influential people" in the world because her company brought ethical investing to the masses. Most importantly, she's also proved that SRIs can be financially beneficial, as the company's Domini 400 Social Index generated almost a 15 percent higher return than Standard & Poor's 500 between 1990 and 2005. Similarly, the Dow Jones Sustainability Index outperformed the S&P 500 in the 1990s by about 15 percent. So, investing with your heart doesn't necessarily lighten your pocketbook.

This SRI trend doesn't show any sign of slowing down, as mainstream investment banks like Goldman Sachs and Smith Barney are now offering legacy-driven investment vehicles. According to Nelson Information's Directory of Investment Managers, more than 600 money managers now provide some form of socially screened investment offerings. And in 2006, the United Nations launched the "Principles of Responsible Investment" campaign with more than 70 institutional investors from 16 countries, representing over $4.5 trillion in assets, joining together to pledge a growing commitment to a core set of environmental, social, and governance principles that legitimize sustainable and responsible investment. Maybe what Dr. Timothy Leary whispered to me all those years ago was spot on: The business world can be the most powerful institution for change that we've ever seen.

PURPOSE DRIVES PROFIT

Before I get too carried away, let me reiterate that the vast majority of investors don't fit this transformational model of investing. But one fact that's hard to argue is that all investors appreciate a company that makes a healthy profit. Numerous studies have shown that the companies most likely to create sustained profits are those that have an enduring purpose that balances the various needs of stakeholders. Collins and Porras demonstrated this in *Built to Last*. A recent Harvard University study found that "stakeholder-balanced" companies showed four times the growth rate of companies that focus only on shareholders. And a sensational new book, *Firms of Endearment: How World-Class Companies Profit from Passion and Purpose,* showed even greater investment performance for these stakeholder-centered companies (an eight-times better return on investment over a 10-year period!). These authors suggest that stakeholder-centered companies are following a successful business model more than a moral code.

Orin Smith, who took over the CEO duties from founder Howard Schultz at Starbucks many years ago, has said that having a purpose, while adding more complexity to their business model, has been one of the primary reasons for their success. He told *Business Ethics Magazine,* "When you have social commitments like making a difference for the environment and for farmers, that builds loyalty, it builds passion for this company." Because Starbucks considers corporate social responsibility (CSR) integral to its success, the company has become a leader in institutionalizing it, like creating an audited social report in 2002 of Starbucks' activities. Smith continued, "It's such an inherent part of the business model, our company can't work without it."

Professional investor George McCown says that while most investors aren't necessarily interested in the legacy of their investments, they are interested in finding companies that have an enduring ability to create great returns. Ironically, many of those companies also have a noble vision and strong values. He explains, "The companies we were most proud of had a quality about them that just made us feel energized when we thought about them. We realized it was because they made a difference in people's lives. They made differences in the industry they were in. They were companies that attracted the best employees. They were companies that the communities wanted to have in their town. They were companies that vendors fought over to have their business. They were the companies that customers wanted to do business with. They were companies where the shareholders loved being shareholders." McCown is a self-actualized investor who has pride of ownership when he invests in private companies.

But McCown isn't your garden-variety investor. Most dyed-in-the-wool institutional investors couldn't tell the difference between a legacy investment and a head of lettuce. Yet, many old-school investors are coming to realize that investing in a company with an aspirational purpose can generate great results. So, the idea of legacy investing is gaining currency in groups far beyond just the Social Venture Network and Business for Social Responsibility crowd.

INVESTING IN COMMUNITY PAYS OFF

Back in Chapter Four, I talked about Joie de Vivre's purchase of what used to be called the Kabuki Hot Springs (now called Kabuki

Springs & Spa), motivated in part because we wanted to provide our employees with a unique perk. But there was a deeper reason for our purchase 10 years ago of America's largest Japanese communal bathhouse and San Francisco's biggest spa.

When it opened in 1971, Kabuki was the crowning glory of San Francisco's Japantown district. Fashioned after the traditional bathhouses found in Japanese cities, Kabuki was founded by a collection of massage practitioners who wanted to introduce shiatsu massage and traditional community bathing into the American lifestyle. Given San Francisco's taste for the exotic and the city's populist roots, the business quickly turned into a well-loved city institution— long before the idea of pampering spas was even a glimmer in some health-minded entrepreneur's dream.

Fifteen years after it opened, the original ownership team sold the business to Kansas City–based AMC Theatres because this mega-multiplex movie company planned to build the city's largest theater next door and call it the AMC Kabuki Theater. So now Kabuki Hot Springs was going to be operated via remote control by a company in Kansas City that had no clue how to run a Japanese bathhouse. This was a classic wrong-owner syndrome, as McCown suggested in Chapter Ten.

I happened to be a regular at Kabuki, as it had become a favorite way to take the edge off at the end of a long workday. While the atmosphere was a little spartan, I appreciated the sense that for an hour or two I could feel like I'd taken a short vacation to Osaka. But AMC's lack of entrepreneurial focus on this business started to become apparent to me and others, especially as a whole new brand of sparkling spas started to open in the 1990s. I began to notice fewer and fewer customers, and there was even talk in Japantown that this community institution, now almost a quarter-century old, might have to close. For nearly five years, I tried to convince the local AMC representatives that owning a large San Francisco communal bath and spa wasn't a good fit for their company, and I asked how I could send that message to their decision makers in Kansas City.

Just when it looked like Kabuki was on its last legs, I got a call from my closest contact at AMC telling me that, given the challenges in the movie theater business at that time, the company decided it was time to shed its nonstrategic assets. After a short negotiation period, AMC sold the Kabuki business to Joie de Vivre and gave us a 20-year tenant commitment (as they still owned the real estate) at a fire-sale price.

So, it was now a matter of raising the few hundred thousand dollars we needed to buy the business and turn around both the aesthetics and the services. In considering investors for this project, I wanted to make sure we had transactional alignment. For example, I wanted them to know this investment could last 20 years, as we had no interest in a short turnaround and flipping of the business. I wanted to make sure we had relationship alignment, which came in many ways, including the fact that two of our largest investors were the interior designer and the contractor for the project who chose to receive much of the compensation for their services in ownership interests.

Finally, I also wanted my investors to realize that we were investing in a community asset with the Kabuki. Although we intended to make a number of changes to improve the guest experience and expand the offering of services, at its core Kabuki Springs & Spa (we chose the new name to clarify there are no mineral hot springs on site) needed to both continue its legacy as the largest Japanese communal bath in the United States and be priced affordably in the Japanese bathhouse tradition. We weren't going to become some kind of exclusive, glamorous, pampering spa. We were going to recreate this local forgotten treasure into a serene respite from our crazy, overmerchandized world.

If you believe that what's scarce is what's valuable, you had to know that in the late 1990s Bay Area dot-com era, serenity was scarce. Whereas most spas peddled product (all kinds of facial creams and the like), we were packaging serenity and an authentic Japanese bathhouse experience (or at least as authentic as one can be in America). That may sound a little ephemeral, which is all the more reason we needed to find the right investors.

As I considered partners for this project, many were enamored with the spa industry, given American demographics and trends toward holistic health. The investors liked the idea of spending a ton of money on this first investment to prove it as a prototype that could then be rolled out across the country. Many of these investors wanted to change our marketing focus to a more upscale clientele (which is typical of most day spas). In fact, the amount of money they wanted to spend on renovation almost necessitated that we go after a high-end customer base, which meant we would have to abandon the democratic principles on which Kabuki had been founded. Many of the prospective investors were more focused on short-term returns than a long-term investment. They were more interested in how they were going to get their money out than how they were going to invest in a legacy.

Fortunately, I had a collection of friends and associates who appreciated my unconventional perspective on this troubled little business. These are the people I chose to be my investors. The net result is that Kabuki Springs & Spa now attracts more than 70,000 customers annually, which is substantially more people than any other day spa in San Francisco. We are doing four times the revenue AMC was doing in exactly the same 10,000 square feet of space, yet with upfront renovation costs of less than $500,000. The collateral benefit for these investors: Kabuki has earned them more than seven times their original investment in cash distributions. Giving back to the community has given back to our investors. Our Kabuki investors have considerable pride of ownership. The only argument they've ever had with me is why we haven't gone out and replicated this successful business model. From my perspective, you can't replicate a legacy.

PEAK PRESCRIPTIONS

Here are some suggestions for how you can seek and satisfy investors who have legacy needs or desires:

1. Recognize that there are two kinds of legacy investors: the progressive hierarchical investor and the philanthropic investor. Some investors are romanced by the legacy of a potential investment, but they still need their transactional and relationship needs met first. In other words, they see the benefits of legacy investing as the icing on the cake. I call these people progressive hierarchical investors because they have progressed up the Investor Pyramid to self-actualization at the top, but they still care about the two levels below. There are other legacy investors who will never look at your annual financial reports, and they won't cash your dividend checks (whether it's because they are thinking of this investment as purely philanthropic or there's some other relationship reason, like they're your parents). I call these people philanthropic investors. It's okay to assume that a philanthropic investor is a progressive hierarchical investor, but never make the reciprocal mistake. I've seen

(continued)

(*continued*)

entrepreneurs take their investors for granted because they wrongly assumed that the investor is purely interested in the change-the-world mission of the company. Such an entrepreneur neglects to send regular financial reports and typically doesn't stay in close contact with investors or make the effort to build the relationship. That entrepreneur shouldn't be surprised when investors start to organize to throw him or her out of the organization. When in doubt, assume all your legacy investors still need the kind of attention that is typical of any investor.

2. Host a visioning session with your investor team about the impact this company can make in the world. Thoreau wrote, "Chop your own wood, and it will warm you twice."[4] This can be applied to your legacy investors who want to not just feel good about what their investment does in the world but also to enjoy the process of chopping the wood or creating the business plan. Collins and Porras talked about the "BHAG" (big, hairy, audacious goals) that "built-to-last" companies create, which gives them a sense of purpose. Often, those of us who run companies segregate our senior leadership team from our investors when we talk about the company's highest aspirations. Thus, when our senior leaders meet with the product development and marketing departments to talk about how this new product is going to revolutionize the world, we don't even imagine that our investors should be at the table (sometimes there is a very good reason why they shouldn't be). But many angel investors who see themselves as legacy investors get great psychic benefit from being at the table to hear the enthusiasm of just how this product might make a difference. And on occasion the investor may have some insightful thoughts that would help the product launch. This is also true with respect to public activities, whether it's press conferences or trade shows, where you are showing the world just why the company is so special. A group of Australian professors cited in their article, "Why Do We Invest Ethically?" that the "fun of participation" is a very relevant need for many investors. Don't forget to include your investors in such events. It won't just satisfy their ego needs. It will also address their more transcendent pride of ownership.

3. Consider the *leader's legacy*. As I mentioned at the start of Part Four, you could apply most of the principles I've outlined in the Investor Pyramid to employees' relationship with their boss. It translates into having clear goals at the base of the pyramid and an engaged collaboration full of humanity in the middle. At the top, a boss's legacy is feeling that they've created a smarter and more effective employee or, in many cases, a future boss who will pass this learning on to others. This same principle applies to some relationships between investors and entrepreneurs. Jay B. Hunt was on the Joie de Vivre board of advisors for a decade, holding my hand through the good times and the bad. Based on conversations we've had, it's apparent to me that one of the greatest benefits he gets from the investment he's made in the company is to see my growth as a leader and to feel like he's had some influence on it. The only other member of our board who's been on as long as Jay B. is my dad, and those sentiments could be tripled when applied to the psychic benefits he's experienced through his investment of time in the company. James M. Kouzes and Barry Z. Posner's book, *A Leader's Legacy*, addresses how leaders want to be remembered. Their book is also relevant to how many investors see themselves.

4. Ask your investors how your company should serve the world. As I mentioned in Chapter Ten, Berkshire-Hathaway does this by letting its investors choose which philanthropic interests the company will pursue. Most of your traditional investors won't care, but it may mean quite a bit to your legacy investors. Each of Joie de Vivre's hotels is responsible for raising $200 per room per month annually for a variety of community causes, which the hotel's management and line-level staff chooses. For a 150-room hotel, that means we're raising $30,000 annually: by giving gift certificates away to local nonprofits, providing free rooms or catered events, or having our employees as a group donate company time to a particular philanthropic endeavor. Most of our hotels choose their nonprofits by engaging their staff in the discussion. But those hotels that have more activated owners or investors may ask the owners which organizations or causes mean the most to them. This gives these owners one more way to invest and to cultivate that pride of ownership.

Developing this Investor Pyramid has completely changed how I view our prospective investors. I know that if we're looking for a long-term investor on a project, we need to look for Legacy Investors. In fact, our senior executives now try to categorize each of our investor or owner groups by which of the three levels of the Investor Pyramid best describes them. But I've come to recognize that some investors can't be easily categorized. We had one investor group that was clearly transactionally minded on one hotel yet viewed another investment as a legacy project. The key lesson here is making sure that the relationships with your investors are properly aligned because if you aren't able to first do this, it could wreak havoc on you and the employees in your business.

Investor pride of ownership. Customer evangelism. Employee inspiration. This is what is created at the transformative peak of the pyramid. Few companies ever scale to the peak of any one of these pyramids, but there is a rare breed that can scale the peak of all three. In the next chapter, I'll illustrate what's ticking at the center of the Relationship Truths for those rare companies.

Recommended Reading

A Leader's Legacy by James M. Kouzes and Barry Z. Posner
Built to Last by Jim Collins and Jerry Porras
Firms of Endearment: How World-Class Companies Profit from Passion and Purpose by David Wolfe, Rajendra Sisodia, and Jagdish Sheth
From Success to Significance by Lloyd Reeb
Halftime by Bob Buford
Purpose by Nikos Mourkogiannis
Socially Responsible Investing by Amy Domini
"Why Do We Invest Ethically?" by Diana Beal, Michelle Goyen, and Peter Phillips, University of Southern Queensland (2005)
"2005 Report on Socially Responsible Investing Trends in the United States: 10 Year Review," Social Investment Forum Industry Research Program (2006)

PART FIVE

PUTTING THE TRUTHS INTO ACTION

CHAPTER THIRTEEN

THE HEART OF THE MATTER

Business is simple. Management's job is to take care of employees.
The employees' job is to take care of the customers. Happy customers
take care of the shareholders. It's a virtuous circle.

JOHN MACKEY, FOUNDER AND CEO, WHOLE FOODS MARKET[1]

We've scaled three pretty impressive peaks so far; I hope you're not too worn out. In the first three parts of the book, we've seen how, by using Maslow's Hierarchy of Needs, we can create a business model that fosters an environment in which employees, customers, and investors can feel more fulfilled and self-actualized. And we've seen how peak experiences for these three constituencies can create peak performance for the company. Like any good climber, I felt a bit of an endorphin high once I'd scaled that third peak—the Investor Pyramid—a few years ago. But as the exhilaration started to wear off, I had to figure out how these three relationship truths fit together and what kind of coherent and enduring whole could come from the sum of these three disparate pyramids.

Frequently, when I've pondered a philosophical business question, I've asked myself, "What would Herb do?" For years, I had a picture of Southwest Airlines founder Herb Kelleher on the wall behind the desk in my office. I've admired him because he was such a role model for visualizing potential in people and turning it into reality. Heck, Colleen Barrett, his secretary during the founding of the airline, ended up becoming president of the company three decades later. Herb served as an entrepreneurial guardian angel for me during the downturn. The cliché that it's "lonely at the top" can be especially on point in tough times. My executive leadership team was very supportive, as were my friends and my family. Yet, in the post-9/11 years, when I was sweating how to make payroll twice a month, sometimes it was all I could do to just try to channel a little bit of Herb (some of my cohorts probably thought I was smoking a little bit of herb when they heard some of my *Herbisms*). Often, I would share Herbisms like "The heart of the service journey is spiritual rather than mechanical," or "Don't think about profit, think about customer service; profit is a by-product of customer service . . . It's not an end in and of itself," or "The customer always comes second; our employees are first," or "There is one key to profitability and stability during either a boom or bust economy: employee morale."[2] My team got used to hearing these pronounce-ments, and because Southwest's corporate culture is so similar to Joie de Vivre's, these Herbisms actually felt true and relevant to our managers and employees.

The fact that our culture is so aligned with Southwest's is not by chance. Five years before Joie de Vivre experienced its thrive or dive post-9/11 drama, our top 35 executives and managers spent a three-day retreat studying Southwest Airlines. We wanted to learn how Southwest consistently set the highest standards of employee satis-faction, customer loyalty, and consistent profitability in its industry. *Money* magazine published a study that showed no U.S. publicly traded company gave a higher return to investors on a dollar-for-dollar basis between 1972 and 2002 than Southwest. Wal-Mart, General Electric, Intel? They were all behind Southwest.

We spent three days pouring over the book *Nuts! Southwest Airlines' Crazy Recipe for Business and Personal Success* and any other documents that could help us understand the reasons for South-west's success. (For a more recent, insightful peek into this rela-tionship-driven company, look for *The Southwest Airlines Way* by Jody Hoffer Gittell; the book's subtitle foreshadows what you'll learn: *Using the Power of Relationships to Achieve High Performance*.) Although there were lots of explanations, including their basic strategy of flying one kind of plane point to point, which helps facilitate maximum utilization of that expensive asset (in other words, their planes are in the air a lot more than those of their competition), the number one message we got was that culture was the glue that held the Southwest organization together. Remarkably, this was true of a company that had one of the highest rates of unionization of any airline (something that most people don't know about Southwest).

And the Southwest culture seemed to get stronger as it got bigger, which is unusual because most companies lose their culture with growth. Clearly, the organizational resilience that allowed Southwest to be the only consistently profitable major airline in the post-9/11 era had a lot to do with the kind of relationships the company created through its unique cultural glue.

THE EMERGENCE OF THE JOIE DE VIVRE HEART

In the mid-1990s, we started to study the idea of corporate culture and how we could harness our Joie de Vivre culture in a way that would allow us to be at our peak. We found studies showing that the culture of an organization, and in particular, the way people feel about their work climate, can account for nearly 30 percent of business performance. In studying positive and negative company cultures, we came to define *culture* as "the standards and values that define how people in an organization are expected to behave, especially in their relationships with each other" or, in other words, "it's the way things are done around here." I also like this definition of culture: "it's what happens when the boss is not around."

Soon after this management retreat, we created what became known as the *Joie de Vivre Heart*, which is illustrated on page 204. It harkens back to a theory I'd learned in business school called the *service-profit chain*, which suggests there is a mutually reinforcing relationship between company culture, employee morale, customer satisfaction, and profitability. This model defines profitability as a lagging—not a leading—indicator of peak performance. To clarify, most standard indicators of financial performance, like an annual profit-and-loss statement, measure results of actions that took place in the past. These are called lagging indicators. Lagging indicators may predict future performance, but it's really the leading indicators that have the greatest influence on where the company is going. Leading indicators measure inputs—the investments of a company—while lagging indicators measure outcomes. For example, whether employees show continued growth in morale based on how the company is investing in its culture is a leading indicator, especially in a service business in which our primary product is the relationship between our customers and our employees. In sum, long-term sustainable profits are a consequence of the three other leading indicators: (1) corporate culture, (2) employee satisfaction, and (3) customer loyalty.

JOIE DE VIVRE HEART

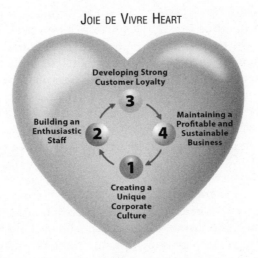

The service-profit chain taught me about the *cycle of capability*. In *The Service Profit Chain,* James Heskett, W. Earl Sasser, and Leonard Schlesinger suggest, "The philosophy behind the cycle of capability is that a satisfied employee is a loyal and productive employee. Their satisfaction stems, at least among the best frontline employees, from their desire and ability to deliver results to customers. In order to deliver results to customers, they must have the ability to relate to customers and solve their problems, the latitude (within well-specified limits) to use their judgment in doing so, the training and technological support needed to do so, and recognition and rewards for doing so." In essence, successful companies create a culture of capability in which employees are well prepared to be empowered. These employees feel a deep resonance with the company culture, and they also appreciate the ability to influence that culture.

Creating the Joie de Vivre Heart was a huge breakthrough for our organization, given the growth we were experiencing in the mid-1990s. It also created a simple symbol that crossed all language and cultural barriers and was a relevant fact to all of our varied hotels, restaurants, bars, and spas. Before creating the heart, I usually stumbled when trying to describe our unique business approach to our employees or to outsiders. Creating the heart diagram helped us to come up with a universal visual icon (hearts and pyramids—we've got an iconic theme here). We all have a heart, right? But this icon is also emblematic of Joie de Vivre's *service from the heart* approach to our customers, as opposed to *service from the employee manual* or *service from the brain.* When our customers feel that our employees are giving service from the heart, they appreciate the emotional connection we are making.

Every new employee learns about the heart in orientation. Many carry a laminated card with this diagram on it. They use the Joie de Vivre Heart to engage with each other about whether we're walking our talk. The basic premise is simple: a unique corporate culture creates happy employees, which leads to greater customer loyalty that, in turn, drives a profitable and sustainable business.

I'll never forget one particular new-hire orientation where I was introducing the idea of the Joie de Vivre Heart and asked the group, "What carries blood through the heart?" A 60-year-old room attendant who had recently emigrated from Vietnam raised her hand. With tears in her eyes (and in broken English), she told us that the arteries carry the blood. She knew this because her husband had gone through heart surgery six months earlier but was now fully recovered.

Her story touched the entire room and prompted a deeper discussion about how we can tell whether the Joie de Vivre Heart is working in each of our businesses. I told her and the group that the most valuable artery in the Joie de Vivre Heart is the link from point number one (corporate culture) to point number two (employees). The role of our senior leadership is to create a unique corporate culture and to help it spread throughout all of our businesses. We enlist our cultural ambassadors (one line-level employee per property who is paid extra for this six-month role) to be cheerleaders and facilitators of culture at their particular property. Point one is where the blood pumps from, but if we have clogged arteries, such that our employees don't feel the positive culture at point two, then we're never going to get that blood to points three and four, and we won't foster customer loyalty or sustainable profits.

Now, I know some of you may find the heart icon to be a bit too Hallmark-y. I understand; when I draw that heart in front of an MBA class or when I'm giving a speech to international CEOs, I initially get a few smirks. But I've yet to find an icon that better defines the virtuous circle associated with the service–profit chain and that does it in a manner that translates across all cultures. If you think it's a little too hokey, don't forget that Southwest's stock market ticket symbol is *LUV.*

CREATING CORPORATE CULTURE

Like those upper reaches of the pyramids, which tend toward the intangible, the subject of corporate culture is one many executives have a hard time getting their hands around. It may seem a little soft or difficult to define. For those of you who want to jump into the deep end of this subject, I recommend *Corporate Culture and Performance*, an academic book that examines why there is a relationship between strong cultures and peak performance. But most of you are probably looking for an easier way to make this subject more tangible. At Joie de Vivre, we decided to use competitive benchmark metrics at points two, three, and four of the heart to help us determine whether what we were doing at point one—the intangibles of culture—was making a difference throughout the rest of the organization.

At point two, we use the details of our annual work climate survey to analyze our trend on various employee satisfaction issues. As well, we can compare our scores versus the industry average. At point three, our monthly customer satisfaction tallies, which are bench-marked against hospitality industry averages, help us determine whether the blood is making it to that part of the heart. In 2010, my last year as CEO, we were proud to score the highest customer satisfaction numbers of any upscale hotel company in the United States. Finally, at point four (as mentioned in Chapter Ten), we have chosen to use market share as our primary definition of sustainable profits because we can compare ourselves with our competition on that metric, but we can't make a profitability comparison because our competition is primarily private companies.

One thing you'll notice is that most of the corporate cultures people admire—from Google's to Whole Foods Market's to Starbuck's—have the imprint of the founders indelibly implanted in the company DNA. Maintaining a great culture is much easier than turning around a bad one. It's not impossible to have a flowering culture sprout from hardened earth, but it helps to have a change in the senior leadership. To change a culture, the leaders have to change the rules of what it means to be part of the organization. It's almost as if the rules for belonging to a club were to change overnight.

Leaders who have been successful in changing their culture did so through tangible changes in organizational behaviors: they literally changed habits. Ken Iverson and his team at Nucor took over one of the most troubled companies in America (Nuclear

Corporation of America) and turned it into a thriving steel-making enterprise with a positive culture. He did this by creating more of a horizontal organization, with senior executives actively building relationships with line-level workers. Then, Iverson preached consistency in staying true to the new habits that he was implementing at Nucor. Similarly, Gordon Bethune inherited a truly awful company when he took over as CEO of Continental Airlines in 1994. Let's look at some of the tangible things Bethune did to turn that culture around.

Before Bethune took over, Continental was simply the worst airline in America on virtually any metrics you could imagine: the worst on-time arrivals, the highest number of mishandled-baggage reports, the greatest number of customer complaints, the lowest customer satisfaction, the least profitable—so much so that the company had gone into Chapter Eleven bankruptcy protection twice in the preceding decade. The company had suffered through 10 leaders in 10 years. While there is no litmus test that would allow us to measure Continental's culture versus its competitors' at that time, I believe that all of these other metrics were the lagging indicators of the simple leading indicator: Continental Airlines had a corrosive culture that dated back to 1983, when Frank Lorenzo bought the airline on the cheap and then operated it in a similar manner while exhibiting a blatant contempt for his employees. To echo a phrase from Chapter Ten, Continental was plagued with the wrong-owner syndrome for quite some time, and that created a truly dysfunctional organization.

In his book *From Worst to First*, Bethune suggests that there was no way Continental could beat the outside competition if they didn't start by dealing with the competitive challenges within the organization. After years of the Lorenzo legacy, no one at Continental trusted anyone else there. Bethune decided to "make it a corporate goal to change how people treated each other: to find ways to measure and reward cooperation rather than infighting, to encourage and reward trust and confidence. That was the only real solution to our problems in the long run." In fact, after Continental had made its turnaround, Bethune said, "We didn't just change the symptoms of what was wrong with Continental. We changed Continental. We changed its corporate culture from top to bottom."[3]

How did Gordon Bethune change the culture, and what does it mean for you and your organization? He started by just listening. What he heard was a demoralized team, one that didn't believe in itself. This is one of the simplest but most overlooked things a new leader can do on joining an organization. He writes, "These people needed to learn that they *could* make a difference before we could expect them to *want* to." One of his most famous solutions was creating a companywide goal that everyone could buy into. Based on customer satisfaction surveys, Continental found that the number one determinant of customer satisfaction was on-time performance (the airplane being at the gate within 15 minutes of the scheduled time of arrival). This on-time metric seemed to make the biggest difference to its customers, and Continental, unfortunately, was in last place among the top 10 airlines. Bethune and his team also found that not being on time was costing the airline $5 million per month (late connections led to housing customers in hotels overnight, paying for their meals, and occasionally giving them free tickets for future travel).

Bethune rallied his senior leaders and boldly suggested something that was antithetical to Continental's divisive and hopeless culture. He vowed that each month that Continental scored in the top five airlines nationally (as measured by the Department of Transportation), they would reward every one of their 40,000 nonmanagers with a $65 bonus (if you do the math, you realize that's a $2.5 million bonus per month if they make their goal). That was a big expenditure for a company that hadn't shown a profit in 10 years. But Bethune thought of it as an investment. If they reached that goal, it would certainly shrink that $5 million monthly cost associated with being late. It would also improve customer satisfaction. Most importantly, though, this group goal might help shift the culture so that a divided company could unify around a common goal.

Remarkably, within three months, Continental went from last to first in on-time performance. Then Bethune upped the ante and started paying all employees $100 per month for each month that the company came in first. And of course, Continental's team made them the consistent on-time performance king for the next few years. Bethune and the management team didn't leave it at that. They made other investments in culture that drove employee satisfaction, from improving lunchrooms to providing a better means of giving managers feedback. They changed the way they conducted employee meetings, including ending the meetings with each employee talking about which improvements they appreciated most in the company.

And when it came to understanding their customers, Bethune even trotted out a little wisdom from our favorite psychologist. In his book, he advises:

> Keep Maslow's Hierarchy of Needs in mind when you're working on your business. For us at Continental, that means we don't want to get so interested in the kind of food we serve that we lose track of getting our planes in on time. We're not going to go too far if we've got one little element right but we're missing the basics. After all, look at our OnePass frequent flyer program, which year after year was voted the best in the business—and all the while we were losing bags, screwing up flights, and losing customers. It's great to have the best frequent flyer program. But we had to have the basics—clean, safe, and reliable flights to places people wanted to go [the food, clothing, and shelter of an airline]—before that was going to get us anywhere.[4]

Changing Continental's culture turned a losing airline into one of the industry's best. Every metric related to employees, customers, performance, and finances shot to the top of the industry. While Continental (now part of United) became one of the most awarded airlines, I think that the most remarkable award is the one Continental received in 2006 as the Most Admired U.S. Airline from *Fortune* magazine. They beat their intrastate rival Southwest (who came in second), which for years had been at the top of the list.

WHAT'S THE RIGHT CULTURE FOR YOUR COMPANY?

The Gallup Organization's "Manage Your Human Sigma" study of sales and service organizations found that a highly engaged employee and customer leads to, on average, 3.4 times more financial productivity. For example, they found that in one luxury retail chain, the stores that scored substantially higher on both employee and customer satisfaction generated $21 more in earnings per square foot of retail space than their remaining stores and that this translated into $32 million in additional profits for the entire chain. This stuff works. Don't take my word for it. Dozens of admired companies have explicitly created their own version of the Joie de Vivre heart. John Mackey's quote at the beginning of this chapter conveys Whole Foods Market's commitment. We know Southwest Airlines believes in the service–profit chain because that's who Joie de Vivre learned it from. And Danny Meyer writes about his version of the service–profit chain theory in his book, *Setting the Table.*

So, what do you, and your company, need to do to ensure you have a culture that will enhance your profits? First, know that the effects of culture are simple, and they come down to the following basic points that are articulated in *The Enthusiastic Employee:*

1. People and their morale matter tremendously for business success, including customer satisfaction.
2. Employee morale is a function of the way an organization is led and the way that leadership is translated into daily management practices.
3. Success breeds success (the feedback loops). The better the individual and organization perform, the greater is employee morale, which, in turn, improves and sustains performance.[5]

There is no one perfect kind of culture. What might work for a biotech company in the San Francisco Bay Area could be completely inappropriate for a Midwestern equipment manufacturing company. Your company's history, location, the nature of your employees and customers, and the nature of your industry will all influence your cultural choices. Any company that focuses closely on the Employee Pyramid (discussed in Chapters Four, Five, and Six) will likely be successful in creating a unique culture that enhances employee performance and customer satisfaction. But beware of the myth that morale or culture has to mean people just getting along. Peter Drucker used to say culture is about "performance not conformance."

I'll use an Herbism to express one more caution. Herb Kelleher said, "The tragedy of our time is that we've got it backwards . . . we've learned to love techniques and use people."[6] Culture is not the same thing as technique. Culture is a framework of values and meaning. It is not a system of specified processes geared specifically to efficiency and results. Culture is authentic and often nonlinear. It doesn't fit into a simple box or some equation. You can't be guaranteed that by taking steps one, two, and three, you will automatically produce a certain result. Yet, when it's incrementally planted, pruned, and harvested, culture develops into a dense and fertile system that yields more than any one leader could have imagined alone.

I've found that culture was at the heart of why Joie de Vivre survived the biggest downturn in the history of American hotels.

And when investment bankers and financiers who've studied our success in the 2001 to 2004 period ask me why we did so well, I always point to the Joie de Vivre Heart.

BRINGING IT ALL TOGETHER

The Joie de Vivre heart was created in 1996. The Employee, Customer, and Investor Pyramids are a manifestation from when my company was suffering through the dot-com-9/11 hangover, as they were created in 2003 to 2004. The connection between these business models wasn't immediately clear to me, although at some point I did arrange the three pyramids into one master pyramid, which created an empty inverted fourth pyramid in the middle (stay with me—I promise this will all make sense in the figure on page 212).

My aha moment came in 2005, when I was speaking to a group of Fortune 500 "leaders of the future" as part of a Global Business Network seminar. This group of leaders, from companies like Ford, Dupont, and IBM, wanted to understand Joie de Vivre's unique business model. I told them the history of the company and how creating the Joie de Vivre Heart helped us to define the importance of culture to our organization. Then I launched into my sad tale of what happened after the turn of the millennium and how Maslow had become an inspiration for me in defining the relationship truths and creating the three pyramids. Looking at the diagram in my presentation, someone in the audience asked me about the empty inverted pyramid in the middle of the other three pyramids. Did I have an operating theory that could fill that space? As I pondered this question and studied the image, a woman in the back of the room politely pointed out that our Joie de Vivre Heart was actually shaped like an inverted pyramid, with a slim base and wide shoulders. Why not drop the heart into the middle of the pyramid?

Have you ever had a moment of reckoning when time stops, the world around you fades, and you just completely lock into something that truly captures you? Maslow called this a "peak experience." Well, I had one in public that day—in front of those 40 ambitious young executives, I got a little teary-eyed when I realized that not only did the heart fit into the pyramid, but the points on the heart also corresponded to each of the contiguous pyramids. Point two on the heart (*Building an enthusiastic staff*, which comes from creating a unique corporate culture) was placed next to the

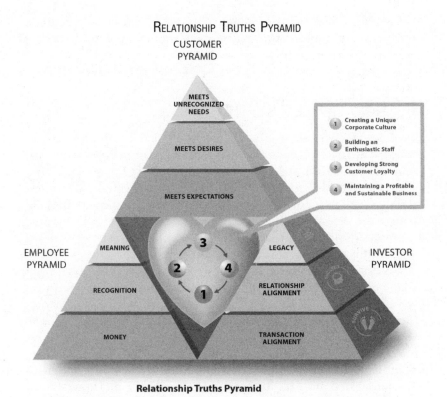

Relationship Truths Pyramid

Employee Pyramid. Point three on the heart (*Developing strong customer loyalty*) was contiguous to the Customer Pyramid. And point four on the heart (*Maintaining a profitable and sustainable business*) was hugging the Investor Pyramid.

Okay, it probably wasn't comparable to when Einstein discovered $E = mc^2$, but I will tell you that it gave me a profound sense of self-actualization. This is what the Joie de Vivre laboratory has taught me. This is what my life's work has been about. This is why I needed to write this book, even though it's meant serious sleep deprivation while running a fast-growing company.

When you or your organization move from the second level of Success on each of these pyramids to the third level of Transformation, a quantum leap occurs. For example, while the initial move from Money to Recognition on the Employee Pyramid may be gradual, the spark that takes an organization from Recognition to Meaning is powerful. It means employees have moved from being externally motivated to internally motivated. Similarly, the quantum leap on the other two pyramids is equally profound and it's really culture that is the organizational glue and firepower that helps a company empower this move up the pyramid toward self-actualization.

In sum, the heart is the core that holds these three pyramids together. No one relationship suffices to bring success in today's competitive environment. It is a combination of these three relationships held together by a unique operating model, like the service–profit chain, that helps create peak performance.

When I conceived of these three Maslow-inspired pyramids, I instinctively knew they had a deeper connection, but adding the heart as the glue that keeps them together has helped Joie de Vivre use the Relationship Truths Pyramid as a comprehensive and holistic approach to how we develop extreme loyalty with our employees, our customers, and our investors.

 RECOMMENDED READING

Corporate Culture and Performance by John P. Kotter and James L. Heskett

From Worst to First by Gordon Bethune with Scott Huler

Reflections on Leadership by Larry Spears

The Enthusiastic Employee by David Sirota, Louis A. Mischkind, and Michael Irwin Meltzer

The Rebel Rules by Chip Conley

The Service Profit Chain by James L. Heskett, W. Earl Sasser Jr., and Leonard A. Schlesinger

Nuts! Southwest Airlines' Crazy Recipe for Business and Personal Success by Kevin Freiberg and Jackie Freiberg

The Southwest Airlines Way by Jody Gittell Hoffer

The Culture Engine: A Framework for Driving Results, Inspiring Your Employees, and Transforming Your Workplace by S. Chris Edmonds

Uncontainable: How Passion, Commitment, and Conscious Capitalism Built a Business Where Everyone Thrives by Kip Tindell

CHAPTER FOURTEEN

PEAK LEADERSHIP PRACTICES

*Practice doesn't make perfect, but it does make public your
commitment to Peak principles. Role model these practices and
you're on the path to peak performance.*

CHIP CONLEY

Doctors and attorneys practice medicine and law. So why
don't business leaders *practice* business? There's practice involved
in sports, the arts, and even religion, but we don't think of our
profession as a practice. We just do it. And, quite often, we do it
rather unconsciously.

The first 13 chapters have prepared you for this one. They
outlined the business model and principles of *Peak* organizations.
But business principles are only as good as the practices that back
them up. And those practices are exhibited by leaders. A leader is a
person who influences a group of people toward a specific result. In
this chapter, we will address how you can improve your capacity to
lead.

In the 10 years since I wrote the original edition of this book,
I've witnessed how effective leaders use the principles of *Peak* in
their everyday leadership practices to drive organizational performance. So, I've developed a set of *Peak* leadership practices that can
assist any leader, or leadership team, to move their organization
from mediocrity to excellence.

When a company embeds these principles and practices into
how they grow their leaders, the end result is *Peak* performance: a
phenomenon of sustained growth—both for the organization and

for those within it. What is unique about these eight practices is they build upon each other and the skills and habits that back them up to help the *Peak* principles come to life. While each practice can stand alone, when combining them together a *Peak* leader unlocks the human potential that's stored in every organization or team so that Peak performance is more likely. More than foundational beliefs, they represent a new way of doing business.

THE PRACTICES
Practice 1: Embody an Inherently Positive View of Human Nature

The principles of *Peak* have their roots in humanistic psychology and a basic belief that man is meant to *be all that he can be.* So, it's not surprising that the fundamental first practice is assuring that a Peak leader believes that humans—at their very core—gravitate to goodness when the right conditions exist for them to flourish.

Creating the right *psycho-hygiene* in a company has a lot to do with focusing on people's best qualities and believing in what's been known for more than a half-century in business as a Theory Y perspective on management versus Theory X. As we discussed in Chapter Two, with Theory X, management assumes employees are inherently lazy, will avoid work if they can, and inherently dislike work. As a result, management believes that workers need to be closely supervised and comprehensive systems of controls should be developed. With Theory Y, management assumes employees may be ambitious, self-motivated, and able to exercise self-control. They believe that the satisfaction of doing a good job is a strong motivator and seek to create the conditions for employees to develop their own strengths to be successful. I often call this creating the right *habitat.*

While this seems straightforward, how much time do we spend trying to change people on our teams rather than allowing them to grow—or, better yet, making sure that you have the right people for your particular kind of habitat? In reality, it takes practice to really embody this perspective and it takes time for it to build the kind of trust that ultimately bears fruit. However, this is the path toward freedom—the path to not needing to be involved in every decision or at every meeting. The command and control structure that defined business for so many years is declining. Yet, for some organizations, chaos is what reigns in its absence. This practice helps leaders to understand the method to tap into their peoples' greatest potential, while still developing a sense of order and mission that can propel the organization forward toward its goals.

It can be truly courageous to operate based upon this practice. Look at Tony Hsieh and Zappos. They chose to develop a whole new approach to their organizational structure and decision-making called *Holacracy*. While controversial, because of the radical nature of some of its processes, Holacracy replaces the top-down predict-and-control paradigm with a new way of achieving control by distributing power. It is a new operating system that instills rapid evolution in the core processes of an organization based on the belief that all employees want to have a stake and a voice in how they operate. It's also based upon the premise that line-level employees, not just managers, should be integrated into decision-making: https:// www.zapposinsights .com/about/holacracy/10-ways-leaders-limit-success/.

John Mackey's approach to empowering small teams at Whole Foods Market has a similar Theory Y perspective. Zappos has had some challenges making this transition, but the company has an impressive track record of trying rebellious, humanistic ideas that become the norm. For example, in 2009, Amazon acquired Zappos and inherited their offer. During their primary training, new employees are offered $4,000 to leave the company (originally, it was $2,000). In his 2014 annual letter to shareholders, Amazon founder Jeff Bezos explained that the company had added a program modeled after the one started by Zappos. After some tweaking, Bezos and Amazon aptly titled the program "Pay to Quit." Old school, Theory X thinking would suggest that employees might try to get a job at Amazon or Zappos just for the bonus to leave. But these two A–Z companies both recognize that helping an employee depart on good terms, and get compensated for it, is better than having them stick around disgruntled and unproductive. Bezos explains the rationale: "The goal is to encourage folks to take a moment and think about what they really want."[1] He writes, "In the long-run, an employee staying somewhere they don't want to be isn't healthy for the employee or the company." While editing this revised edition, Amazon purchased Whole Foods Market and it will be interesting to see how the fresh grocer evolves.

Here are a couple tips you can consider to address the premise behind Douglas McGregor's quotation that opened Chapter Two: *"Behind every managerial decision or action are assumptions about human nature and human behavior."*

- Make a list of a dozen different examples of your employment practices—from time clocks to vacation policies—and then grade them on a one-to-five basis of how they fit on the Theory X (1) and Theory Y (5) spectrum. What was your average score and how can you create more practices that veer in the direction of Theory Y? Or, take McGregor's direction as outlined in Chapter Two: "Next time you attend a management staff meeting at which a policy problem is under discussion, or some action is being considered, try a variant on the pastime of doodling. Jot down the assumptions (beliefs, opinions, convictions, generalizations) about human behavior made during the discussion by the participants. Some of these will be explicitly stated. Most will be implicit, but fairly easily inferred." Engage a conversation of your top leaders about the risks and rewards of developing a more positive view of human nature. Is it possible for you to test some new, human-centric approaches in some part of your company to see what the effect is on employee engagement and customer satisfaction?

- Peter Mullin is one of the wisest men I know. He started M Financial more than 35 years ago and it grew into one of the preeminent life insurance and financial services firms in the world. His underlying Theory Y belief is that his employees are smart problem-solvers, but they just haven't been coached to properly exercise that muscle. So, when an employee comes to Peter with a problem looking for a solution from him, he'll say, "You've been thinking about this a lot, what do you think is the best solution?" He waits for an answer, even if there's a long, awkward pause. Often, the employee comes up with an answer that isn't very plausible so Peter will ask them their number two and three ideas, which brings a panic to the face of the employee. Peter then suggests the employee go back and think through a few solutions with the idea that a week later they will review these together. When that future meeting happens, the vast majority of the time, the employee has developed two or three credible solutions that Peter can help tweak a little so that the employee feels a greater self-confidence in the ability to problem solve as well as the boss.

Practice 2: Create the Conditions for People to Live Their Calling

Abe Maslow wrote, "One can set up the conditions so that peak experiences are more likely, or, one can perversely set up the conditions so that they are less likely."[2] Great leaders understand there are only three relationships you can have with your work. You can have a job, a career, or a calling. When you're living a calling, it energizes you, while a job tends to deplete you. Great companies create the conditions for employees to live their calling.

Most employees live in the bartering world of work. The company gives them a compensation package and recognition and, in return, the employee gives their time and energy. Yet, those who are living their calling have moved from external motivation to internal motivation. And, quite often, these employees are less focused on the specific collection of tasks they perform and more focused on the impact or purpose of what they do. This is true of all employees whether they be hotel housekeepers, tech engineers, or airline flight attendants. And, yet, there's a real skill as a leader in creating the environment where employees are compelled by a purpose as opposed to discouraged by task-driven rules.

Gary Kelly, the CEO of Southwest Airlines, explains that one of the principal reasons his company didn't start charging for baggage—like all the other airlines did when oil prices spiked in 2008 during the Great Recession—was because he recognized this decision would negatively affect the sense of calling his flight attendants have in their work. One key differentiator for Southwest is the friendly, casual, and genuine service the company's flight attendants provide. Yet, if passengers were now going to bring dramatically more baggage on the plane to avert the baggage charges (which is what ended up happening at the other airlines), this could affect the happiness and engagement of his customer-serving airplane personnel.

Southwest initially got beaten up by Wall Street analysts because they didn't pursue the short-term profits of extra fees for bags. But the airline's on-time performance vastly improved during this era, while their competitors were delayed due to all the extra bags being carried on and then escorted out of the passenger section of the plane. Southwest saw fast growth in their market share partly due to its decision not to mess with the happiness of their flight attendants.

Great leaders face difficult decisions. They holistically consider how their decision-making will impact the employee work climate and their employees' ability to aspire to living a calling. Here are two questions a *Peak* leader can ask themselves and their team to assure they're applying this practice:

- As you make any significant operational or strategic decision for the company, who on your team will be most affected by this decision, what is the potential collateral damage that could arise out of this decision, and how can you mitigate it if you are going to pursue this path?

- How are you regularly gathering insights from your various job functions in the company to determine what gives each of them the greatest sense of meaning in their job, as dishwashers will likely have different answers than bartenders but both work in the same restaurant? Once you've identified this mojo-creator, how can you amplify more of that kind of experience in that particular job classification?

Practice 3: Promote and Measure the Value of Intangibles

In business, we're taught that leadership is all about managing what you can measure, but what's most easily measurable is the tangible in life. It's easier to answer the question of whether your stomach is hungry (a basic physiological need) than whether your soul is famished (a self-actualization need). No doubt, the tangible is important. In business, the metrics that track the tangible are well known: your profitability, your cost structure, and your market share. Yet, in reality, these tangible metrics are the result of a series of intangibles that drive excellence: brand loyalty and reputation, employee engagement, customer evangelism and word of mouth, ability to innovate and create intellectual capital, or company culture. These intangibles are the inputs that truly drive the tangible output most companies use to evaluate their performance.

These intangibles drive business success and yet they are much more difficult to measure. Just because something is more intangible and difficult to measure, we often mistake it to be less valuable. Or, even more likely, we neglect it because it doesn't fit as easily onto an Excel spreadsheet. Yet, modern leaders recognize that the intangibles tend to be the ultimate differentiators of their company and brand.

In a world that is increasingly driven by the value of the intangible, *Peak* leaders are able to rise above their colleagues by tapping into a set of practices that values what truly counts in business, and, in life. A quote often attributed to Einstein reads "Not everything that can be counted counts and not everything that counts can be counted"[3]; yet Einstein never ran a business in the twenty-first century. Today, our visionary yet practical business leaders know that intangibles matter, but they also have to prove this with a new set of meaningful metrics that drive organizational performance.

I had the good fortune of traveling to the Himalayan kingdom of Bhutan in 2009 to meet the prime minister and the country's Gross National Happiness Commission. Back in the early 1970s, Bhutan's young king, sounding like a *Peak* leader, asked why all countries are fixated with gross national product (GNP) when spreading happiness should be the aspiration of every effective governmental leader. With nearly 40 percent of the world's population on its tiny borders, like a tiny start-up surrounded by mature competitors, Bhutan has created the ultimate disruptive metric, a global currency of well-being, which has now been adopted in over 50 other countries. I came back from this transformative trip and gave a TED talk about learning to measure what makes life worthwhile: https://www.ted .com/talks/chip_conley_measuring_what_makes_life_worthwhile.

There are so many opportunities to create meaningful metrics in your company. At Airbnb, our recruiting team tracks the number of online applicants to jobs available each year as a means of understanding our popularity as an employer. This popularity index grew by more than 50 percent in 2016, after the company won the award—overtaking Google—in 2015 for being the best place to work (according to the anonymous online employee review site Glassdoor). Other companies track unique metrics like the percentage of employees involved in company philanthropic activities, or the percentage of employees referring friends or family to work in the company (with no financial bounty attached), as a means of evaluating the intangible of employee engagement. Kickstarter, the crowdfunding platform, chose to become a public benefit corporation (known as a B-Corp) because they appreciated the metrics that B-Corps have to live up to while some other companies use WorldBlu's Scorecard as a means to track the democratic design of an organization.

Steps you can take to give greater attention to the intangible in your organization:

• Create a small task force of diverse employees in your company focused on the question, "What is valuable for our employees, customers, or community that we currently don't measure and need to start counting?" Airbnb has taken this question seriously and is looking at the variety of ways it can measure *Beyond*

Anywhere, the company's mission for our guests and employees. We charted the *Belong Here Transformation Journey* that charts the moments and influences that help our employees belong at work and we redesigned the check-in experience to help employees feel that sense of belonging on their new teams almost immediately. Finally, we added a question to our twice-annual employee engagement survey asking their perspective on "I feel a sense of belonging."

- Create your own meaning index in the Notes app on your smartphone. Each day, when you experience a moment of *joie de vivre*, make a note of what prompted it—whether it be someone complimenting your action plan that was just distributed or feeling accomplished about a meeting you just led. At week's end, gather the list of meaningful moments and start developing a list of categories that these moments fall into. Over the course of a few weeks, you will better understand what gives you meaning and can start developing an operating strategy for how you can seek more of that in your work life as well as a sustained way of measuring it.

Practice 4: Ability to Move Fluidly Between Being a *Transactional* and a *Transformational* Leader

Transactional leaders lead from the bottom of the pyramid, while transformational leaders lead from the top. Most management decisions require only transactional thinking because the goal is purely to optimize existing resources. But, in an era of constant change, transformational leaders visualize potential and actualize it into reality. And they do so in a manner that energizes and inspires the organization to greatness. A *Peak* leader is able to move fluidly between addressing people's foundational needs, while also helping them to see beyond the short-term, which motivates a compelling vision to help transcend their momentary challenges.

I call someone with this fluidity a *Golden Eagle Leader*. No other bird can fly to 10,000 feet or one of the fastest horizontal speeds, 80 miles per hour, like the golden eagle can. Yet, like a visionary who is able to dive deep into an operational challenge when he or she spots it, the golden eagle has the fastest vertical drop speed of any bird, 150 miles per hour. These leaders are adept at the left-brain, right-brain tango and able to shift from logic to creativity in a moment's notice.

I appreciate that many of the people I've worked with see me as a Golden Eagle Leader. But, I've witnessed those with considerably more fluidity than me. Barry Sternlicht, who created Starwood Hotels, could be rapping on the phone about a complex real estate deal one minute, and addressing a designer in his office with a critique of a new hotel room style the next (as he did when he launched the W and 1hotel brands). He could fly high or low in multiple disciplines of business.

Similarly, I've enjoyed flying side-by-side with Airbnb CEO Brian Chesky. His visionary perspective on making the company the "superbrand" of travel is matched by his superhuman ability to sit in on a design meeting to make small, essential changes to the Airbnb app. Many have compared him to Steve Jobs in his capacity to be both transactional and transformational.

Julie Hanna, the Egyptian-born technologist, entrepreneur, and executive chair of the board of Kiva, iteratively asks the Peter Drucker question "What business are we in?" to ensure Kiva is being guided by its mission to democratize access to capital. A peer-to-peer lending pioneer, and the world's largest crowdfunding marketplace for global entrepreneurs, Kiva targets underserved borrowers, most of whom are in the developing world. When the Great Recession hit in 2008, they saw a need and opportunity to also fund U.S. small business entrepreneurs who had largely been abandoned by traditional banks. Kiva received quite a bit of grief from stakeholders (lenders and employees) who believed it had strayed from its mission. The Drucker question helped give the leadership team the comfort to think more expansively about their mission.

If Julie and the team hadn't shifted from their transformational vision to the transactional question of how to address the pushback from stakeholders, this new direction might have died. By practicing what she calls "radical empathy" and going deep to understand what wasn't resonating in hearts and minds, they uncovered a hidden unconscious bias that blinded stakeholders to the unmet capital needs of small businesses in the United States. Once Kiva demonstrated that extreme lending cutbacks (44 percent drop with 8 out of 10 loan applicants being turned down) meant tens of billions of dollars—that used to fuel the U.S. economy and job growth while helping communities thrive—had been eviscerated meant they were able to shift and unite the market toward a *Think Global, Act Local* mindset.

Julie's actionable tips for moving fluidly between transactional and transformational leadership:

- If you tend to operate in a visionary way, make sure to always do a spot check around buy-in. Especially with teammates responsible for execution. Can they link their on-the-ground operating reality to what the company is trying to achieve? What do they need to succeed and what's blocking them?
- At least once a year, and as much as quarterly, ask your teams to do the following exercise as a group. Answer the question "How does our day-to-day work enable the organization's top line goals and reason for being?" In Chapter Six, we reviewed the idea that employees can have meaning *in* work and *at* work. This exercise helps to make sure your people feel they have meaning in their sense of impact, which supports the company's purpose. It can be a simple way of identifying gaps for teams between *in* and *at*. It also helps team members at all levels cultivate their capacity to become Golden Eagle Leaders themselves.

Practice 5: Nurture, Value, and Evolve Corporate Culture as Your Ultimate Differentiator

Transformational leaders can't do it alone. Studies show that approximately 30 percent of the difference in results between competing companies with similar products or strategies can be traced to the quality of the corporate culture of each organization. Corporate culture—or, in other words, the way things are done around here—is like a pond. There can be vibrant life under the surface or a stench from dead water. Throw a stone into the pond and it creates ripples, just as organizations are contagious with emotions. The number one emotion affecting most companies? Fear. But a healthy culture is your corporate inoculation against an epidemic of fear that can paralyze your organization.

Great leaders know that company culture is their secret weapon, that it needs to be nurtured and valued, and that it must evolve with the times. It takes years to create a compelling culture, yet you can lose it with just a few bad decisions. This isn't solely an HR department concern. It's relevant to all leaders within an organization because, just like overall corporate culture, there's also departmental culture that can either propel or stymie a team.

The most valuable lesson in this practice is to become more conscious about what constitutes your current culture and what steps you can take to move that in the direction most appropriate for your long-term corporate or departmental goals.

When investor Peter Thiel made his $150 million investment in Airbnb, he famously said, "Don't fuck up the culture"[4] to the three cofounders. Cofounder and Chief Product Officer Joe Gebbia took that advice seriously and interviewed hundreds of employees to understand what would give them a greater sense of belonging, and then he took a lead role in evolving the company's core values as a result. Joe says, "The more you have a vibrant culture that everyone buys into, the less process you need in the org."

Airbnb's investment in culture takes many forms. There's a collection of *core values interviewers* who do their normal jobs in various departments of the company—from engineers to lawyers—but are also trained to interview new candidates for their core value fit with the company. A core values interviewer can veto a candidate if they don't think this person understands and appreciates the culture. There's also a Core Values Council that considers business issues that arise that may be at odds with the core values of Airbnb. The company also has a sizable Ground Control team whose exclusive role is to create a vibrant culture for the employees of each of the more than 20 global offices, but in a way that fits the local culture of that part of the world.

Airbnb's biggest investment in culture is likely its biennial One Airbnb and Airbnb Open. Imagine bringing every one of your 3,000 employees globally to the mothership to reconnect with the mission of the company. This requires a big commitment of time, money, and logistical prowess because you still have a company to run while this retreat is taking place. Similarly, due to the sizable success of this all-employee event, I took the lead in developing the Airbnb Open, which is our way of investing in the culture of our global host community. This movable feast has taken place in San Francisco, Paris, and Los Angeles, where in 2016, we had 20,000 enthusiastic evangelists from more than 100 countries tap into the culture. No doubt, this is a differentiator; as one host said to me, "I can't imagine Expedia [through HomeAway, their home-sharing subsidiary] or Booking.com putting this on for their host community. For that matter, they don't even have this kind of host community."

How are you being an advocate for your culture? Here are a couple of ways you can ensure this practice in your company:

- One of the most important questions a *Peak* leader can ask when faced with challenging economic circumstances is "What do I want our culture to look like when we come out of this difficult time?" If you're leading during a recession, a merger, or some major reorganization, make sure this question is asked amongst your leadership team at least monthly during your regular meetings. If you want to emphasize how important culture is, put it in the title of the CEO. Liderman's CEO (profiled in Chapter Four) Javier Calvo Perez Badiola includes the title "Guardian of the Culture" on his business card and Airbnb CEO Brian Chesky has added "Head of Community" to his CEO title.
- Just like people have personalities, companies have cultures. The more clear and intentional you are in defining your culture the better. This is also true of various departments within a company that have subcultures. At a company retreat, ask employees to name an animal that first comes to mind when thinking of your company culture, along with a few adjectives that define the animal and culture. Converse about this as a group to understand commonalities. Then, break into functional departmental groups and define the personality of your team or department. At Airbnb, we even have graphic animals on large signs defining the workspaces of the various teams.

Practice 6: Calibrate the Balance Between *Conscious* and *Capitalism*

Business has quite often been seen as a zero-sum game. One person's win is another person's loss. Taken to a global level, some believe that capitalism's short-term gains are often to the long-term detriment of the environment and to certain communities. Yet, there's been a paradigm shift in the past decade, most noticeably evidenced by America's largest retailer, Wal-Mart. Peak-performing companies have to become conscious capitalists as the world has become much more transparent and companies have become more accountable. Many companies today believe that you can do well by doing good, but they also believe *sustainability* isn't just about being eco-friendly. It's also about having a sustainable business model, which assures you're in business next year.

My initial title for this book was *Karmic Capitalism* and John Mackey used the now ubiquitous term *Conscious Capitalism* for his. How does a great business teach the practice of conscious capitalism to their key leaders? Teaching leaders the value of leading with a long-term, systemic perspective is foundational to this practice. No doubt, leadership is all about balancing priorities. In the twenty-first century, the most profound leadership question will be how to balance being conscious about how your decisions impact those around you, and the world, while focusing on maximizing financial return for the organization. That may sound like the kind of concern only a CEO has to consider but, in reality, on a daily basis, midlevel leaders are faced with questions about how a financially motivated decision might affect the culture of their department, the motivation of those who work with them, or the company's reputation in the community. Think of the United Airlines gate agents who in April 2017 decided to send police officers onto a plane to drag Dr. David Dao from his seat because they were overbooked—a classic *un*-conscious capitalism case study. This practice helps create a leadership paradigm for leaders throughout an organization to use.

John Zimmer, cofounder and president of Lyft, is a great role model for this practice. A graduate of the Cornell Hospitality School, he says he was heavily influenced by a quotation on a plaque at Cornell: "Life is service. The one who progresses is the one who gives his fellow men a little more—a little better service." This human-minded ethos is part of the reason Lyft's moral compass is often seen as more admirable than that of its chief rival, Uber.

How does this approach to conscious capitalism show up in Lyft's business practices? They value their drivers more by offering more humane education and mentorship options, allowing drivers to receive tips (more than $200 million has been collected as of mid 2017), which Uber doesn't allow its drivers, creating a driver community forum, encouraging passengers to round-up their fare to make a donation to charity, and the company is frequently more collaborative with municipal regulators. It's no surprise that more than 75 percent of Lyft drivers are satisfied with their experience while this number is less than 50 percent for Uber drivers. This conscious approach to being a disruptor has created great brand value to Lyft and, while they are today only a fraction of the size of Uber, their momentum and market share is growing because of their reputation.

Here are a couple of ways you can put this conscious capitalism practice to good use:

- Read the book *Conscious Capitalism* by Whole Foods Market CEO John Mackey and Raj Sisodia, review the website www .consciouscapitalism.org, and consider going to their annual conference or getting involved in a local chapter.
- Move beyond the typical platitudes of corporate social responsibility. What are the specific things your company is doing to operate from a broader stakeholder perspective that none of your competitors are doing? How can you engage your employees to take a more active role in deciding which causes you'll support, and what operational changes can you make in your business to make it more conscious?

Practice 7: Disrupt the Customer Pyramid with Consistent, New Innovations at the Peak

The sixth practice helps a *Peak* leader look beyond the borders of their company, and this seventh practice furthers that expansive thinking. Transformational companies and leaders can often be contrarian by focusing on the higher needs of their obvious primary customers, but also with customers that their competitors hadn't ever considered.

Peak leaders often understand what the customer wants even before the customer has articulated it, and they realize that customer experience innovation requires a certain amount of mind reading and cultural anthropology. Like Amazon, this means finding new ways to observe your customers. Part of the reason Amazon is now creating physical stores is that Jeff Bezos likes his insights team to observe the interplay between shoppers and the company's digital platforms such as Kindle and Alexa.

The faster change is happening in your industry, the faster an unrecognized need becomes a desire, and then gravity shifts it to an expectation. This means you need to be constantly scaling the customer pyramid with innovations that could disrupt your core business, as Netflix's Reed Hastings did with its streaming product that hurt their DVD-by-mail cash cow.

Fred Smith learned this when he started FedEx. Initially, he introduced a product—overnight package delivery around the United States—that was unfathomable at the time. It led to FedEx becoming the leader in the industry until this unique product offering became a commodity and Fred and his company had to imagine his customers' newest needs. Fred ultimately realized that the new differentiator was minute-by-minute electronic tracking of the packages being delivered. FedEx moved into the *peace of mind* business from just being in package delivery. *Peak* leaders are constantly imagining what new customer needs may pop-up once their existing need has been satisfied.

Amazon was named Fast Company's number one innovative company in the world for 2017, partly because, while they're huge, they're also a start-up at heart and constantly scaling the customer pyramid to offer new products to address unrecognized needs. Often, they do this by taking the learning from one product offering and applying it to another. Amazon's Echo smart speaker rose from learning from the Fire Phone system, which wasn't all that successful. The latest version of its streaming music service, Amazon Music Unlimited, was hatched out of its initial music store, Amazon MP3. And their new media studio, which is winning all kinds of Emmys, sprouted from the crowdsourcing platform they created in 2010 for aspiring screenwriters. Be on the lookout for Amazon Go, a new kind of convenience store that retires the idea of waiting in a cash register checkout line.

A relentless commitment to innovation means that you're tirelessly climbing that customer pyramid to the peak, over and over again, knowing that gravity will take hold of any new products you launch and turn them into customer expectations. Here are a couple of ways you can *seek the peak* with new product and service inventions:

• Determine how you can become the world's best mind reader with respect to the unrecognized needs of your core customers. At Joie de Vivre, we used our process of defining a magazine and five adjectives to help us determine the *identity refreshment* we could offer to our bull's-eye psychographic customer. Intuit uses its *follow-me-home* ethnography approach to understanding the latent needs of its customers. Amazon is creating retail stores as insight centers. Create a persona with a name for your primary core customers and regularly refresh your definition of who they are and what new products in the marketplace are delighting them.

• Make a commitment that a certain percentage of your future revenues (let's say five years from now) will come from products, services, or businesses that don't exist today. Be careful, as these are empty words if they're not followed up with a roadmap for how you'll accomplish this. Making this kind of commitment internally and externally helps accelerate your momentum in building an organization that's constantly refreshing itself with new innovation, and it will likely force you to look at new pools of customers you haven't historically served.

Practice 8: Lead to Peak (In Other Words, You're Always a Role Model and a Sherpa)

Just as a Sherpa does in the Himalayas, great leaders meet their people where they are on the pyramid and help them to see the natural path up to the peak. *Peak* leaders embody loyalty and build an *emotional bank account* with their employees by championing personal development in tandem with corporate development. They understand the synergistic effect of having a self-actualized individual in the workplace. *Peak* leaders also unconsciously calculate the lifetime value of their customer, employee, and investor relationships knowing that investing in relationships builds trust, which is the ultimate lubricant for a well-run business.

Most importantly, *Peak* leaders embody authentic leadership by being, not just by doing. The essence of who they are helps incubate a collection of other leaders who see them as a role model and are loyal to them—both as a leader and as a person they admire. Ping Fu came to the United States at age 24 with just $80 in her pocket after being expelled from her homeland, China, because she spoke out about infanticide due to the strictly enforced one-child policy. Her path to acclimating in this new place wasn't easy but, ultimately, many years later, she started a 3-D printing company called Geomagic that was sold to a public company for tens of millions of dollars. Part of her success as a leader has to do with her *presence*—the sense that she was not just an awake leader, but she was also an inspired human who had scaled many peaks in her life.

Kip Tindell, cofounder, chairman, and past CEO of the Container Store, uses the metaphor of a wake, the trail of water left by a boat, to define this practice. Just like a boat's wake has an effect on everything behind it, each person also has a wake, and their decisions impact those around them more than they realize. He says, "Your wake, my wake, everybody's wake is far more vast and powerful than you think it is. It makes you realize how big and influential we are, and how much impact we have on the companies around us and the world around us. We're not just one grain of sand on the beach. In an organization mindful of their wake, good things tend to happen—it becomes an unassailable business advantage."[5] Kip's approach to role modeling the leaders' wake is part of the reason the Container Store is regularly on Fortune's list of the Best Companies to Work For.

Conscious people pay attention. It's true of spiritual leaders. And it's true of business leaders. *Peak* leaders pay attention to the higher needs while not neglecting the base needs that provide a foundation for their organization. Leadership is all about making conscious choices and knowing that the higher you are in the company, the more magnified your decisions and behavior will be throughout the organization. At the end of the day, a great leader has a profound impact far beyond their little end of the pond.

When I was leaving my day-to-day role at Airbnb, I was humbled at receiving nearly a hundred unsolicited notes from employees, hosts, and guests in our community. You might think that the primary message would have been an expression of thanks for some specific thing I'd done for them. But, far and away, the summarized messages say something like "You are an inspiring human being who expresses your radiant spirit universally, no matter who the audience is. You've helped me to see that being a great leader means being a great human."

Here are a couple of ways you can hone your practice of being a role model and Sherpa:

- *Leaders are the emotional thermostats of those they lead.* The moment you truly own that sentence, you realize you're a role model. Stop calling yourself a *leader* and start calling yourself a *role model*. Truly, try this for a week. Ask your *role model team* (not your *leadership team*) what it feels like to be addressed in this new way. I'm sure it will be awkward initially, but you'll find it magical over time as being a role model forces you to realize the impact you have on others.

* Read Robert Greenleaf's classic book, *Servant Leadership: A Journey into the Nature of Legitimate Power and Greatness,* and look at all the ways you and your role model team can practice the principles that are outlined in this book.

In Sum

The eight practices that define *Peak* leaders can be summarized in one simple paragraph.

Peak leaders believe humans are basically good (Practice 1). Work is a powerful means for one to live their calling (Practice 2). Yet, what's most valuable in life and business is often elusive (Practice 3). Great leaders know that these elusive intangibles are found higher up on the Hierarchy of Needs pyramid and they try to lead from that transformational place (Practice 4). A healthy company culture can be transformative in helping a leader and an organization pay attention to higher needs (Practice 5). But, in the interdependent and transparent world we live in, *Peak* leaders recognize that they have to be conscious of higher needs beyond their organization (Practice 6). Delivering on the unrecognized needs of your customers—or your community—requires a relentless commitment to innovation (Practice 7). *Peak* leaders develop loyalty with all their stakeholders by operating as if they're a role model all of the time (Practice 8). Being a humanistic role model takes a leader back to Practice 1.

Leadership practice isn't something you miraculously learn by reading a book. It isn't something you learn in business school. It is an ability that develops throughout one's career and one's life. And it must be practiced to be learned. One of the aspects of a practice is that it has us bring our attention to something, make it more conscious than it might have been otherwise, and it breaks the unconscious or habitual cycle in which most of us languish. But these practices aren't confined to our business life, which is why we finish the book with a chapter on how to integrate *Peak* into your personal life.

RECOMMENDED READING

- *Conscious Capitalism: Liberating the Heroic Spirit of Business* by John Mackey and Raj Sisodia
- *Delivering Happiness: A Path to Profits, Passion and Purpose* by Tony Hsieh
- *Emotional Equations: Simple Truths for Creating Happiness + Success in Business + Life* by Chip Conley
- *Servant Leadership: A Journey into the Nature of Legitimate Power and Greatness* by Robert Greenleaf
- *Start with Why: How Great Leaders Inspire Everyone to Take Action* by Simon Sinek
- *Tribal Leadership: Leveraging Natural Groups to Build a Thriving Organization* by Dave Logan, John King, and Halee Fischer-Wright
- *Uncontainable: How Passion, Commitment, and Conscious Capitalism Built a Business Where Everyone Thrives* by Kip Tindell and Casey Shilling
- *Work Rules!: Insights from Inside Google That Will Transform How You Live and Lead* by Laszlo Bock

CHAPTER FIFTEEN

CREATING A SELF-ACTUALIZED LIFE

We fear our highest possibilities. We are generally afraid to become that which we can glimpse in our most perfect moments, under conditions of great courage. We enjoy and even thrill to the godlike possibilities we see in ourselves in such peak moments. And yet we simultaneously shiver with weakness, awe, and fear before these very same possibilities. Obviously the most beautiful fate, the most wonderful good fortune that can happen to any human being, is to be paid for doing that which he passionately loves to do.

ABRAHAM MASLOW[1]

Peter Drucker once wrote, "We know nothing about motivation. All we can do is write books about it." While I'm a huge fan of Drucker and his legacy of leadership wisdom, I beg to differ with him on this point.

I think most of us have a clue about what motivates and inspires ourselves and others. Yet, while we may understand the various pieces of motivational theory, I'm not sure we've had a proper container—a global framework—to help integrate and make use of what we intuitively know. My hope is that this book provides an operating model that you and the leaders in your company can use to do a little consciousness-raising. The Relationship Truths Pyramid can help you converse about the underlying motivations of your employees, customers, and investors.

Abe Maslow believed that a self-actualized workplace could make a better world. I believe that creating a fulfilled workplace is a meaningful way of giving back to the world—subscribing to the karmic capitalist philosophy that doing good will help your business do well.

But before this becomes too much of a *kumbaya* moment, let's talk about integrating what we've learned in the past 14 chapters. What I want to accomplish with this last chapter is to move from the philosophy of the workplace to the habits of your own life. How can you live the principles of self-actualization? What shifts do you need to make to truly be fulfilled, not just in the workplace but throughout all components of your life? Maslow's quotation that started this chapter hints at his concern that humans have a "fallacy of insignificance," what he also called "the Jonah Complex," based on the biblical figure who ran from his higher calling and ended up inside the belly of a whale. Maslow would frequently ask his students, "Which of you believe that you will achieve greatness?" When they stared at him blankly, he would follow up with "If not you, *who* then?" That question can be posed to your company and, certainly, to you.

I found a little enlightenment on this subject on the golf course in my early teens. My grandfather, Lauren Conley (whom I called *Potka*), was a straitlaced banker who desperately tried to get me to love the game of golf. Each summer he would take me out to his country club, we'd hit a bucket of balls at the driving range, and then we would hoof it for 18 holes with me hacking a few dozen divots along the way.

I remember one particularly sunny afternoon when I was hitting the divots farther than the balls. Being the competitive type, I threw down my club and shouted, "I'm never going to be Arnold Palmer!" Potka, who typically wasn't much of a philosopher, slowly picked up the club, handed it to me, and said softly with steely conviction, "Having a high handicap doesn't mean you'll have low enjoyment in life. There are all kinds of scorecards you can have. How many squirrels you see on the course, how many cloud formations you see in the sky, how many times you can get your grandpa to crack a smile with one of your silly jokes. Just remember, you can decide which scorecard you want to use in life."

Clearly, nearly 50 years later, those out-of-character words from Potka still resonate with me. What am I *handicapping* in my life by being preoccupied with some irrelevant scorecard? That particular day with Potka, I was certainly missing the experience of noticing the beauty of nature because I was distracted with my sorry golf score. Years later, I was reminded of this in the midst of the economic downturn, when I didn't pay myself for more than three years, and I had just a few hundred bucks in the bank. I was having dinner with a friend and exhibiting a little self-pity because I'd just come back from my Stanford Business School 20-year reunion, where I felt like a pauper compared with my rich classmates.

My friend asked me a pointed question that reminded me of Potka's scorecard: "What's really most important to you in your work life?" I answered something about having the freedom to create soulful, unique hotels while bringing together a collection of individuals in the company who are truly fulfilled by working together. This friend rocked me when he responded, "Chip, get it through your thick skull. Your calling in life is to be an artist posing as a businessman. In fact, prior to this downturn, and for the past decade, you were probably the best-paid 'artist' in San Francisco. Your work—both in the hotels you create and in your Joie de Vivre corporate culture—is admired by so many. You are *rich*, but just in a different way than most of America defines that word."

What a wake-up call! How are you measuring success? What scorecard are you using? What is your calling? Everything is relative in life. I have investors who think Joie de Vivre is one-tenth the size it should be, while I have friends who don't see me enough and think I've grown the company way too big. Ultimately, it really doesn't matter what they think. I've spent a good part of my life honing my external antenna trying to read the crowd, but I've learned that tapping into my internal antenna is what truly gives me a sense of fulfillment. So, let's revisit the idea of how you connect with why you're on this planet and how you can find your calling.

JOB, CAREER, CALLING

You may have heard the parable about three stonecutters who were working at the side of a road. When asked what they were doing, the first replied, "I am making a living." The second said, "I am doing the best job of stonecutting in my country." And the final one proclaimed, "I am building a grand cathedral."

These three responses relate to what we talked about in Chapter Six: the three kinds of subjective orientation people often have with their work. Those with *jobs* tend to focus more on the financial rewards of working than on any pleasure or fulfillment. Many of these individuals may find their true enjoyment outside of their nine-to-five existences. Those with *careers* focus primarily on growing their talent and advancement. While they may gain quite a bit of satisfaction in their work, it is often associated with the esteem that comes from external sources (like recognition or raises). The lucky few who pursue a *calling* find their work fulfilling in its own right, without regard for money or advancement. Those pursuing their calling would recognize Maslow's statement in their own life: "One must respond to one's fate or one's destiny or pay a heavy price. One must yield to it; one must surrender to it. One must permit one's self to be chosen."

You can see in the figure below that each of these three approaches to work correspond to a different level of the Transformation Pyramid (survive, succeed, transform) and the Employee Pyramid (money, recognition, meaning).

THREE APPROACHES TO WORK

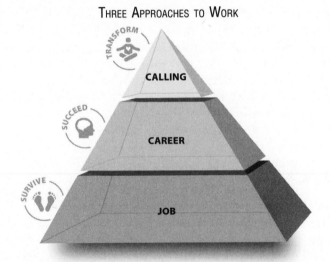

How do you know which level you, your friends, family, or work associates would be placed on this pyramid? Take the following test, although beware that your answers will be influenced by your current state of mind, which means you may want to take the test twice, at least one week apart, to really gauge your accurate score. Read each of the following statements and place a check next to the five that best describe your relationship with your current work. Be careful, as it's easy to think broadly about how certain statements *should* reflect your work life. What we're looking for here are the statements that actually reflect your work life today:

1. While I enjoy what I do at work and am very good at it, I often feel like I've topped-out, and I have to look elsewhere—my home, my spiritual life, my friends, my hobbies, my community service—for inspiration or fulfillment.
2. I tend to lose myself in my work. I just feel like I'm in the flow, and I lose all sense of time.
3. I like what I do, but I don't expect a lot from my work. It just provides what I need to do the other more important things in my life. I enjoy my leisure life more than my work life.
4. My work truly makes a difference in the world.
5. The greatest experience I have at work is when I'm truly recognized by others for what I've accomplished.
6. If I had to choose between receiving a 10 percent raise at work or finding a new best friend at work, I would probably choose the raise.
7. I often feel like the work I'm doing is coming from some greater source than just me. It's like I'm channeling this energy or talent, and I'm amazed by its power.
8. I'm often not that excited to go to work on Monday morning.
9. My goal in life is to rise to the top of my field.
10. There are moments when I think to myself, "If I were independently wealthy, I'd probably still be doing this work." I do what I do because I just love it.
11. I've thought pretty deeply about where my work will take me the next 10 years and what I need to do to excel in this field.
12. I'm pretty conscious to use my vacation time and sick days off so that I can create more balance and ensure that work doesn't dominate my life.
13. I often feel like my work allows me to show the *real me*. My work lets me use my deepest creative gifts.
14. I think work is overrated when you consider what percentage of our lives we spend working as compared to enjoying life. I don't think much about work when I'm not there.
15. I will do what it takes to become a success in my work.

Okay, I know that wasn't easy. You may have had a hard time trimming down to just five, or you may have found it difficult finding five statements that represent your perspective on your work. Here's how we'll score them. The following statements reflect someone who has a *job* perspective: 3, 6, 8, 12, and 14. The *career* statements are 1, 5, 9, 11, and 15. The *calling* statements are 2, 4, 7, 10, and 13.

How many did you have in each category? Your dominant category will tell you a lot about your relationship with your work. If your dominant category wasn't *calling*, don't be alarmed because most people find their calling outside of their work, whether it's as a Girl Scout leader, a gardener, a triathlete, a devoted friend, or an ardent political activist.

Michael Novak has written a fascinating book, *Business as a Calling*, that examines both the religious underpinnings of the idea of a calling and the characteristics that define a calling. He identifies four qualities that best define the experience of a calling:

1. *"Each calling is unique to each individual."*
   This suggests there are subtleties as customized as our fingerprints in how we are called by our inherent gifts.
2. *"A calling requires certain preconditions. It requires more than desires; it requires talent."*
   Not everyone can have a particular calling; it must fit our abilities. And there must be a willingness to put up with what some might see as the monotony associated with living out this calling. Essayist Logan Pearsall Smith once wrote, "The test of a vocation is the love of drudgery it involves."
3. *"A true calling reveals its presence by the enjoyment and sense of renewed energies its practice yields us."*
   Some activities drain us, and others fill us up. While following a calling can create fatigue in the moment, especially when the activity is intensive, the called person typically feels renewed and refreshed by pursuing this activity.
4. *"They are not usually easy to discover."*
   Callings don't tap you on the shoulder and say, "I'm here." Public education doesn't even speak this language, so quite often we get disconnected early in life from our true callings. Those who have found their calling are more likely to be what Maslow called "peakers."[2]

Although Novak's book has a strongly religious bent to it, the reality is that secular folks are just as likely to feel disappointed by not finding their calling. Others have a sense of their calling but are preoccupied with the mundane commitments we all have in our lives. Don't despair if you haven't found or pursued your calling in work. For some, it is just a matter of timing. Both Colonel Sanders and McDonald's Ray Kroc were nearly 60 years old when their empires were born. As was the controversial capitalist Armand Hammer. And we all know about late-blooming artist Grandma Moses, but perhaps it is not as widely known that Laura Ingalls Wilder was 65 when *Little House on the Prairie* was first published. And Mary Baker Eddy founded *The Christian Science Monitor* at the age of 87.

Mihaly Csikszentmihalyi is an authority on the idea of *flow,* the state in which people find themselves when everything just seems to come together perfectly. Often, the idea of flow is compared with the self-actualized place a person pursuing a calling may be in. He cites in his book *Good Business* that the Gallup Organization found that "between 15 percent and 20 percent of adults never seem to experience flow, while a comparable number claim to experience it every day. The other 60 percent to 70 percent report being intensely involved in what they do anywhere from once every few months to at least once a week."[3] These results are encouraging, as it suggests that a large percentage of us have the capacity to transcend to the higher levels of the pyramid once we find our special place in life.

THE QUALITIES OF A SELF-ACTUALIZED PERSON

Maslow seemed to agree with the Gallup survey when he wrote 40 years earlier, "What seems to distinguish those individuals I have called self-actualizing people, is that in them these episodes (peak experiences) seem to come far more frequently, and intensely and perfectly than in average people. This makes self-actualization a matter of degree and of frequency rather than an all-or-none affair."[4] Maslow believed that those living out their calling spent more of their time in a self-actualized place. He listed a number of qualities that define the "peaker" in a state of self-actualization:

- "For the transcenders, peak experiences . . . become the most important things in their lives, the high spots, the validators of life, the most precious aspect of life."
- "Peakers cultivate periods of quiet, meditation" and getting out of their day-to-day normal life in order to see the world in a new way and as a way to "try to recover the sense of the miraculous about life."

- "They seem somehow to recognize each other, and to come to almost instant intimacy and mutual understanding even upon first meeting."
- When in a state of a peak experience, the peakers have a lessening of fears, a giving up of ego, a spontaneity and sense of seeking, and a fusion of feeling "one with the world."

Edward Hoffman's biography on Maslow, *Future Visions*, is a great source of recommendations for how to cultivate a state of self-actualization. In the book, he lists more than 40 suggestions Maslow made for achieving this state. Viktor Frankl in his landmark book *Man's Search for Meaning* has a relevant suggestion that will help give you the courage to seek your calling: "Live life as if you were living for the second time and had acted as wrongly the first time as you are about to act now."[5]

USING PYRAMIDS TO SET PRIORITIES

As we've found in this book, pyramids are powerful. They represent a unique organizing principle that suggests some things in your life are foundational, and others are at the peak. Maslow's Hierarchy of Needs is akin to the principle of homeostasis, which is how your furnace thermostat works. When it gets too cold, the thermostat turns the heat on. When it gets too hot, the heat switches off. In the same way, when our bodies, minds, and souls are lacking a certain substance, they develop a hunger for it. When we get enough of it, the hunger stops, and we move up the pyramid.

With this way of thinking, I have been able to define both work and personal priorities using the pyramid. I know I have some base hungers that need to be fed sufficiently in order to seek the peak. You can use the pyramid, too. All it takes is a willingness to be conscious about the priorities that you're seeking. Here are a couple of simple exercises: Think of the way you set your New Year's resolutions with respect to work. You may have some base-level needs you want to meet that are related to a raise or achieving some kind of financial incentive. I won't belabor this point because there are dozens of books that can help you get clear on how to manifest your financial goals. Your midlevel need may be winning some kind of recognition in your company or in your industry through excellent performance. You will have greater effectiveness in achieving that honor if you become conscious of that esteem goal at the start of the year and then develop an action plan that will help you succeed. Finally, at the peak of your work resolutions for the year could be something truly meaningful, like taking the lead in volunteering your company to philanthropically support some community program that is well aligned with your company's values and mission. While these three ideas on the three different levels aren't earth shattering, they do provide you with a means of understanding your hierarchy of priorities in the workplace.

As another example, imagine you're going on a family vacation. You and your spouse have been working crazy hours, and it's finally that time of year when you've coordinated your schedules to take a break together. Where should you go? What should you do? What kind of pyramid would define your Hierarchy of Needs on this family vacation? I would imagine at the base you might be looking for an affordable place that's comfortable for your family. As you move up the pyramid, you and your family might make a list of all the other things you would be seeking. Then you can prioritize them as level one, two, or three needs, knowing that the lowest level (one) is foundational—the *must haves*, even though they might be a little mundane, because without them the higher needs may not be relevant—like making sure you have insect repellant for a camping trip. At the top of your pyramid would be the peak experiences you might be seeking on this vacation. These are the moments that you are most likely to remember, like when your kids cooked their first campfire meal.

Many friends and work associates are now regularly using the pyramid to help prioritize their lives. But often they get a little tripped up with the hierarchy of priorities—in other words, at which level of the pyramid a particular priority should be placed. As a guide, I often refer them to the Transformation Pyramid we discussed in Chapter Two. Take a look at whether this activity or priority is a *survival* need (something that will help provide basic sustenance or comfort), a *success* need (something that will enhance the performance or experience), or a *transformation* need (something less predictable, more intangible, and ultimately, most satisfying or memorable). My number one recommendation for those who are using a pyramid to define their peak experience is to make sure you are climbing the right mountain. A midlife crisis is perhaps the natural result of someone realizing they've perhaps climbed the wrong peak.

CLIMBING HIGHER

Using the pyramids as a guide requires a certain amount of introspection and mindfulness. It not only requires getting conscious about what you want or need; it also obligates you to create an order of priorities for those wants or needs. An insightful book called *Power vs. Force* helped me to look at this hierarchy in an even more metaphysical way, as I came to the conclusion that there are three states of being involved in how we interact with life. And of course, the three steps can be depicted on a pyramid, as shown below.

THE THREE STATES OF BEING

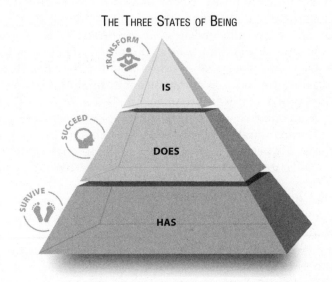

You can see these three steps manifested in both how a culture evolves and how humans often mature. The base needs are typically *has* needs: what material things we want in our life to give us safety, comfort, pleasure, or status. As humans and societies age, they move beyond the *has* to the *does* needs. As our material needs are met, what one does for a living becomes a more relevant symbol of our identity. At some point, relentless *doing* no longer carries currency, at which point the *is* needs predominate at the peak of the pyramid. You see this in wise men and women and in cultures that have learned that having and doing carry you only so far. When someone or something just *is*, it feels pure, essential, powerful, and magnetic. There is a strong sense of presence that accompanies this state of being. As for me, I spent my early years growing Joie de Vivre and focusing on how big we might become. My scorecard was defined by how many hotels we had in the collection. And, at times, I gauged my definition of success by the things I could buy for myself and for the company. At some point, I transcended *has* up to *does* and became more focused on my role as the CEO, enjoying the esteem associated with how people perceived me in that role. More recently, I have found myself moving more into an *is* place, going beyond my possessions and my role so that I can just try to be a voice of change for how the business world can be. I know that I'm on a self-actualized path when it feels like I'm almost channeling the message from the master, Abraham Maslow. You know you've moved to that *is* place when you realize that how you show up in the world has great impact on those who are learning from you. Great leaders don't count their successes by the number of cars in their garage or by the impressiveness of their job title. Great leaders know their success is defined by the personal impact they've had on others. Business is typically considered hard-edged and unemotional. But in more than two decades of running my own business, I found it to be a remarkable exercise in humanity. It has helped me change my life and understand myself and others better than 20 years of therapy ever would. Maslow has been a great guide for me. He's the first well-known psychologist to study healthy people as opposed to sick people. His insights about human motivation are relevant not just in our work life but even more so in our personal life.

Great business leaders create transformation: in themselves, their companies, and their people. And if they're truly transformational, they likely create peak experiences for their customers and investors, as well. Great leaders aren't afraid of scaling the peaks that few others are willing to climb. They recognize that while the ascent to the top may be strenuous, the feeling of accomplishment and, most importantly, the understanding that *this is the real me* will create both a soaring high and a deep sense of well-being that are unmatched.

My role with this book has been to act like a Himalayan Sherpa who guides you up to the rarified summits of Nepal or Tibet. I hope you have enjoyed the journey. I wish you the best on your path. I'll look forward to seeing you again at the peak.

RECOMMENDED READING

Business as a Calling by Michael Novak
Conscious Business by Fred Kofman
Future Visions by Edward Hoffman
Pathfinders by Gail Sheehy
Power vs. Force by David R. Hawkins
Presence by Peter Senge, C. Otto Scharmer, Joseph Jaworski, and Betty
  Sue Flowers
The Farther Reaches of Human Nature by Abraham Maslow
The Laws of Lifetime Growth by Dan Sullivan and Catherine Nomura

APPENDIX

PEAK MANAGERIAL ASSESSMENT

Peak **Managerial Assessment**

> *Behind every managerial decision or action are assumptions about human nature and human behavior.*
>
> - Douglas McGregor, *The Human Side of Enterprise*

What level of the pyramid do you pay attention to as a manager? Answer the following questions to indicate how frequently or infrequently you engage in each behavior.

---

1 = NEVER   2 = SOMETIMES   3 = OFTEN   4 = CONSISTENTLY

_____ I understand and can communicate how my organization's compensation package ranks vis-à-vis our competitors'.

_____ I encourage socialization and host unique events to help employees feel more connected to each other and their workplace.

_____ I initiate conversations with my employees about their role and responsibilities and how they might wish to modify them in order to feel more fulfilled by their jobs.

_____ I educate and coach managers on the importance and value of informal recognition.

_____ I initiate discussions with senior management regarding employee compensation packages, including nonmonetary incentives.

_____ I know each of my employees' life aspirations or what their sense of calling might be.

_____ I have introduced a way that employees (on my team or in my department) can express appreciation and recognition for one another.

_____ I am aware of employees' current states of mind regarding their compensation packages and ask them what types of nonmonetary benefits they most value.

_____ I encourage employees to pursue activities outside of their immediate job tasks (e.g., organization committees, philanthropic efforts) that are meaningful to them and beneficial to the department and/or organization.

(*continued*)

_____ I understand and can communicate the ways in which our organization internally monitors compensation equity.

_____ I give employees personalized, 1:1 feedback and appreciation about their contributions.

_____ I educate or inform employees about their entire compensation package, including nonmonetary perks.

_____ I am aware of the type of recognition that is most meaningful for each of my employees and employee groups.

_____ I create opportunities for my employees to hear directly from our customers about the impact they are having.

_____ I deliberately make space for employees to share their highlights or meaningful moments with the team and/or department.

Scoring:

Look at the three following categories, which correspond to each of the 15 statements. Tally your scores by category to determine what level of awareness you have for each level of the employee pyramid.

MONEY	**RECOGNITION**	**MEANING**
1, 5, 8, 10, 12	2, 4, 7, 11, 13	3, 6, 9, 14, 15
Total: ___	Total: ___	Total: ___

HIGH: 16–20   *MED: 11–15*   *LOW: 5–10*

Often your tendency as a manager mirrors your own personal needs or desires. It is helpful to remember that although people have the same needs, not everyone is at the same place on the pyramid. For example, if you score high on recognition and meaning but low on money, you will want to ensure that you are not underestimating the compensation needs of your employees. Or, if you score high on money and recognition and low on meaning, you'll want to pay attention to how you can help your employees discover their meaning in and at work.

(*continued*)

(*continued*)

When looking at your results, how evenly distributed are the points? Is there a dominant or low-scoring category?

_____

_____

Based on this assessment, which level of the pyramid do you operate from most as a manager? What needs do you tend to emphasize and why do you suppose that is?

_____

_____

_____

_____

_____

Which level of the pyramid (and corresponding actions) do you tend to not pay as much attention to as a manager? Why do you think that is?

_____

_____

_____

_____

_____

What, if any, shift would you like to make? Which area or areas do you wish to focus on in the future? (List them on the following lines.)

_____

_____

_____

_____

_____

NOTES

INTRODUCTION

1. Personal communication.
2. Gibran Kahlil, "On Work," *The Prophet* (New York: Knopf, 1923).

PREFACE

1. Frederick F. Reichheld, *Loyalty Rules: How Today's Leaders Build Lasting Relationships.* (Boston: Harvard Business School Press, 2003).

CHAPTER ONE

1. Abraham H. Maslow, *The Farther Reaches of Human Nature* (New York: Penguin/Arkana, 1993).
2. Abraham H. Maslow, *Motivation and Personality* (New York: Harper, 1954).
3. Jim Collins, "Foreword" in Maslow with Stephens and Heil, 1998. Available online: http://eqi.org/maslow.htm.
4. Abraham H. Maslow, *Motivation and Personality* (New York: Harper, 1954).
5. Abraham H. Maslow, *The Farther Reaches of Human Nature* (New York: Penguin/Arkana, 1993).
6. Ibid.
7. Abraham H. Maslow, *Maslow on Management* (New York: John Wiley & Sons, 1998).
8. Ibid.
9. Interview with Malcolm Gladwell, *New York Times*, Feb. 5, 2006. Audio file available at http://www.nytimes.com/audiosrc/books/gladwell-function.mp3.

CHAPTER TWO

1. Douglas McGregor, *The Human Side of Enterprise* (New York: McGraw-Hill, 1960), p. 33

2. Abraham H. Maslow, *Maslow on Management* (New York: John Wiley & Sons, 1998).

3. Douglas McGregor, *The Human Side of Enterprise* (New York: McGraw-Hill, 1960), pp. 6–7.

4. Stephen R. Covey, *The 7 Habits of Highly Effective People* (New York: Free Press, 1989).

5. John C. Bogle, *The Battle for the Soul of Capitalism* (Collingdale, PA: DIANE Publishing Company, 2005).

6. Alan B. Goldberg and Bill Ritter, "Costco CEO Finds Pro-Worker Means Profitability", abc News, August 2, 2006, Available at http://abcnews.go.com/2020/Business/story?id=1362779.

7. Mihaly Csikszentmihalyi, *Good Business: Leadership, Flow, and the Making of Meaning* (New York: Penguin Books, 2003).

8. Abraham H. Maslow, Deborah C. Stephens (ed.), *The Maslow Business Reader* (New York: John Wiley & Sons, Inc.), p. 130.

9. Fred Reichheld, *The Loyalty Effect* (Brighton, MA: Harvard Business School Press, 1996).

10. Abraham H. Maslow, *Eupsychian Management: A Journal* (Homewood, IL: R. D. Irwin, 1965).

11. Quoted in *A Thousand Shades of Green: Sustainable Strategies for Competitive Advantage* by Peter Winsemius, Ulrich Guntram (London, UK: Earthscan Publications Ltd, 2013), p 185.

12. John Locke, *Two Treatises of Government* (London, UK: Awnsham Churchill).

13. Dennis Bakke, *Joy at Work: A Revolutionary Approach To Fun on the Job* (Edmonds, WA: Pear Press).

14. James MacGregor Burns, *Leadership* (New York: Harper Perennial Modern Classics, 2010).

15. Quoted in Dan Millman, *Living on Purpose: Straight Answers to Universal Questions* (Novato, CA: New World Library, 2000).

CHAPTER THREE

1. Margaret J. Wheatley, *Leadership and the New Science: Discovering Order in a Chaotic World* (San Francisco: Berrett-Koehler Publishers, 1999).

2. Ranjay Gulati and David Kletter, "Shrinking Core, Expanding Periphery: The Relational Architecture of High-Performing Organizations" in *California Management Review* (Spring 2005).

3. Daniel Goleman, *Emotional Intelligence: Why It Can Matter More Than IQ* (New York: Bantam Books, 1995).

4. Frederick F. Reichheld, *The Loyalty Effect: The Hidden Force Behind Growth, Profits, and Lasting Value* (Brighton, MA: Harvard Business School Press, 1996).

5. Jody Hoffer Gittell, *The Southwest Airlines Way: Using the Power of Relationships to Achieve High Performance* (New York: McGrawHill Professional, 2003).

6. Jill Rosenfeld "Here's an Idea!," *Fast Company*, March 31, 2000. Available at https://www.fastcompany.com/39461/heres-idea.

7. Abraham H. Maslow, *Eupsychian Management: A Journal* (Homewood, IL: R. D. Irwin, 1965).

Part Two

1. Studs Terkel, *Working: People Talk About What They Do All Day and How They Feel About What They Do,* (New York: New Press, 1997).

Chapter Four

1. Zig Ziglar, *Great Quotes from Zig Ziglar* (Wayne, NJ: Career Press, 1997).

2. Isadore Sharp, "How to Create a Great Workplace Anywhere in the World," keynote address at the 2006 Great Place to Work® Conference, April 7, 2006, Boston, MA.

3. Abraham H. Maslow, *Motivation and Personality* (New York: Harper, 1954).

4. Personal communication.

5. Peter F. Drucker, M*anagement Challenges of the 21st Century* (New York: Harper Business, 2001).

6. Frederick Herzberg, "One More Time: How Do You Motivate Employees?" (Personnel Policies column), *Harvard Business Review*, January 2003. Available at https://hbr.org/2003/01/one-more-time-how-do-you-motivate-employees.

7. Rich Teerlink and Lee Ozley, *More Than a Motorcycle: The Leadership Journey at Harley-Davidson* (Brighton, MA: Harvard Business Review Press, 2000).

8. Martin E. P. Seligman, *Authentic Happiness: Using the New Positive Psychology to Realize Your Potential for Lasting Fulfillment* (New York: Simon & Schuster, 2002).

9. Ricardo Semler, *The Seven-Day Weekend: Changing the Way Work Work* (New York: Portfolio, 2004).

Chapter Five

1. Quoted in Jack Wiley and Brenda Kowske, *RESPECT: Delivering Results by Giving Employees What They Really Want* (San Francisco, CA: Pfeiffer, 2011), p. 35.

2. https://www.goodreads.com/quotes/23215-the-deepest-principle-in-human-nature-is-the-craving-to

3. Maribeth Kuzmeski, *The Connectors: How the World's Most Successful Businesspeople Build Relationships and Win Clients for Life* (Hoboken, NJ: John Wiley & Sons, 2009).
4. Marcus Buckingham and Curt Coffman, *First, Break All the Rules: What the World's Greatest Managers Do Differently* (New York: Simon & Schuster, 2014).
5. Tony Schwartz, "Life/Work—Issue 40" in *Fast Company*, October 31, 2000. Available at https://www.fastcompany.com/40847/life-work-issue-40.
6. Jody Hoffer Gittell, *The Southwest Airlines Way: Using the Power of Relationships to Achieve High Performance* (New York: McGrawHill Professional, 2003).

CHAPTER SIX

1. Jim Collins, *Good to Great: Why Some Companies Make the Leap . . . and Others Don't* (New York: HarperCollins, 2001).
2. C. William Pollard, *The Soul of the Firm* (Grand Rapids, MI: Zondervan, 1996).
3. Lance Secretan, *Inspirational Leadership: Destiny, Calling & Cause* (Caledon, ON, Canada: The Secretan Center Inc., 1999).
4. Peter Katz, *The New Urbanism: Toward an Architecture of Community* (New York: McGrawHill Education, 1993).
5. Lance Secretan, *Inspire!: What Great Leaders Do* (Caledon, ON, Canada: The Secretan Center Inc., 2004).
6. Viktor E. Frankl, *Man's Search for Meaning* (Boston: Beacon Press, 2006 [original publication 1946]).
7. Quoted in ibid.
8. C. William Pollard, *The Soul of the Firm* (Grand Rapids, MI: Zondervan, 1996).
9. Betsy Morris, "Genentech: The best place to work now," *Fortune*, January 20, 2006, Available at http://money.cnn.com/2006/01/06/news/companies/bestcos_genentech/.
10. Richard E. Boyatzis and Annie McKee, *Resonant Leadership: Renewing Yourself and Connecting with Others Through Mindfulness, Hope, and Compassion* (Brighton, MA: Harvard Business Review Press, 2005).

PART THREE

1. David Lewis, *The Soul of the New Consumer* (London: Nicholas Brealey, 2000).

CHAPTER SEVEN

1. Theodore Levitt, "Marketing Myopia," *Harvard Business Review,* July-August 1960.

2. "Branding on the Beach," ContraBrand website, Available at https://contrabrand.wordpress.com/2003/07/01/branding-on-the-beach/.

3. Harry Beckwith, *Selling the Invisible: A Field Guide to Modern Marketing* (London, UK: Orion Business, 1999).

4. Abraham Maslow, *The Psychology of Science: A Reconnaissance* (Washington, DC: Gateway Editions, 1969).

5. Fred Reichheld, *The Ultimate Question: Driving Good Profits and True Growth* (Brighton, MA: Harvard Business School Press, 2006).

6. Patrick Barwise and Sean Meehan, *Simply Better: Winning and Keeping Customers by Delivering What Matters Most* ((Brighton, MA: Harvard Business Review Press, 2004).

7. Amy Zipkin,"Out of Africa, Onto the Web," *New York Times*, December 17, 2006. Available at http://www.nytimes.com/2006/12/17/jobs/17boss.html.

8. Bo Burlingham, *Small Giants: Companies That Choose to Be Great Instead of Big* (New York: Portfolio, 2007).

9. Patrick Barwise and Sean Meehan, *Simply Better: Winning and Keeping Customers by Delivering What Matters Most* ((Brighton, MA: Harvard Business Review Press, 2004).

10. Fred Reichheld, *The Ultimate Question: Driving Good Profits and True Growth* (Brighton, MA: Harvard Business School Press, 2006).

CHAPTER EIGHT

1. Abraham Maslow, *Maslow on Management* (New York: John Wiley & Sons, Inc., 1998).

2. Diana LaSalle and Terry A. Britton, *Priceless: Turning Ordinary Products Into Extraordinary Experiences* (Brighton, MA: Harvard Business School Press, 2003).

3. Don Peppers and Martha Rogers, *Return on Customer: Creating Maximum Value From Your Scarcest Resource* (New York: Crown Business, 2005).

4. Ibid.

5. Danny Meyer, *Setting the Table: The Transforming Power of Hospitality in Business* (New York: HarperCollins, 2009).

CHAPTER NINE

1. https://hbr.org/2011/08/henry-ford-never-said-the-fast.

2. Reicheld, *Loyalty Rules:How Today's Leaders Build Lasting Relationships.* (Boston: Harvard Business School Press, 2003).

3. "Profile your customers—don't build requirements!," Toolbox.com, July 12, 2005. Available at http://it.toolbox.com/blogs/bridging-gaps/profile-your-customers-dont-build-requirements-10466.

4. Gerald Zaltman, *How Customers Think: Essential Insights into the Mind of the Market* (Brighton, MA: Harvard Business School Press, 2003).

5. William C. Taylor and Polly LaBarre, *Mavericks at Work: Why the Most Original Minds in Business Win* (New York: William Morrow, 2006).

6. Diana LaSalle and Terry A. Britton, *Priceless: Turning Ordinary Products Into Extraordinary Experiences* (Brighton, MA: Harvard Business School Press, 2003).

7. Alex Williams, "Planet Google Wants You," *New York Times* October 15, 2006. Available at http://www.nytimes.com/2006/10/15/fashion/15google.html.

8. Susan Dominus, "The Starbucks Aesthetic," *New York Times* October 22, 2006. Available at http://www.nytimes.com/2006/10/22/arts/22domi.html.

9. Guy Kawasaki and Michele Moreno, *Rules for Revolutionaries: The Capitalist Manifesto for Creating and Marketing New Products and Services* (New York: HarperCollins, 1999).

10. Pamela N. Danziger, *Let Them Eat Cake: Marketing Luxury to the Masses—as Well as the Classes* (New York: Kaplan Trade, 2005).

PART FOUR

1. Deborah Stephens, ed., *The Maslow Business Reader* (New York: John Wiley & Sons, 2000).

CHAPTER TEN

1. Marcus Aurelius, *Meditations* (New York: Hackett Publishing Company, Inc., 1984).

2. Fred Kofman, *Conscious Business: How to Build Value through Values* (Louisville, CO: Sounds True, 2006).

3. Stephen M. R. Covey, *The Speed of Trust: The One Thing That Changes Everything* (New York: Simon & Schuster, 2006).

4. Robert F. Hurley, "The Decision to Trust," *Harvard Business Review*, September 2006. Available at https://hbr.org/2006/09/the-decision-to-trust.

5. Warren Buffet, *The Essays of Warren Buffet: Lessons for Corporate America* (New York: Cardozo Law Review, 1997).

6. Ibid.

7. Ibid.

8. Bill George, *Authentic Leadership: Rediscovering the Secrets to Creating Lasting Value* (San Francisco: Jossey-Bass, 2003).

9. Betsy Morris, "New rule: Admire My Soul—Old Rule: Admire My Might," *Fortune*, July 11, 2006. Available at http://money.cnn.com/sales/executive_resource_center/articles2/rule7.fortune/index.htm.

10. Bill George, *Authentic Leadership: Rediscovering the Secrets to Creating Lasting Value* (San Francisco: Jossey-Bass, 2003).

11. Jim Collins, *Good to Great: Why Some Companies Make the Leap . . . and Others Don't* (New York: HarperCollins, 2001).

CHAPTER ELEVEN

1. Ken Iverson, *Plain Talk: Lessons from a Business Maverick* (New York: John Wiley & Sons, 1997).
2. Ibid.
3. Carrie Coolidge, "Follow the Leader," *Forbes*, June 6, 2005. Available at https://www.forbes.com/free_forbes/2005/0606/138.html.
4. Warren Buffet, *The Essays of Warren Buffet: Lessons for Corporate America* (New York: Cardozo Law Review, 1997).
5. Jim Collins, *Good to Great: Why Some Companies Make the Leap . . . and Others Don't* (New York: HarperCollins, 2001).

CHAPTER TWELVE

1. Personal communication.
2. Bob Buford, *Halftime: Changing Your Game Plan from Success to Significance* (Grand Rapids, MI: Zondervan, 1997).
3. Quoted in Bob Buford, *Finishing Well: The Adventure of Life Beyond Halftime!* (New York: HarperCollins, 2004).
4. Henry David Thoreau, *Walden* (Boston: Beacon Books, 2004).

CHAPTER THIRTEEN

1. Steven Shapin, "Paradise Sold: What Are You Buying When You Buy Organic?", *The New Yorker*, May 15, 2006. Available at http://www.newyorker.com/magazine/2006/05/15/paradise-sold.
2. Kevin Freiberg and Jackie Freiberg, *Nuts!: Southwest Airlines' Crazy Recipe for Business and Personal Success* (New York: Broadway Books, 1996).
3. Gordon M. Bethune and Scott Huler, *From Worst to First: Behind the Scenes of Continental's Remarkable Comeback* (New York: John Wiley & Sons, 1998).
4. Ibid.
5. David Sirota, Louis A. Mischkind, and Michael Irwin Meltzer, *The Enthusiastic Employee: How Companies Profit by Giving Workers What They Want* (New York: Prentice Hall Professional, 2005).
6. Kevin Freiberg and Jackie Freiberg, *Nuts!: Southwest Airlines' Crazy Recipe for Business and Personal Success* (New York: Broadway Books, 1996).

CHAPTER FOURTEEN

1. Martha C. White, "Amazon Will Pay You $5,000 to Quit Your Job," *Time*, April 11, 2014. Available at http://time.com/58305/amazon-will-pay-you-5000-to-quit-your-job/.
2. Abraham H. Maslow, *Toward a Psychology of Being*, 3rd ed. (New York: John Wiley & Sons, 1998).
3. http://quoteinvestigator.com/2010/05/26/everything-counts-einstein/.
4. Kristine Kern, "Peter Thiel's One Piece of Advice for Airbnb: 'Don't Mess Up Culture,'" *Slate*, May 3, 2014. Available at http://www.slate.com/blogs/moneybox/2014/05/03/brian_chesky_airbnb_co_founder_peter_thiel_s_one_piece_of_advice_for_entrepreneurs.html.
5. Shalene Gupta, "The Container Store's CEO Unpacks His Business Philosophy," *Fortune*, October 19, 2014. Available at http://fortune.com/2014/10/19/the-container-stores-ceo-unpacks-its-business-philosophy/.

CHAPTER FIFTEEN

1. Abraham Maslow, *The Farther Reaches of Human Nature* (New York: Penguin/Arkana, 1993).
2. Michael Novak, *Business as a Calling: Work and the Examined Life* (New York: Free Press, 1996).
3. Mihaly Csikszentmihalyi, *Good Business: Leadership, Flow, and the Making of Meaning* (New York: Penguin, 2004).
4. Abraham H. Maslow, *Toward a Psychology of Being*, 3rd ed. (New York: John Wiley & Sons, 1998).
5. Viktor E. Frankl, *Man's Search for Meaning* (Boston: Beacon Press, 2006 (original publication 1946).

REFERENCES

"The 100 Best Companies to Work for 2006," *Fortune,* January 23, 2006.

"2005 Report on Socially Responsible Investing Trends in the United States: 10 Year Review," Social Investment Forum Industry Research Program, 2006.

Autry, James A. *Love and Profit: The Art of Caring Leadership* (reprint). New York: Harper Paperback, 1992.

Bains, Gurnek, et al. *Meaning, Inc.: The Blueprint for Business Success in the 21st Century.* London, UK: Profile Books, 2007.

Bakke, Dennis. *Joy at Work: A Revolutionary Approach to Fun on the Job.* Seattle: PVG, 2005.

Barrett, Richard. *Liberating the Corporate Soul: Building a Visionary Organization.* Boston: Butterworth-Heinemann, 1998.

Barwise, Patrick, and Sean Meehan. *Simply Better: Winning and Keeping Customers by Delivering What Matters Most.* Boston: Harvard Business School Press, 2004.

Bayus, Barry. *Understanding Customer Needs.* Chapel Hill: Kenan-Flagler Business School at the University of North Carolina, 2005.

Beal, Diana, Michelle Goyen, and Peter Phillips. "Why Do We Invest Ethically?" *Journal of Investing* 14, no. 3 (2005): 66–77.

Beatty, Jack. *The World According to Peter Drucker.* New York: Free Press, 1998.

Beckwith, Harry. *Selling the Invisible: A Field Guide to Modern Marketing.* New York: Warner Books, 1997.

Bethune, Gordon, with Scott Huler. *From Worst to First: Behind the Scenes of Continental's Remarkable Comeback.* New York: John Wiley & Sons, 1999.

Bogle, John. *The Battle for the Soul of Capitalism.* New York: Yale University Press, 2005.

Boyatzis, Richard, and Annie McKee. *Resonant Leadership: Renewing Yourself and Connecting with Others Through Mindfulness, Hope, and Compassion.* Boston: Harvard Business School Press, 2005.

Brown, John Seely, and Paul Duguid. *The Social Life of Information.* Boston: Harvard Business School Press, 2002.

Buckingham, Marcus, and Curt Coffman. *First, Break All the Rules: What the World's Greatest Managers Do Differently.* New York: Simon & Schuster, 1999.

Buffett, Warren E. *The Essays of Warren Buffett: Lessons for Corporate America* (Lawrence A. Cunningham, Ed.). New York: Cunningham Group, 2001.

Buford, Bob. *Halftime: Changing Your Game Plan from Success to Significance.* Grand Rapids, MI: Zondervan, 1997.

Burlingham, Bo. *Small Giants: Companies That Choose to Be Great Instead of Big.* New York: Portfolio, 2005.

Burns, James MacGregor. *Leadership,* New York: Harper & Row, 1978.

Cameron, Kim, Jane E. Dutton, and Robert E. Quinn. *Positive Organizational Scholarship.* San Francisco: Berrett-Koehler, 2003.

Cascio, Wayne F. "The High Cost of Low Wages," *Harvard Business Review,* December 2006.

Chouinard, Yvon. *Let My People Go Surfing: The Education of a Reluctant Businessman.* New York: Penguin Press, 2005.

Christensen, Clayton M. *The Innovator's Dilemma: The Revolutionary Book That Will Change the Way You Do Business* (reprint ed.). New York: HarperCollins, 2003.

Collins, Jim. "Foreword" in *Maslow* with Stephens and Heil, 1998. Available online: http://eqi.org/maslow.htm

——— *Good to Great: Why Some Companies Make the Leap . . . and Others Don't.* New York: HarperCollins, 2001.

Collins, Jim, and Jerry Porras. *Built to Last: Successful Habits of Visionary Companies.* New York: HarperCollins, 2004.

Conley, Chip. *The Rebel Rules: Daring to Be Yourself in Business.* New York: Fireside Books, 2001.

Conley, Chip, and Eric Friedenwald–Fishman. *Marketing That Matters: 10 Practices to Profit Your Business and Change the World.* San Francisco: Berrett-Koehler, 2006.

Covey, Stephen M. R. *The Speed of Trust: The One Thing That Changes Everything.* New York: Free Press, 2006.

Covey, Stephen R. *The 8th Habit: From Effectiveness to Greatness.* New York: Free Press, 2004.

——— *The 7 Habits of Highly Effective People.* New York: Free Press, 1990.

Crawford, Fred, and Ryan Mathews. *The Myth of Excellence: Why Great Companies Never Try to Be the Best at Everything.* New York: Three Rivers Press, 2003.

Csikszentmihalyi, Mihaly. *Flow: The Psychology of Optimal Experience.* New York: Harper Perennial, 1990.

——— *Good Business: Leadership, Flow, and the Making of Meaning.* New York: Penguin, 2003.

Danziger, Pamela N. *Let Them Eat Cake: Marketing Luxury to the Masses—as Well as the Classes.* Chicago: Dearborn Trade, 2004.

Dodd, Dominic, and Ken Favaro. "Managing the Right Tension," *Harvard Business Review,* December 2006.

Dodd, Dominic, and Ken Favaro. *The Three Tensions: Winning the Struggle to Perform Without Compromise*. San Francisco: Jossey-Bass, 2007.

Domini, Amy. *Socially Responsible Investing*. Chicago: Kaplan Business, 2000.

Dominus, Susan. "The Starbucks Aesthetic," *New York Times*, October 22, 2006.

Donadio, Rachel. "The Gladwell Effect," *New York Times*, February 5, 2006.

Edmonds, S. Chris. *The Culture Engine: A Framework for Driving Results, Inspiring Your Employees, and Transforming Your Workplace*. San Francisco: John Wiley & Sons, 2014.

Erickson, Gary, and Lois Lorentzen. *Raising the Bar: Integrity and Passion in Life and Business: The Story of Clif Bar & Co.* San Francisco: Jossey-Bass, 2004.

Fleming, John H., Curt Coffman, and James K. Harter. "Manage Your Human Sigma," *Harvard Business Review*, July–August 2005.

Fox, Matthew. *The Reinvention of Work: A New Vision of Livelihood for Our Time*. New York: HarperCollins, 1994.

Frankl, Viktor. *Man's Search for Meaning*. New York: Pocket Books, 2000.

Freiberg, Kevin, and Jackie Freiberg. *Nuts! Southwest Airlines' Crazy Recipe for Business and Personal Success*. Austin, TX: Bard Press, 1996.

Friedman, Milton, John Mackey, and T. J. Rodgers. "Rethinking the Social Responsibility of Business," *Reason Magazine*, October 2005.

George, Bill. *Authentic Leadership: Rediscovering the Secrets to Creating Lasting Value*. San Francisco: Jossey–Bass, 2003.

Gilbert, Matthew. *The Workplace Revolution: Restoring Trust in Business and Bringing Meaning to Our Work*. Boston: Conari Press, 2005.

Gittell, Jody Hoffer. *The Southwest Airlines Way: Using the Power of Relationships to Achieve High Performance*. New York: McGraw-Hill, 2002.

Goble, Frank G. *The Third Force: The Psychology of Abraham Maslow*. Chapel Hill, NC: Maurice Bassett, 2004.

Goffee, Rob, and Gareth Jones. *Why Should Anyone Be Led by You?* Boston: Harvard Business School Press, 2006.

Goldberg, Alan B. and Ritter, Bill. "Costco CEO Finds Pro-Worker Means Profitability", abc News, August 2, 2006. Available at: http://abcnews.go.com/2020/Business/story?id=1362779

Goleman, Daniel. *Emotional Intelligence*. New York: Bantam, 1995.

——— *Working with Emotional Intelligence*. New York: Bantam, 1998.

Gostick, Adrian, and Chester Elton. *Managing with Carrots*. Salt Lake City: Gibbs Smith, 2001.

——— *The Carrot Principle: How the Best Managers Use Recognition to Engage Their Employees, Retain Talent, and Drive Performance*. New York: Free Press, 2007.

Gulati, Ranjay, and David Kletter. "Shrinking Core, Expanding Periphery: The Relational Architecture of High-Performing Organizations," *California Management Review*, Spring 2005.

Handy, Charles. *The Hungry Spirit: Beyond Capitalism. A Quest for Purpose in the Modern World.* New York: Broadway, 1998.

Hartman, Darrell. "Virtual Hospitality," *Travel+Leisure,* January 2007.

Hawkins, David R. *Power vs. Force: The Hidden Determinants of Human Behavior.* Carlsbad, CA: Hay House, 2002.

Heil, Gary, Warren Bennis, and Deborah C. Stephens. *Douglas McGregor, Revisited.* New York: John Wiley & Sons, 2000.

Heil, Gary, Tom Parker, and Deborah C. Stephens. *One Size Fits One.* New York: John Wiley & Sons, 1996.

Herzberg, Fred. "One More Time: How Do You Motivate Employees?" *Harvard Business Review,* 1968.

Herzberg, Frederick, Bernard Mausner, and Barbara Bloch Snyderman. *The Motivation to Work.* New Brunswick, NJ: Transaction, 1993.

Heskett, James L., Thomas O. Jones, Gary W. Loveman, W. Earl Sasser Jr., and Leonard A. Schlesinger. "Putting the Service-Profit Chain to Work," *Harvard Business Review,* March–April 1994.

Heskett, James L., W. Earl Sasser, Jr. and Leonard A. Schlesinger. *The Service Profit Chain.* New York: Free Press, 1997.

Hewlett, Sylvia Ann, and Carolyn Buck Luce. "Extreme Jobs: The Dangerous Allure of the 70-Hour Workweek," *Harvard Business Review,* December 2006.

Hey, Kenneth, and Peter D. Moore. *The Caterpillar Doesn't Know: How Personal Change Is Creating Organizational Change.* New York: Free Press, 1998.

Hoffman, Donna. "Planet Google Wants You." *New York Times,* October 15, 2006, Fashion & Style.

Hoffman, Edward (Ed.). *Future Visions: The Unpublished Papers of Abraham Maslow.* Thousand Oaks, CA: Sage, 1996.

Hoffman, Edward. *The Right to Be Human: A Biography of Abraham Maslow* (revised ed.). New York: McGraw-Hill, 1999.

Huba, Jackie, and Ben McConnell. *Creating Customer Evangelists.* Chicago: Dearborn Trade, 2002.

Hurley, Robert F. "The Decision to Trust," *Harvard Business Review,* September 2006.

Iverson, Ken. *Plain Talk: Lessons from a Business Maverick.* New York: John Wiley & Sons, 1997.

Kahlil, Gibran. "On Work." *The Prophet,* New York: Knopf, 1923.

Katz, Peter. *The New Urbanism: Toward an Architecture of Community.* New York: McGraw-Hill, 1993.

Kawasaki, Guy. *Rules for Revolutionaries: The Capitalist Manifesto for Creating and Marketing New Products and Services.* New York: Harper Business, 1999.

Kazanjian, Kirk. *Exceeding Customer Expectations: What Enterprise, America's #1 Car Rental Company, Can Teach You About Creating Lifetime Customers.* New York: Currency, 2007.

Kelly, Marjorie. "The Legacy Problem." *Business Ethics Magazine,* Summer 2003.

Kofman, Fred. *Conscious Business: How to Build Value Through Values.* Boulder, CO: Sounds True, 2006.

Kotter, John P., and James L. Heskett. *Corporate Culture and Performance.* New York: Free Press, 1992.

Kouzes, James M., and Barry Z. Posner. *A Leader's Legacy.* San Francisco: Jossey-Bass, 2006.

LaSalle, Diana, and Terry A. Britton. *Priceless: Turning Ordinary Objects into Extraordinary Experiences.* Boston: Harvard Business School Press, 2002.

Lashinsky, Adam. "Search and Enjoy (The 100 Best Companies to Work for)," *Fortune,* January 22, 2007.

Lepsinger, Richard, and Antoinette Lucia. *The Art and Science of 360 Degree Feedback.* San Francisco: Pfeiffer, 1997.

Levitt, Theodore. "Marketing Myopia," *Harvard Business Review,* July–August 1960.

Lewis, David. *The Soul of the New Consumer.* London: Nicholas Brealey, 2000.

Long, Karl. "Customer Loyalty and Experience Design in E-Business," *Design Management Review,* Spring 2004.

Lowry, Richard J. (Ed.). *The Journals of A. H. Maslow.* Monterey, CA: Brooks/Cole, 1979.

Mariampolski, Hy. *Ethnography for Marketers.* Thousand Oaks, CA: Sage, 2005.

Maslow, Abraham. *Eupsychian Management: A Journal.* Homewood, IL: R. D. Irwin, 1965.

——— *Motivation and Personality* (3rd ed.). New York: HarperCollins, 1987.

——— *The Farther Reaches of Human Nature* (reprint) New York: Penguin, 1993.

——— *Religion, Values and Peak Experiences* (reprint) New York: Penguin, 1994.

——— *Toward a Psychology of Being* (3rd ed.). New York: Wiley, 1999.

Massie, Hugh."Feeling Your Way to Wealth: Emotional Intelligence in Investing." www.raymondjames.com.

Max, D. T. "Happiness 101," *New York Times Magazine,* January 7, 2007.

McGregor, Douglas. *The Human Side of Enterprise.* New York: McGraw-Hill, 2005.

Meyer, Danny. *Setting the Table: The Transforming Power of Hospitality in Business.* New York: HarperCollins, 2006.

Moore, Geoffrey A. *Crossing the Chasm: Marketing and Selling Disruptive Products to Mainstream Customers* (revised ed.). New York: HarperCollins, 2002.

Morris, Betsy. "New Rule: Admire My Soul. Old Rule: Admire My Might," *Fortune,* July 11, 2006.

Mourkogiannis, Nikos. *Purpose: The Starting Point of Great Companies.* Hampshire, UK: Palgrave Macmillan, 2006.

Nelson, Bob. *1001 Ways to Reward Employees.* New York: Workman, 2005.

Norton, David W. "Toward Meaningful Brand Experiences," *Design Management Journal,* Winter 2003.

Novak, Michael. *Business as a Calling.* New York: Free Press, 1996.

Pattakos, Alex. *Prisoners of Our Thoughts.* San Francisco: Berrett-Koehler, 2004.

Peppers, Don, and Martha Rogers. *Return on Customer: Creating Maximum Value From Your Scarcest Resource.* New York: Currency, 2005.

Pine, Joseph, II, and James Gilmore. *The Experience Economy.* Boston: Harvard Business School Press, 1999.

Pollard, C. William. *The Soul of the Firm.* Grand Rapids, MI: Zondervan, 1996.

Putnam, Robert. *Bowling Alone: The Collapse and Revival of American Community.* New York: Simon & Schuster, 2001.

Rath, Tom, and Donald O. Clifton. *How Full Is Your Bucket?: Positive Strategies for Work and Life.* New York: Gallup Press, 2004.

Reeb, Lloyd. *From Success to Significance.* Grand Rapids, MI: Zondervan, 2004.

Reichheld, Fred. *The Loyalty Effect: The Hidden Force Behind Growth, Profits and Lasting Value.* Boston: Harvard Business School Press, 2001.

————— *Loyalty Rules: How Today's Leaders Build Lasting Relationships.* Boston: Harvard Business School Press, 2003.

————— *The Ultimate Question: Driving Good Profits and True Growth.* Boston: Harvard Business School Press, 2006.

"Rethinking the Social Responsibility of Business," *Reason Magazine,* October 2005.

Ridderstrale, Jonas, and Kjell Nordstrom. *Karaoke Capitalism.* Westport, CT: Praeger, 2005.

Roberts, Kevin. *Lovemarks: The Future Beyond Brands.* New York: Powerhouse Books, 2005.

Sanders, Tim. *Love Is the Killer App: Daring to Be Different in a Copycat World.* New York: Crown Business, 2002.

Secretan, Lance. *Inspirational Leadership: Destiny, Calling and Cause.* Toronto, Ontario: Macmillan Canada, 1999.

————— *Reclaiming Higher Ground: Creating Higher Organizations That Inspire the Soul.* New York: McGraw-Hill, 1997.

Seligman, Martin E. P. *Authentic Happiness: Using the New Positive Psychology to Realize Your Potential for Lasting Fulfillment.* New York: Free Press, 2002.

Semlar, Ricardo. *Maverick.* New York: Warner Books, 1995.

——— *The Seven-Day Weekend: Changing the Way Work Works*. New York: Portfolio, 2004.

Senge, Peter, C., Otto Scharmer, Joseph Jaworski, and Betty Sue Flowers. *Presence*. Cambridge, MA: Society for Organizational Learners, 2004.

Sheehy, Gail. *Pathfinders*. New York: Bantam, 1982.

Silverstein, Michael J., and John Butman. *Treasure Hunt: Inside the Mind of the New Consumer*. New York: Portfolio, 2006.

Silverstein, Michael J., and Jay Fiske. *Trading Up: Why Consumers Want New Luxury Goods and Companies Create Them*. New York: Portfolio, 2004.

Sirota, David, Louis A. Mischkind, and Michael Irwin Meltzer. *The Enthusiastic Employee*. Philadelphia: Wharton School, 2005.

Spears, Larry. *Reflections on Leadership: How Robert K. Greenleaf's Theory of Servant-Leadership Influenced Today's Top Management Thinkers*. New York: John Wiley & Sons, 1995.

Statman, Meir. "What Do Investors Want?" *Journal of Portfolio Management*, 2004.

Stephens, Deborah C. (Ed.). *The Maslow Business Reader*. New York: John Wiley & Sons, 2000.

Stephens, Deborah C., and Gary Heil (Eds.). *Maslow on Management*. New York: John Wiley & Sons, 1998.

Sullivan, Dan, and Catherine Nomura. *The Laws of Lifetime Growth: Always Make Your Future Bigger Than Your Past*. San Francisco: Berrett-Koehler, 2006.

Taylor, William C., and Polly LaBarre. *Mavericks at Work: Why the Most Original Minds in Business Win*. New York: Morrow, 2006.

Teerlink, Rich, and Lee Ozley. *More Than a Motorcycle: The Leadership Journey at Harley-Davidson*. Boston: Harvard Business School Press, 2000.

Taulane, Anne. "The Second Coming," *Lodging Magazine*, January 2007.

Terkel, Studs. *Working: People Talk About What They Do All Day and How They Feel About What They Do*. New York: New Press, 1997.

Tindel, Kip. *Uncontainable: How Passion, Commitment, and Conscious Capitalism Built a Business Where Everyone Thrives*. New York: Grand Central Publishing, 2014.

Van Boven, Leaf, and Thomas Gilovich. "To Do or to Have? That Is the Question," *Journal of Personality and Psychology* 85, no. 6 (2003).

Van Osnabrugge, Mark, and Robert J. Robinson. *Angel Investing: Matching Start-Up Funds with Start-Up Companies—The Guide for Entrepreneurs, Individual Investors, and Venture Capitalists*. San Francisco: Jossey-Bass, 2000.

Wheatley, Margaret. *Leadership and the New Science*. San Francisco: Berrett-Koehler, 2006.

Whitmore, John. *Need, Greed or Freedom: Business Changes and Personal Choices*. Dorsett, UK: Element Books, Ltd., 1997.

Wipperfurth, Alex. *Brand Hijack: Marketing Without Marketing*. New York: Portfolio, 2005.

Wolfe, David, Rajendra Sisodia, and Jagdish Sheth. *Firms of Endearment: How World-Class Companies Profit from Passion and Purpose.* Philadelphia: Wharton School, 2007.

Wrzesniewski, Amy, and Jane Dutton. "Crafting a Job: Revisioning Employees as Active Crafters of Their Work," *Academy of Management Review,* April 2001.

Zaltman, Gerald. *How Customers Think: Essential Insights into the Mind of the Market.* Boston: Harvard Business School Press, 2003.

Zander, Rosamund Stone, and Benjamin Zander. *The Art of Possibility: Transforming Professional and Personal Life.* New York: Penguin, 2002.

ACKNOWLEDGMENTS

What a long, strange trip it has been! Writing two books in barely more than a year while running a company that's growing by leaps and bounds is not for the faint of heart. I could not have done this without the support of so many friends and colleagues. First off, I can't say enough about Debra Amador DeLaRosa, my research partner, editor extraordinaire, publicist, and good friend who was my midwife through this birthing process. This was our second collaboration, and I still feel so lucky to have her unfailing support in all my endeavors. My executive committee and home office colleagues (especially my assistant Rachel Carlton) at Joie de Vivre put up with many Monday morning arrivals by a very sleep-deprived Chip—after my weekends were spent writing by candlelight. Of course, none of this would be possible without the labors of love that more than 3,000 Joie de Vivre employees put into their work every day. Thanks to all of you for putting up with my experiments in how to implement Maslow's principles in our workplace. And a very special thank you to Rachel Carlton. Before she came along, I'd never had an executive assistant. I am now deeply spoiled, as Rachel keeps more balls in the air than I do—and she does it with real grace, efficiency, and smarts.

There are so many others who helped contribute ideas or editing to this process. Alan Webber read my initial concept for the book and bluntly told me, "The world doesn't need another business book." His advice helped me to make *Peak* more of a personal story. My close friend Drew Banks and I regularly jump into the deep end discussing the philosophy of business. More than anyone else other than Debra, Drew helped me find my voice in interpreting Maslow's work (and he also came up with the title for this book). My former colleague Eric Sinoway, who's now running the Worth media empire, gave me numerous editing suggestions that helped to clarify some essential points. Eric has a true knack for understanding how to take my New Age nuggets and turn them into mainstream musings. My best friend Vanda fed me full of inspiration. And Sue Funkhouser became the world's foremost expert on how to apply *Peak* principles in organizations. She was very helpful in adding material to this updated edition.

All of the following people made valuable contributions to this work, and I thank them from the bottom of my heart: Jim Oakley, Peter Sims, Seth Godin, MeiMei Fox, Mike Faith, Andrew Greenberg, Fran Conley (yes, my mom!), Laura Galloway, Eugene Dilan, Athena Katsaros, Christian Forthomme, Rob Delamater, Dave Norton, Lenny Nash, Paul Coury, Stephen Mitchell, Yosi Amram, Lindsay Nelson, Chris Anderson, Steven Addis, Johanna Vondeling, Tris Brown, Russ Silva, David Erickson, Michael Scribner, Mark McCormick, Robin Beers, Lowell Selvin, Zern Liew, Matthew and Tercis Englehart, Nancy Murphy, Scott Bovard, Peter and Cathleen Schwartz, Mary Jane Ryan, Kristin Cobble, David Cragg, William Powanda, Jamie Danziger, Mark Dwight, Gary Muszynski, Jack Crawford Jr., Katherine von Jan, Kirsten Hassert, Jan Lapidoth, Srikumar Rao, Gregg Britt, Denise Corcoran, and Larry and Ann Wheat. Also, a big thanks to the folks at the Ritz-Carlton Half Moon Bay who took care of me during my last week of writing hibernation. They reminded me of how a business can help its customers reach self-actualization. And my Vizsla, Sugar Ray (my writing companion), showed me that even bird dogs could have peak experiences when they chase seagulls on the beach.

And there are those unique business leaders who so generously spent time talking with me about my theory. These individuals demonstrate daily that Maslow's influence goes way beyond my little company. Thanks to Mort Meyerson, Danny Meyer, Robert Stephens, Bill George, Lee Ozley, Walter Robb, Dave Pottruck, Marc Benioff, George Zimmer, Reed Hastings, Ron Johnson, Arthur Gillis, George McCown, Bill Price, Kent Thiry, John Donohoe, Michael Gross, Peter Mullin, Bill Linton, Tudor Havriliuc, Joe Gebbia, Ping Fu, Julie Hanna, Kip Tindell, Ben Silbermann, and Mike Meldman.

Then there's the literary brigade. Amy Rennert, my agent, knew I had this book cooking and has been trying to gently pry it out of me for a half-dozen years. And thanks to the team at Jossey-Bass/ Wiley. I heard from a lot of New York publishers that Joie de Vivre isn't a household word (except for maybe in Marseilles), but the San Francisco–based Jossey-Bass folks knew who I was and what the potential impact of this book could be. Thanks to senior editor and

"Chip-believer" Susan Williams, who gave birth to her own baby in the middle of my writing and put me in the care of Byron Schneider, who came to the rescue and did a masterful job of guiding my thinking and writing. And thanks to Liz Gildea, my associate editor, who helped me hone and deliver this newest edition, along with Jocelyn Kwiatkowski, Jeanenne Ray, and Danielle Serpica. And Anne Digges for improving *Peak*'s pyramids. Carolyn Carlstroem, Erik Thrasher, Rob Brandt, Amie Wong, Amy Packard, Adrian Morgan, Kathe Sweeney, Rebecca Browning, Mark Karmendy, Genoveva Llosa, and Jan Andersen helped *Peak* reach its peak.

Finally, I need to say a big thank you to Deborah Stephens, the leading expert on how Abraham Maslow's theories are used in the workplace. Deborah is one of the coeditors of *Maslow on Management* and *Douglas McGregor, Revisited* and author of *The Maslow Business Reader*. As I started developing my book proposal for *Peak*, I reached out to Deborah, not knowing how she might respond to this Maslow-channeling CEO. Deborah graciously welcomed my interpretive inquiry of Maslow, and she truly appreciated how we'd adapted the Hierarchy of Needs within Joie de Vivre. Without Deborah's support, I'm not sure I would have started scaling this *Peak*.

THE AUTHOR

Chip Conley is a high-profile entrepreneur and *New York Times* best-selling author. He is the founder and former CEO of Joie de Vivre Hospitality. Between 2013 to 2017, Chip provided full-time leadership counsel to the founders and CEO of Airbnb. So, he disrupted his beloved hospitality industry twice: first as a boutique hotelier, and 30 years later as the Head of Global Hospitality and Strategy for the world's largest home sharing company. He is the author of *The Rebel Rules: Daring to Be Yourself in Business* (Fireside), *Marketing That Matters: 10 Practices to Profit Your Business and Change the World* (Berrett-Koehler), *Emotional Equations: Simple Truths for Creating Happiness + Success in Business + Life* (Atria), and *Wisdom@Work: The Making of a Modern Elder* (Crown) forthcoming in 2018. Chip received his BA and MBA from Stanford University. He has an honorary doctorate in psychology from Saybook University. He is a long-time board member of the Burning Man Project and the Esalen Institute. Chip lives in San Francisco and on the coast of Baja California Sur. You can contact him at www.chipconley.com.

INDEX

A

Accountability, 24
AES, 27
Affinity programs, 74
Air Canada, 152
Airbnb, *xiv–xvi, 38,* 101, 114
  leadership fluidity at, 223
  popularity metrics of, 221
  recognition culture at, 73
"Airfinity," 74
Ally McBeal, 61
Amazon, 114
  customer commitment
      of, 125–126
  innovation at, 229–230
  mass customization
      approach, 132
  small teams at, 217
  technology harnessing
      by, 124–125
Amazon Echo, 229
Amazon Go, 229
Amazon Music Unlimited, 229
AMC Theaters, 193
American Psychological
      Association, 10
Amtrak, 106
Anchoring, 164
Anthropologie, 146
AOL, 123
Apple, 11, 38, 82
  customer service at, 139–140

halo effect, 149
historical context of, 138–139
iPod creation by, 152
mantra of, 86
retail stores, 139
transformation of, 137
Ash, Mary Kay, 63
Aspirational needs, 11
AstraZeneca, 56
Aurelius, Marcus, 159, 162
Authentic Happiness
      (Seligman), 53
Authentic Leadership
      (George), 166, 170
Autodesk, 70
Ava Maria Mutual Funds, 190

B

B-Corp. *See* Public Benefit
      Corporation
Baby boomers, 190
Badiola, Javier Calvo Perez, *xvii,*
      51, 226
Bailey, George, 22
Bain & Company, 24, 35
Bakke, Dennis, 27
Bakken, Earl, 83
Bank of America, 149, 154
Banks, Drew, 179
Barrett, Colleen, 201
Barrett, Richard, 66
Barwise, Patrick, 106

*The Battle for the Soul of
Capitalism,* 23
Bayus, Barry, 147
Beckwith, Harry, 101–102,
107
Behaviorism, 8
*Belong Here Transformation
Journey,* 222
Bennis, Warren, 7, 164
Berkshire Hathaway, 23, 166,
185, 197
Best Buy, 89, 93, 126–127, 132,
140
Bethune, Gordon, 207–209
Beyond Anywhere, 221–22
Bezos, Jeff, 125, 217
BHAG (big, hairy, audacious
goals), 196
Big Gulp, 45–46
"Bleisure" trend, *xv–xvi*
Bleustein, Jeffrey, 141
Blink (Gladwell), 12
Blockbuster, 107
Bogle, John, 23
Boise Cascade, 171–172
Booz Allen Hamilton, 105
Bottom line, 164
Boutique hotels, 108–111,
136–137
Bowl-a-rama event, 82
"Bowling Alone" (Putnam), 82
Boyatzis, Richard, 89
Bradshaw, Terry, 180
Brands
building, *xi*
company culture and, *xii*
do-gooder, 151–152
high-touch, 126–128
Branson, Richard, 3, 72
Britton, Terry, 122, 147
Buckingham, Marcus, 63–64

Buffett, Warren, 23, 165–166,
180–181, 184
Buford, Bob, 190
Built to Last (Collins, Porras), 7,
22, 191
Burlingham, Bo, 108
Burning Man, *xvii*
Burns, James MacGregor, 28
Business Ethics Magazine, 192
Business plans, 166
Business Week, 91, 111
Businesses. *See also* Corporate
culture
cash need by, 168
economic denominators
in, 168–169
great causes at, 82–83
growth of, 24
mantras at, 86
maximizing profits at,
173–174
misaligned owners of, 172
off-site retreats, 88
philosophical question
for, 201
psychology of, 12–13
short-term focus of, 21–24
transformation of, 12–13
transparency in, 167
wellness, *xiii–xiv*

C
Cafe Gratitude, 153
*California Management
Review,* 33
Calling. *See also* Career; Job
finding, 77
focus of, 238
impact of, 219
pyramid level of, 238
qualities defining, 240

statements, 238–239
transformative effect of, 80
Capitalism
  conscious, 226–228
  democratic, 120
  fundamentalist, 22
  karmic, 17–19, 21, 30
Career. *See also* Calling; Job
  focus of, 38–39, 238
  path of, 80
  pyramid level of, 238
  statements, 238–239
Carreiro, Toni, 148–149
Category needs, 106
Chesky. Brian, *xiv–xv*, 223,
    226
Chihuly, Dale, 91
Chouinard, Yvon, 26
Christensen, Clayton, 101
Christian Science Monitor, 241
The Citizen, 120
Classic economic theory, 19
Clif Bar, 57
Coffman, Curt, 63–64
Collaborative partnerships, 38,
    179–181
Collins, Jim, 7, 22–23, 77, 168,
    173, 185, 191, 196
Colonel Sanders, 240–241
Compensation
  benchmarking tool for, 54
  competitive, 48–49
  consideration of, 47–49
  creative, 55–56
  employee retention and,
    51–53
  full, 36–37
  policy pillars, 52
  prescriptions for, 57–59
  recognition and, 75
  recommended reading, 60

Complaints, 49
Concept, 120, 131–132, 160
Condé Nast, 109–110
Conley, Lauren, 236–237
Conscious Business
    (Kofman), 164
Conscious Capitalism
    (Mackey), 227–228
Container Store, 231
Continental Airlines, 207–209
Cook, Scott, 146–147
Cornell Hospitality School,
    227
Corporate culture. *See also*
    Businesses
  banding and, *xii*
  basis of, 19
  creation of, 206–209
  effects of, 210
  nurturing of, 224–226
  performance and, 203
  profits and, 209–211
  recognition, 64–65, 67–73
  recommend reading for,
    213
Corporate culture and
    Performance, 206
Corporate social responsibility
    (CSR), 192, 228
Costanoa, 160–162
Costco, 23, 59
Covey, Stephen, 7, 21,
    165
Cragg, David, 86
Crawford, Jack, Jr., 179–180
Crossing the Chasm
    (Moore), 101
Csikszentmihalyi, Mihaly, 23,
    241
Cultural Ambassadors,
    87–88

Culture. See also Corporate
    culture; Recognition
    culture
  characteristics of, 210
  defined, 203
  growth and, 203
  service, 128–134
  tech/touch, 126–128
Customer Pyramid, 111
  Apple's, 138–140
  base of, 105, 116
  creation of, 142–145
  employee pyramid
    connection, 101
  Harley-Davidson's, 140–141
  innovations at peak,
    228–230
  middle level, 126
  origins of, 211
  overview of, 100–102
  prescriptions for, 153–155
  progression on, 102–103
  recommend reading for, 134,
    156
  rising to peak of, 138
  Starbucks', 150–151
  top, themes at, 148–156
  Whole Foods', 141–142
Customers
  customization of, 114
  desires, 121–126, 130–133
  disappointed, 106, 111
  engagement of, 131
  expectations of, 37, 104–107,
    114–116
  goal achievement, 148–149
  good will of, 25
  gratitude of, 153
  loyalty, 123–124, 137, 205
  loyalty, creation of, 106–108,
    123–124

  matching product to,
    113–114
  middle income, 116
  mood of, 155
  motivation, 116
  needs focus, 102–104
  needs of, 34
  one-size-fits-one, 123
  recommended reading, 117
  repeat, 123–124
  safety of, 103–104
  satisfaction tools, 114
  self-actualization of, 149–151
  self-transcendence of, 151
  social responsibility and,
    151–152
  surveys, 114–115
  unrecognized needs of, 38,
    144–148, 152
Cycle of capability, 204

D
Dao, David, 227
DaVita, 66–67
"The Decision to Trust"
    (Hurley), 165
Declaration of
    Independence, 26
DeLaRosa, Debra Amador, xviii
Dell, 139
Deming, W. Edward, xiii
Devo, 18
Differentiation, 168
Digges, Anne, 269
"Digital nomads," xv
Directory of Investment
    Managers, 191
DirecTV, 152
Discovery Land, 180
Diversity programs, 74
Do-gooder brands, 151

Dodd, Dominic, 168
Domini, Amy, 190
Domino's Pizza, 190–191
Dot.com bubble, 4
Dow Jones Stock Index, 84
Dow Jones Sustainability
    Index, 191
Dream sessions, 131
Dreammaker program,
    154–155
Drucker, Peter, 7, 52, 128, 137,
    153, 210, 223, 235
Duke University, 82

E
Eddy, Mary Baker, 241
Effectiveness, 168–171, 215
Einstein, Albert, 10
Eisenhower, Dwight D., 102
Eisner, Michael, 3–4
Eli Lilly, 54
Elton, Chester, 66
Emotional bank accounts,
    21–22, 230
Emotional connections, 150,
    181–186
Emotional Equations
    (Conley), *xiv*
Emotional intelligence, 34–35,
    176–178
Emotional thermostats,
    231–232
Employee Pyramid
    base of, 47–49
    customer pyramid
        connection, 101
    focus of, 14
    foundation of, 53–57
    Google example, 49–51
    hourly workers in,
        59–60

managers' understanding
    of, 93–94
money on, 51–53
motivation and, 80
origins of, 211–212
peak of, 95
recognition and, 68
recommended reading
    for, 60
top level of, 37
Employees
    basic needs of, 48
    categorization of, 133
    company strategy and, 88
    complaints of, 49
    disengaged, 94
    heroes, 83
    hourly, 59–60
    morale growth of, 203
    motives of, 36
    perspective expansion, 90–91
    satisfied, 204
    sense of community, 93
    Spanish-speaking, 88–89
    union representation of, 33
    work value of, 51–53
Engagement forums, 119–120
Engelhart, Matthew, 153
Engelhart, Tercis, 153
Enlightened hospitality, 86
Enterprise Rent-a-Car, 24, 126
The Enthusiastic Employee
    (Sirota, et al.), 210
Entrepreneurs
    accountability of, 162–163
    investors and, 197
    new thing fixation of, 179
Environmental factors, 52
The Epiphany. *See* Nobu
Erickson, Gary, 57
Ernst & Young, 56

Enron, 21
Esalen Institute, *xvii*
ESI (Emotional and Social
    Intelligence)
    Bootcamp, 50
The Essays of Warren Buffett:
    Lessons for Corporate
    America, 165–166
Estaff retreat, *xv*
Ethnographers, 146–147, 229
Eupsychian Management
    (Maslow), 11, 25
Everfest, *xiv*
Expedia, 111–112
Extraordinary Service award, 71

F
Facebook, 50, 132
Fairfield Inn, 109
Favaro, Ken, 168
Fear
    defense against, 224
    impact of, 34
    possibilities, 235
Fear of regret theory, 164
FedEx, 38, 126
Fest300, *xiv*
Financial DNA Resources, 177
Fire Phone system, 229
Firms of Endearment: How World-
    Class Companies Profit from
    Passion and Purpose
    (Collins, Porras), 191
First, Break All the Rules
    (Buckingham,
    Coffman), 63
Flickr, 93
Flockhart, Calista, 61
Focus groups, 38
Folds, Ben, 132
Follow-me-home approach, 229

Ford, Henry, 135
Fortune magazine, 54, 58, 166,
    209
Four Seasons Hotel and
    Resorts, 47
Frankl, Viktor, 83–84
Freud, Sigmund, 7–8
Friedman, Milton, 22
Fringe benefits, 55–56
From Worst to First
    (Lorenzo), 207
Fundamentalist capitalism, 22
Funkhouser, Sue, 74
Future Visions (Hoffman), 242

G
Galleria Park Hotel, 111
Gallup, 63–64, 209
Gamez, Peter, 21
Gap, 115
Gateway, 139
Geek Squad, 89, 93, 152
Gen Xers, 190
Genentech, 54
    employee benefits at, 14
    "purity of purpose" at, 86–87
    revenue growth at, 166–167
    scientific breakthroughs
        at, 82
General Electric, 131
General Motors, 105
Genius Bar, 139
Geolo Capital, *xiv*
Geomagic, 230
George, Bill, 82–83, 166, 167,
    170
Gibran, Khalil, *xvii–xviii*
Gittell, Jody Hoffer, 35–36, 69,
    202
Gladwell, Malcolm, 12
Glass Door, 221

Goals
  BHAG, 196
  customers', 148
  short-term, 21, 23
  strategic, 66
  transactional, 164, 166–167
Golden Eagle Leader, 222
Goldman Sachs, 191
Goleman, Daniel, 34–35, 176
"Goaltender" tool, 148
Good Business (Csikszent-
    mihalyi), 23, 241
Good to Great (Collins), 7, 77,
    168, 185
Good will, 22
Google, 14, 40, 221
  customer engagement
    by, 148
  employee pyramid of,
    49–51
  mindfulness programs, 50
  owners' imprint on, 206
  talent retention by, 93–94
"Googleplex," 49
Gostick, Adrian, 66
Gottman, John, 75
Gramercy Tavern, 127
Grandma Moses, 241
Gratitude journals, 94
Graves, Michael, 138
Greenleaf, Robert, 232
Greyhound, 106
Gross National Happiness
    Commission, 221
Gross, Michael, 143
Growth
  culture and, 203
  relationships and, 24
  revenue, 169, 182
  sustained, 215
  types of, 99

Growth industries, 99
Gulati, Ranjay, 33–34, 105

H
Halftime (Buford), 190
Hammer, Armand, 241
Hanna, Julie, 223–224
Hanover Insurance, 25
Harley Owner Group
    (H.O.G.), 132, 141
Harley-Davidson, 114
  cult of, 38
  employee loyalty at, 53
  H.O.G program at, 132, 141
  leadership team at, 52
  renaissance of, 11
Harvard Business Review, 165
Hastings, Reed, 107, 228
Havriliuc, Tudor, 50
Hay, Thomas, 150
Hayne, Richard, 146
"Heavenly Bed," 116
Herbisms, 202, 210
Hero awards, 71–72
Herzberg, Frederick, 52
Heskett, James, 204
Hewlett-Packard, 131
Hierarchy of Needs, xvii, 25
  application of, 27–30
  business model from, 201
  corporate embrace of, 11–12
  countries, 53
  customer motivation
    and, 116
  customer needs and, 102–104
  essential levels of, 36
  evolution of, 9
  increased levels for, 189
  presumption of, 8
  priority setting with, 242–243
  reliance on, xxi

Hierarchy of Needs (*Continued*)
  self-transformation in, 29
  states of being in, 28–29
  workplace relationships
    and, 29–30
Hilton Hotels, 101, 108–109
Hoffman, Donna, 148
Hoffman, Edward, 242
Hoke, John R. III, 91
Holacracy, 217
Holiday Inn, 103, 108–109,
    116
Holloman, Karlene, 170–171
Home Depot, 148
Homeostasis, 242
Hotel Avante, 136
Hotel Carlton, 64
Hotel chains, 108–109
Hotel Heroes award, 71–72
Hotel Rex, 136
Hotel Vitale, 128–130, 145
How Customers Think: Essen-
    tial Insights into the
    Mind of the Market
    (Zaltman), 145
Howard, Jane, 64
Hsieh, Tony, 59, 217, *xii*
Huggies Pull-Ups theme, 147
Human nature, 19
  assumptions, 20
  "growing tip" of, 10
  higher ceiling of, 8
  investors, 163–164
  needs of, 244–245
  positive view of, 216–218
  tangibility of, 24–25
  theory of, 20
  traditional view of, 7
  work and, 19
Human potential movement,
    81–92

The Human Side of Enterprise
    (McGregor), 17, 248
Hunger, 63
Hunt, Jay B., 197
Huntting, Gabe, *xviii–xix*
Hurley, Robert, 165
Hurricane Katrina, 70–71

I
Identity refreshment, 104, 110,
    229
Immelt, Jeff, 131
Inc. magazine, *xv*
Individual Development
    Plan, 75
The Innovator's Dilemma
    (Christensen), 101
Inspiration, 77–79
Inspirational Leadership
    (Secretan), 79
Inspired Speakers Series, 88–89
Intangibles, 220–222
Internet, 105, 111–116
Interstate highway system,
    102–103
Introspection, 244
Intuit, 24, 146
Investor Pyramid
  base of, 163, 165
  bottom line of, 164
  conventional wisdom
    and, 187–189
  development of, 198
  employees and, 162
  focus of, 14
  middle level, 179–181
  origins of, 211
Investors. *See also* Legacy
    investors
  attracting, 165–167
  communication with, 175

emotional connection with, 181–186
emotionally intelligent, 176–178
entrepreneurs and, 197
foundational needs of, 164
goal alignment with, 159–162
humanity of, 163–165
legacy-driven, 189–191
motivations of, 184
needs of, 38
short-term perspective of, 177–178
social needs of, 184
survey of, 172
transactional alignment, 167–168
trust development in, 164–165
iPod, 101, 152
It's a Wonderful Life, 22
Iverson, Ken, 178, 206–207

J
James, William, 63
Jefferson, Thomas, 26
Jerry Maguire, 170
Jet Blue, 152, 154
Job. *See also* Calling; Work
crafting, 90
feedback, 69
focus of, 237–238
meaning of, 81, 94
mojo creator in, 220
path of, 80–81
perception of, 92–93
performance, 75
pyramid level of, 238
security, 71
statements, 238–239
Job crafting, 90

Jobs, Steve, 121, 138–139
"Jonah Complex," 236
Johnson, Ron, 138–140
Joie de Vivre (JdV) Heart, 203–205, 210–213
Joie de Vivre (JdV) Hospitality, 5, 14, 54, 114, 149, 181
benchmark metrics at, 206
Bowl-a-rama at, 82
capital calls by, 181–183
cash loses of, 46
challenge of, 111
charity of, 197
coastal property investment by, 160–162
compensation at, 55
culture of recognition at, 64–65, 70
customer loyalty strategy of, 137
customer needs focus by, 102–103, 229–230
Customer Pyramid, 143
Dreammaker program, 136
e-marketing, 113–114
employee perspective at, 90–91
growth of, 3
holiday party at, 71
hotels created by, 110–111
industry downturn and transformation, 29
Internet challenge of, 111–116
investor perks, 185
jobs at, 80–81
Kabuki purchase by, 192–198
loss of, 5
mantra of, 86
market share data for, 170

Joie de Vivre (JdV) Hospitality
(*Continued*)
meaningfulness at, 85–87
meeting customer expecta-
tions at, 105–106
mission statement, 85
ownership of, 32–33
philanthropy at, 87–88
Phoenix purchase by, 100
recognition awards at, 71–72
redefining effectiveness
at, 169–170
revenue decline at, 169
revival of, 13
service culture at, 129–130,
204–205
size of, 237
Southwest Airlines' influence
on, 201–203
success defined at, 245
survival of, 21, *xiii–xiv, xxi*–xii
T-shirt concept, 181–183
theme song of, 62
town hall meetings, 120–121
turnover at, 47
vision for, 6
work climate survey, 53
Joie de Vivre (JdV) University,
99–89
Jones Soda Company, 149–150

K
Kabuki Springs & Spa, 192–198
Kanter, Rosabeth Moss, 61
Karaoke Capitalism
(Kendrick), 25
Karmic capitalism
application of, 21
inspiration for, 17–19
reading list for, 30
recommended reading, 50

Katz, Peter, 82
Kawasaki, Guy, 151
Kay, Andrew, 11
"Keep the Change"
program, 149
Kelleher, Herb, 72, 201
Kelly, Gary, 219
Kendrick, Jonathan, 25
Kennedy, John F., Jr., 17
Kenny, Jack, 64, 72, 86, 181
Kimberly-Clark, 147
Kimpton Group, 128, 135
Kimpton, Bill, 109,
135–136
Kiva, 223
Kletter, David, 33–34, 105
Koch Industries, 11
Koch, Charles, 11
Kofman, Fred, 164
Konica, 147
Kouzes, James M., 197
KPMG, 188–189
Kroc, Ray, 240–241
Kwiatkowski, Jocelyn, 269

L
LaBarre, Polly, 146
Lagging indicators, 203
LaSalle, Diana, 122, 147
Leader's Legacy (Kouzes,
Posner), 197
Leaders. *See also* Managers
accountability of, 162–163
authentic, 230
business plans, 166
decision making by,
219–220
effective, 215
humanizing, 132–133
inspirational, 79
legacy of, 196–197

transactional/transformational, 222–224
value creation by, 166
Leadership
  authentic, 166, 170
  mindful, 50
  paradigm, 227
  types of, 28
Leadership (Burns), 28
Leadership and the New Science
    (Wheatley), 31
Leadership practices
  conscious-capitalism
    balance, 226–228
  corporate cultural
    evolution, 224–226
  Customer Pyramid
    innovations, 228–230
  intangible promotion/
    measurement, 220–222
  living a calling creation,
    218–220
  moving from transactional
    to transformational,
    222–224
  overview of, 215–216
  Peak,
    Practice 1: Embody an
      Inherently Positive View
      of Human Nature, 216
    Practice 2: Create the
      Conditions for People to
      Live Their Calling, 218
    Practice 3: Promote and
      Measure the Value of
      Tangibles, 220
    Practice 4: Ability to Move
      Fluidly Between Being
      a Transactional and a
      Transformational
      Leader, 222

Practice 5: Nurture, Value,
  and Evolve Corporate
  Culture as Your Ultimate
  Differentiator, 224
Practice 6: Calibrate the
  Balance Between
  Conscious and
  Capitalism, 226
Practice 7: Disrupt the
  Customer Pyramid with
  Consistent, New Innova-
  tions at the Peak, 228
Practice 8: Lead to Peak
  (In Other Words, You're
  Always a Role Model and
  a Sherpa), 230
positive view of human
  nature, 216–218
recommend reading for, 233
role modeling, 230–232
summary of, 232
Learning relationships, 124
Leary, Timothy, 18–19, 110
Legacy companies, 108
Legacy investors
  benefits of, 192–198
  firms offering, 191
  history of, 189–190
  market size, 189–190
  prescriptions for, 195–197
  recommended reading
    for, 198
  types of, 195–196
Let My People Go Surfing
    (Chouinard), 26
Levinson, Arthur, 166,
  167
Levitt, Theodore, 99, 100, 106,
  137
Lewis, David, 97
Lewis, Peter, 153

Liberating the Corporate Soul (Barrett), 66
Liderman, xvi–xvii, 50–51, 226
Life@Facebook, 50
Limbic system, 35
Lincoln, Abraham, 10
Linden Lab, 131
Linton, Bill, xvii
Liquidity timing/strategy, 167–168
Lithium Technologies, 133
Little House on the Prairie (Wilder), 241
Locke, John, 26
Lokey, Houlihan, xvi–xvii
Lorenzo, Frank, 207
Love, Courtney, 17
Loyalty
    customer, 123–124, 137, 205
    employee, 63
    profits and, 35
    unprecedented, 40
The Loyalty Effect (Reichheld), 24, 35
Lululemon Athletica, 148
"Luv Lines," 70–71
Lyft, 106, 227–228

M
M Financial, 218
Mackey, John, 26, 201, 209, 217, 227
Macy's, 151–152
Madoff, Bernie, 21
Malone, Margarett, 188
Man's Search for Meaning (Frankl), 83
Managers. See also Leaders
    assessment of, 93–94, 248–240
    hundred-year, 23

    influence of, 20
    peak assessment of, 93–94
Managing with Carrots (Gostick, Elton), 66
"Manage Your Human Sigma" study, 209–210
Mantras, 86
Market Matrix, 62, 88
"Marketing Myopia" (Levitt), 100–101
Marriott, 109
Mary Kay Cosmetics, 63
Maslovian model, xvi
Maslow on Management, 1, 12
Maslow, Abraham, xvii, xxi, 27, 105, 189
    on achieving greatness, 236
    on basic needs, 48
    biography of, 242
    on consumers, 24–25
    drawing inspiration from, 12–13
    early exposure to, 6–7
    on employee complaints, 49
    on enlightened management, 23
    on entrepreneurial opportunity, 157
    on fear of possibilities, 235
    on gratitude, 94
    on heroism, 83
    on human growth, 3
    on hunger, 63
    Leary on, 18–19
    legacy of, 15
    on living a calling, 218–219
    on motivation, 79, 245
    on new enterprise creation, 14
    primer on, 7–10

pro-technology
    statement, 121
recommended reading, 15
on self-actualized peo-
    ple, 241–242
on transformation, 40–41
on work conditions, 19
work experience of, 10–12
on workplace
    environments, 20
Massie, Hugh, 176–177
Maverick (Semlar), 27, *xxi*
Mavericks at Work (Taylor,
    LaBarre), 146
McCown, George, 171–172,
    192–193
McDonald's, 108, 240
McEwen, William, 180
McGregor, Douglas, 17, 20,
    217–218, 248
McKee, Annie, 89
Mead, Margret, 146, 187
Meaning, 92–93
Meaning index, 84–85
Meaning, Inc., 95
Meaningful workplace
    components of, 83–89
    creation of, 81–83
    day-to-day approaches, 89–95
    prescriptions for, 91–94
    reasons for, 81–62
    recommended reading
        for, 95–96
Medtronic, 14, 82–83, 166, 170
Meehan, Sean, 106
Meetings
    community, 120
    with customers, 105
    employee, 208
    executive committee, 65–66
    expectations for, 134

management, 218
monthly, 73, 92
Meldman, Mike, 180, 185
Memory, 123–124
Merrill Lynch, *xvi*
Methodists, 190
Meyer, Danny, *xxi*, 86, 127, 129,
    209–210
Millennials, 108, 190
Millennium restaurant,
    188–189
Mindfulness, 50, 244
Mission alignment, 190
Mission statements, 85
"Mission and Medallion"
    ceremony, 83
Mojo
    defined, 13
    relational, 40
    relationship with, 14
Monaghan, Tom, 190
Money, *xvii. See also*
    Compensation
    investors, 178, 194
    meaning in, 37
    motivational aspects of,
        52–53
    recognition scoring, 249
    relevance of, 59–60
Money-Recognition-Meaning
    pyramid, 48
Montgomery Ward, 105
Moore, Geoffrey, 101
More Than a Motorcycle
    (Ozley), 52
Morgan Stanley, 6
Motivation
    alignment, 179
    base, 45–47
    customer, 116
    employee, 80

Motivation (*Continued*)
  inspiration *vs.*, 79
  theory of, 19
  true, 36, 41
Motivation and Personality
    (Maslow), 10
Mullin, Peter, 218
Munger, Charlie, 184
Murrow, Edward R., 47

N
Nader, Ralph, 153
"Name Your Favorite Shop,"
    91–92
"Naming it" concept, 86
Nanus, Burt, 164
Nelson Information, 191
Nelson, Bob, 66, 69
Net promoter score (NPS), 24,
    115
Netflix, 107–108, 114,
    132, 228
New York Times, 107,
    148, 150
New Yorker, 110
The New Urbanism (Katz), 82
Nietzsche, Friedrich, 84
Nike, 91
Nin, Anaïs, 30
Nirvana, 18
Nixon, Richard, 18
Nobu, 148
Nokia, 137
Non-Linear Systems (NLS),
    10–11
Nonpeakers, 10
Novak, Michael, 240
Nucor, 206–207
*Nuts! Southwest Airlines' Crazy
    Recipe for Business and
    Personal Success,* 202

O
O'Brien, Bill, 25
O'Connell, Patrick, 155
O'Connor, Sinead, 17
Ogilvy & Mather, 101
Ogilvy, David, 101
Oliver, Mary, 5
Omidyar, Pam, 189–190
Omidyar, Pierre, 189–190
One-size-fits-one customers, 123
"100 Best Companies to Work
    For" list, 54–55, 58, 87
1001 Ways to Reward Employees
    (Nelson), 69
Open Table reservations, 127
Organizational Recognition
    Assessments for
    Managers (ORAM), 73
Ozley, Lee, 11, 52

P
Patagonia, 26, 151
Peakers, 10
Pearl Jam, 18
Peppers, Don, 123–124
Performance
  culture and, 206, 210
  effective, 168–171
  financial, 66, 203
  on-time, 208
  reviews, 74–75
Personal transformation, 12–13
Petite Auberge, 143
Philanthropy Task Force, 87
The Phoenix
  grand opening party at, 100
  marketing of, 109–110
  offbeat quality of, 136
  original vision for, 17–18
  personality of, 109–110
Pinterest, 11

Pioneer Fund, 190
Plain Talk (Iverson), 178
planet go "Planet Google Wants You" (Hoffman), 148
Plato, 15
Plemons, Jill, 62
Pollard, C. William, 79
Pompei, Ron, 146
Pop, 3–4
Porras, Jerry, 22–23, 191, 196
Positive Organizational Scholarship, 25
Posner, Barry Z., 197
Potka. *See* Conley, Lauren
Pottery Barn, 115
Power vs. Force, 244
Presence, 230
Price, Bill, 175, 177
Priceless (LaSalle, Britton), 122, 147
PricewaterhouseCoopers (PwC), 57
Priority setting, 242–243
Pritzker, John, *xiv*
Procare, 139
Product differentiation, 112–113
Progression, 40
Progressive Insurance, 152–153
Promega, *xvii*, 50, 74
Pseudo-loyalty, 123
Psychohygiene, 35, 216
Public Benefit Corporation, 221
Putnam, Robert, 82

Q
Quach, Vivian, *xviii*
Quakers, 190
QuickBooks, 146–147
Quicken, 146

R
"Radical empathy," 223
Radisson, 116
Raising the Bar (Erickson), 57
Rate of return, 167
Ray, Jeanenne, 269
The Rebel Rules: Daring to Be Yourself in Business (Conley), 3
Recognition
   broad view of, 36–37
   compensation and, 75
   culture of, 64–65, 67–73
   examples of, 61–65
   formal, 67, 71–72
   strategic approach to, 65–67
Recognition culture
   employee Pyramid and, 68
   formal, 67, 70–71
   informal, 68–70
   at Joie de Vivre, 64–65
   loose, 68
   recommended reading for, 76
   traditional, 67–68
   training and, 69
Red Hot Chili Peppers, 18
Reichheld, Fred, *xxi–xxii*, 24, 35, 106, 115
Relationship alignment
   collaboration in, 179–181
   emotional connection for, 181–184
   emotional intelligence and, 176–178
   long-term focus of, 176
   overview of, 175–176
   prescriptions for, 183–184
   recommended reading for, 186

Relationship Truths Pyramid
  defined, 13–14
  effects of, 213
  focus of, 15
  introduction of, 36–39
  investors needs in, 38
  job orientation on, 237–241
  overview of, 31–32
  power of, 39–41
  recommended reading
    for, 41
  underlying motivations
    and, 235
Relationships
  defining, 34
  functional, 22–23
  growth and, 24
  learning, 124
  value of, 33–36
  web of, 32–33
Religious investors, 190
Resonant Leadership (Boyatzis,
    McKee), 89
Retire-a-Little, 56–57
Return on Customer (Peppers,
    Rogers), 123
Rider's Edge Program.
    See Riding Academy
Riding Academy, 140
Ritz-Carlton, 109
Robb, Walter, 142–143
Roberts, Julia, 3–4
Rogers, Martha, 123–124
Rogers, Myron, 79
ROI (return on investment)
  focus on highest, 163
  outcome, 165
  overemphasis on, 178
Role models, *xxi*
  characteristics of, 10,
    230–231

companies as, 184–185, 227
managers as, 133
visualizing potential,
    201–202
Rolling Stone magazine, 110
Ronstadt, Linda, 17
Roosevelt, Eleanor, 10
Rotten, Johnny, 18
*Rules for Revolutionaries: The
    Capitalist Manifesto for
    Creating and Marketing
    New Products and Services*
    (Kawasaki), 151
Rush Hour MBA, 56

S
Saga Corporation, 11, 121
Salary. *See* Compensation
San Francisco Business Times,
    183
San Francisco Examiner, 100
Sarbanes–Oxley, 167
SARS (severe acute respiratory
    syndrome), 5
Sasser, W. Earl, 204
Saunders, Anne, 150
Schlesinger, Leonard, 204
Schrager, Ian, 109, 136–137
Schultz, Howard, 150, 192
Search Inside Yourself Leader-
    ship Program, 50
Sears, 105
Second Life, 131–132
Secretan, Lance, 79
Self-actualization, 8
  of customers, 149–151
  defined, 7
  Harley customers, 141
  impulse to, 19
  Leary on, 18
  overview of, 235–237

qualities of, 241–242
recommending reading
   for, 246
Self-transcendence, 151
Seligman, Martin, 53
Selling the Invisible
   (Beckwith), 101
Semco, 27
Semlar, Ricardo, *xxi*, 27, 56
Senior executive team, 59
Serpica, Danielle, 269
Servant Leadership
   (Greenleaf), 232
The Service Profit Chain
   (Heskett, et al.), 204
Service culture, 128–134
Service from the heart
   approach, 204–205
Service-profit chain, 203–204
Setting the Table (Meyer), *xxi*,
   127, 210
The Seven-Day Weekend
   (Semlar), *xxi*, 27
*The 7 Habits of Highly Effective
   People* (Covey), 21, 56
Sharing economy, *xiv*
Sharp, Isadore, 47
Sherpa model, 230–232
A Simpler Way (Wheatley,
   Rogers), 79
Simply Better (Barwise,
   Meehan), 106, 115
Sinegal, James, 23
Sisodia, Raj, 228
Skinner, B.F., 8
Small Giants (Burlingham), 108
Smith Barney, 191
Smith Travel Research, 170
Smith, Frederick W., 38, 229
Smith, Logan Pearsall, 240
Smith, Orin, 192

Smucker, J.M., 54
Social Investment Funds, 190
Social media, 132
Social responsibility, 151–152
The Social Life of Information
   (Brown), 36
Socially responsible investments
   (SRIs), 189–191
Sony, 101
The Southwest Airlines Way
   (Gittell), 35, 69, 202
Southwest Airlines, 82
   company newsletter, 70–73
   culture at, 201–203
   low fares at, 106
   organizational practices
      at, 35–36
   sense of calling at, 219–220
   service-profit chain at, 209
Spanish language classes, 88–89
The Speed of Trust (Covey), 165
Spiderwebs, 31
Spotify, 114
The Soul of the New Consumer
   (Lewis), 97
Stage one companies, 102–103,
   107
Stage three companies, 102
Stage two companies, 102
Standard & Poor's, 191
Stanford University, 6, 11
Starbucks, 40, 150–151, 192, 206
Starwood Hotels, 116, 131–132,
   223
States of being, 28–29, 244
Stay Interview, 75
Stephens, Deborah, 12, 123
Stephens, Robert, 89, 93
Sternlicht, Barry, 223
Story Gardener, xviii
Strobel, Christian, 72

Success
  company culture and, 204,
    206
  intangible aspects of, 30
  Maslow's ideas and, 13
  measuring, 27, 245
  on pyramid, 212, 238
Success needs, 121, 243
Summa Health System of
    Akron, Ohio, 89–90
SuperUser, 133
Survival needs, 243

T
Target, 115, 138
Task Force Delta, 8
Taylor, William C., 146
Technology
  for concept testing, 131–132
  culture of, 126–128
  harnessing, 123–126
Teerlink, Rich, 11, 52
Telecommuting, 55
Terkel, Studs, 43
Theory X management, 20,
    216–217
Theory Y management, 20, 27,
    216–217
Think different approach, 139
Think Global, Act Local
    mindset, 223
Thiry, Kent, 66
Thoreau, Henry David,
    196
360–conversation, 74
The Three Tensions (Dodd,
    Favaro), 168
Timberland, 54
Time magazine, 190
Tindell, Kip, 231
The Tipping Point (Gladwell), 12

"Total Compensation State-
    ment," 58
Touch culture, 126–128
Toward of Psychology of Being
    (Maslow), 6
Town and Country, 110
Training, 69, 73
Transactional alignment
  collaboration and, 179–181
  creation of, 167–168
  need for, 38
  prescriptions for, 171–183
  recommended reading
    for, 174
  YPO example, 176
Transformation
  corporate, 12–13
  creation of, 29, 245
  need, 243
  occurrence of, 40–41
  personal, 12–13
Transformation Pyramid
  application of, 12
  customer's desires and, 121
  investor needs on, 164
  as life model, 30
  succeed/survival levels
    in, 29–30
Transformative effect, 80
Transparency, 167
Travel & Leisure, 102
Travelocity, 111–112
Trust
  building, 173, 181
  development of, 164
  rewarding, 207
  types of, 165
"Trust Index," 54
TV and radio personalities, 15
TWA, 108
Twitter, 132

U

Uber, 106, 227–228
Ullman, Tracey, 61
The Ultimate Question
    (Reichheld), 106,
    115
Union Square Hospitality
    Group, 86, 127
Unions, 33
United Airlines, 227
USA Today, 3, 109, 161

V

Values
    core, 22, 55, 225
    as differentiator, 224
    intangible, 220
    intrinsic, 23
    leading with, 227
    long-term, 24, 234–235
    perception of, 51
van Stolk, Peter, 149–150
Vanguard Group, 23
Vanity Fair, 111
Venture capitalists, 179
Voice of the customer
    program, 131

W

Walgreen, 168
Walkman, 101
Wall Street Journal, 64
Walmart, 59, 226
Walton, Sam, 72
Wang Computers, 108
We Are Here, 67
Webb, Peter, 184
Wegman, Danny, 145
Wegmans, 145
Westin Hotels, 116
WeWork, 143–144

What the World's Greatest
    Managers Do Differently
    (Buckingham,
    Coffman), 63
Wheat, Ann, 188–189
Wheat, Larry, 188–189
Wheatley, Margaret, 31, 79
Whelmers, 127–128
Whitman, Meg, 131
Who Moved My Cheese, 8
Whole Foods Market, 206,
    209
    business model of, 26
    customer profile, 142–143
    senior leadership at, 11
    small team concept at, 217
Wilder, Laura Ingalls, 241
Wired, 110
"Woodstock of Capitalism," 184
Work. *See also* Job
    break from, 57
    as a calling, 80
    day-to-day, 89–91, 224
    defined, 143
    hollow, 79
    meaning in, 37, 43, 89–91
    purpose of, 12
Working (Terkel), 43
Workplace. *See also* Meaningful
    workplace
    crucial relationships in,
    29–30
    Google's, 49–50
    happiness at, 25–27
    mirrors, 19–21
    relationships in, 33–36, 51
    supervision of, 216
WorldBlu Scorecard, 221
Wrong-owner syndrome, 171
Wrzesniewski, Amy, 90
Wyatt, Watson, 165

Y
Young Presidents Organization
    (YPO), 175–176
YouTube, 132
YPO. *See* Young Presidents
    Organization
    (YPO)

Yvette, the Hotel Matchmaker,
    113

Z
Zaltman, George, 145–146
Zappos, *xi–xii*, 59, 217
Ziglar, Zig, 45